KIDNAP IN CRETE

KIDNAP IN CRETE

*The True Story of the
Abduction of a Nazi General*

Rick Stroud

BLOOMSBURY

NEW YORK · LONDON · NEW DELHI · SYDNEY

Bloomsbury USA
An imprint of Bloomsbury Publishing Plc

1385 Broadway   50 Bedford Square
New York   London
NY 10018   WC1B 3DP
USA   UK

www.bloomsbury.com

First published in Great Britain 2014
First U.S. edition 2015

ISBN: HB: 978-1-63286-193-1
ePub: 978-1-63286-194-8

LIBRARY OF CONGRESS CATALOGING-IN-PUBLICATION DATA HAS BEEN APPLIED FOR.

2 4 6 8 10 9 7 5 3 1

Typeset by Hewer Text UK Ltd, Edinburgh
Printed and bound in the U.S.A. by Thomson-Shore Inc., Dexter, Michigan

To find out more about our authors and books visit www.bloomsbury.com.
Here you will find extracts, author interviews, details of forthcoming events,
and the option to sign up for our newsletters.

Bloomsbury books may be purchased for business or promotional use.
For information on bulk purchases please contact Macmillan Corporate
and Premium Sales Department at specialmarkets@macmillan.com.

For Constantinos E. Mamalakis

ΟΙ ΗΡΩΕΣ ΠΑΝΕ ΦΥΛΑΚΗ
Prison is for heroes
(Cretan saying)

Contents

A Note on the Names

I am very grateful to Dr Stavrini Ioannidou and Mr Constantinos E. Mamalakis for helping me find my way through this minefield. Dr Ioannidou sent me the United Nation's *Romanization Systems for Geographical Names* and very generously spent time going through the manuscript to correct my versions of Greek proper nouns. Mr Mamalakis was equally helpful. He went through the manuscript three times making corrections and even convened a small, impromptu conference of philologists in Heraklion to debate the issue.

Even so it has been difficult to come to a consensus. Rather than Anglicise the names (apart from a few instances like that of *Micky Akoumianakis* whom everyone, whether Cretan or British, seemed to call Micky) or revert to the nicknames given to the Cretans by the SOE, I wanted the names used in the book to reflect the person or place to which they belong. When in doubt I have followed the advice of Mr Mamalakis, a native Cretan who probably knows more about life on wartime Crete than anyone else who helped with my research.

In most cases I have opted for the accusative form for Christian names and have almost always rendered 'Φ' as 'F'. I hope my decisions have done justice to the people of Crete and their beautiful island.

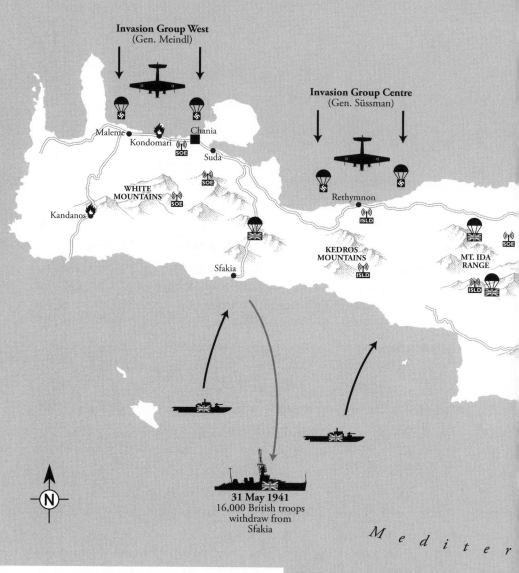

The Island of Crete

Invasion Group West
(Gen. Meindl)

Invasion Group Centre
(Gen. Süssman)

Maleme

Kondomari

Chania

Suda

WHITE MOUNTAINS

Kandanos

Rethymnon

KEDROS MOUNTAINS

MT. IDA RANGE

Sfakia

31 May 1941
16,000 British troops
withdraw from
Sfakia

Mediterr

N

Allied Activity Post-invasion, 1941–43

Radio (Inter Service Liaison Department)

Radio (Special Operations Executive)

Parachute supply point

Submarine and motor launch access to beaches

British seaborne evacuation

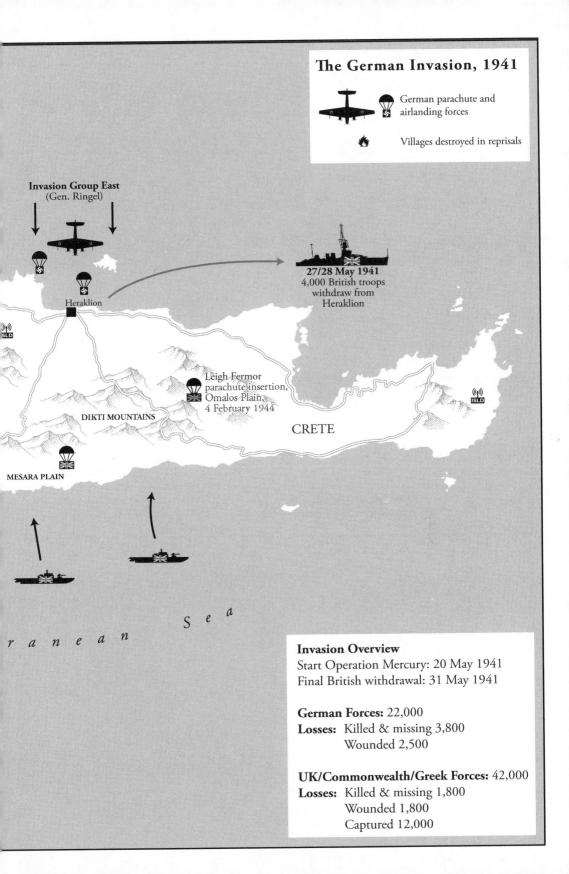

The German Invasion, 1941

German parachute and airlanding forces

Villages destroyed in reprisals

Invasion Group East
(Gen. Ringel)

Heraklion

27/28 May 1941
4,000 British troops
withdraw from
Heraklion

ISLD

Leigh Fermor
parachute insertion,
Omalos Plain,
4 February 1944

DIKTI MOUNTAINS

ISLD

CRETE

MESARA PLAIN

Mediter~~ranean~~ Sea

Invasion Overview
Start Operation Mercury: 20 May 1941
Final British withdrawal: 31 May 1941

German Forces: 22,000
Losses: Killed & missing 3,800
 Wounded 2,500

UK/Commonwealth/Greek Forces: 42,000
Losses: Killed & missing 1,800
 Wounded 1,800
 Captured 12,000

Kidnap: Operational Route from Landing to Escape, 4 April – 14 May 1944

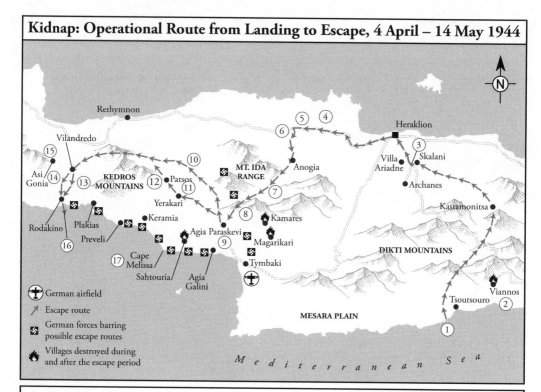

German airfield

Escape route

German forces barring possible escape routes

Villages destroyed during and after the escape period

1 4 April Moss/Paterakis team arrive by motor launch	10 PLF/Tyrakis route
2 Viannos destroyed in 1943	11 Amari Valley, Lotus Land
3 Point A, kidnap junction	12 PLF Group & Kreipe Group reunite
4 Kreipe Team head for hideout near Anogia	13 Guard team take fast dangerous route to sea
5 Yeni Gave, leave car	14 Kreipe team take safe difficult route to sea
6 PLF & Giorgios abandon car and go to Anogia	15 Asi Gonia, Ciclitira hideout
7 Hideout, 1st rendezvous for all teams after kidnap	16 14 May Escape to Egypt by motor launch
8 30 April/1 May at night and by luck kidnappers slip through German cordon	17 Cape Melissa, original pick-up point
9 PLF & Tyrakis set off to find radio	

Map based on War Office issued MDR 630/10099 (G.S.G.S..4410) Drawn by 512 Fwd. Survey Coy. RE. 1941/1943. Using Greek and German maps and Allied aerial photographs. Reissued 1944. The map was the property of Patrick Leigh Fermor and was heavily annotated by him to show operational route and main events on way

Route of kidnap car through Heraklion on the night of 26 April 1944

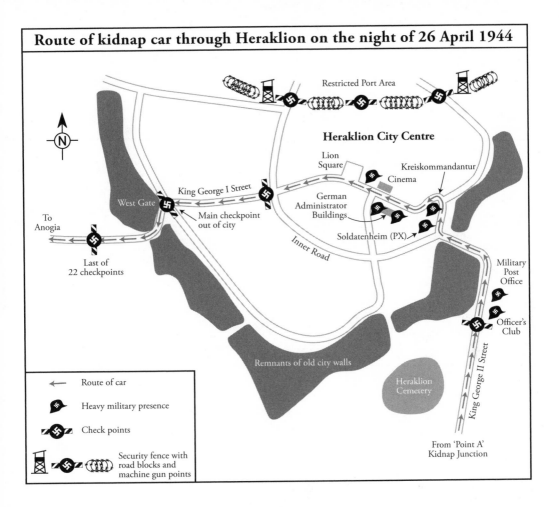

Heraklion City Centre

Restricted Port Area

Lion Square

Kreiskommandantur

Cinema

King George I Street

West Gate

German Administrator Buildings

Main checkpoint out of city

To Anogia

Soldatenheim (PX)

Inner Road

Last of 22 checkpoints

Military Post Office

Officer's Club

Remnants of old city walls

Heraklion Cemetery

King George II Street

From 'Point A' Kidnap Junction

Route of car

Heavy military presence

Check points

Security fence with road blocks and machine gun points

Prologue

On 1 March 1944, a German Junkers 52 transport plane flew over the bright blue Mediterranean towards Crete. Among those on board was *Generalmajor* Heinrich Kreipe, the newly appointed commander of the 22nd *Luftlande* Division, who was about to become the second in command of the island.

Forty-eight years old and unmarried, the army was Kreipe's life. He joined up as German forces rolled across Belgium and into France at the outbreak of the First World War. By the end of hostilities, Kreipe had earned a reputation for bravery and wore an Iron Cross at his throat. At the start of the next war he was a lieutenant colonel, and in the spring of 1940 once more marched into France as a senior officer in a conquering army. By January 1942, Kreipe was in the disorientating cold outside Stalingrad, feeling the full force of a Russian armoured counterattack. Over the course of the next year he fought on the Eastern front, caught in the mincing machine that was the Red Army, the impossible supply lines and the Russian weather. Although his health was badly affected by the stress and conditions of the Eastern front, when Kreipe finally came home in late 1943 he had won the Knight's Cross of the Iron Cross, the highest award for bravery on the battlefield that an officer of the Wehrmacht could win. It was awarded to men of outstanding leadership. There was only one higher distinction, the Grand Cross of the Iron Cross, held by one man: Hermann Göring. But it was his first Iron Cross, won in the mud of the trenches, which Kreipe wore round his neck as he headed for Fortress Crete.

The Junkers circled over the airfield at Maleme. Through the windows of the unpressurised aircraft Kreipe could see almost nothing but the mountains, which were the refuge for the resistance, known on the island as the 'andartes'. The resistance, he was assured, was made up of bands of disorganised, poorly disciplined peasants – mainly shepherds who had been cowed by the brutality of his predecessor General Friedrich-Wilhelm Müller, 'The Butcher of Crete'. The andartes were nothing to worry about; Kreipe's command was going to be what soldiers all over the world call a 'cushy number', a rest-cure after the torments of the Russian Steppes.

The plane bounced to a halt, a door in the side opened and light flooded the gloomy, utilitarian military interior. The small honour guard on the tarmac crashed to attention, the soldiers rigid under their helmets, their boots gleaming in the sun. Kreipe climbed from the aircraft; a soft breeze wafted the smell of thyme across the runway. At the foot of the steps stood an escorting officer who saluted him and led the way to a shining black Opel staff car where the driver held the door open, staring straight ahead in respectful anonymity. The wings of the car already bore pennants showing the general's rank. Kreipe sank back into the leather seats; his escorting officer climbed into the front next to the driver, the doors slammed and the car pulled away, heading first to the German headquarters in the port of Heraklion and then on south to his new home, the Villa Ariadne, built by British archaeologist Sir Arthur Evans.

On the outskirts of the town they came to a huge guarded arch, the West Gate. The men on duty saw the flags on the car's wings and stiffened to attention, waving it past the barriers. Through the windows Kreipe could see tidied-up evidence of the fierce battles that had been fought in 1941, when the largest airborne force in history had invaded the island: whole streets were lined with remnants of buildings destroyed by shellfire and aerial bombardment. Local people milled about, stepping aside to let the big car pass – women wearing long black dresses that looked heavy and uncomfortable, swarthy-looking men who did not appear to have shaved for weeks.

Invisible among the unkempt civilians were resistance fighters, watching the progress of the car as carefully as they watched all the comings and goings of the invaders, noting the badges of identity on their uniforms, the regimental plates on their vehicles, the positions of guard posts and the routine of the soldiers that manned them. The information was recorded, collated and analysed, turned into lists, drawn into maps and sent by radio and motor launch to SOE Balkans office, known as Force 133, in Cairo. One of the key figures in this work was Mihalis Akoumianakis (codename 'Minoan Micky'), who had been recruited to Force 133 SOE as head of counter-intelligence. He was the son of the caretaker of the archaeological dig at Knossos; his father had been killed in the first three days of the German invasion.

Covert operations had been conducted on Crete since before the first German soldiers arrived on the island, and coordinated by British SOE officer John Pendlebury. The networks he started had grown in size and efficiency, sending back information that had helped the Allies defeat Rommel in the Western Desert. Many of the Desert Fox's supply ships were sunk in the Mediterranean, depriving him of petrol, ammunition and reinforcements, because of intelligence gleaned by the men and women whom the Germans dismissed as disorganised peasants. Members of the resistance risked their property, their lives and those of their families; many had already been caught, tortured and executed; whole villages on the island had been destroyed in reprisals.

The general's car stopped at the Kreiskommandantur, a large administration building on the edge of Heraklion's Liberty Square, where he was to take his lunch. He stepped inside and was met by a pretty young Cretan woman who greeted him with a warm smile and offered him real coffee. She too was an undercover agent who for months had been smuggling secret documents out

of the building to be photographed; the pictures were sent to
Cairo and the documents returned to the files from which they
had been taken.

In the afternoon Kreipe continued on his journey to the Villa
Ariadne, next to which stood the small house where Akoumianakis's
late father had lived. Micky stood in the garden, talking to his
sister – another valued member of the resistance, though the
soldiers guarding the villa thought she was just a charming flirt.
The security measures round the villa itself were impressive: barriers, layers of coiled barbed wire, some of it electrified, machine-
gun nests, armed guards. Kreipe was greeted by a soldier-servant
who fussed with the general's luggage and ordered it to be taken
to the ground-floor bedroom of the villa, where his new master
was to sleep. Kreipe was pleased to see that the only staff allowed
to work inside the building were German soldiers. He was shown
through the cool hall and into his study. Another servant brought
him more coffee. Tomorrow he must go to his headquarters in
Archanes to meet and take charge of his new command.

Through the open door of the study he heard his staff talking
quietly and the front door closing. Outside a guard patrolled in
the dusty garden which was scattered with carved stones and exca-
vating equipment from the now abandoned archaeological dig.
Everything was in order, quiet and safe. The general took off his
heavy uniform jacket and sat in a chair beside the desk, sleepy
from the journey. As a schoolboy he had attended the Latin School
at Greussen in Thuringia; he had enjoyed learning about the clas-
sical world, and now looked forward to visiting some of the island's
ancient sites. He sat drowsy and musing, happily unaware that he
had entered a trap that in less than five weeks would spring shut,
ruin his career, destroy his reputation and nearly cost him his life.

An Island of Heroes

The general's new home was then, as it is still, a land of contrasts: violence and feuding coexist with passionate friendship and overwhelmingly generous hospitality. Cretan mountain men have been described as living 'in a past where a young man only attains his majority when he has stolen his first goat or abducted a girl or drawn blood in a family feud'. Blood vendettas over family honour or sheep can go on for decades. Cretans, especially those who live in the mountains, have an inbuilt distrust of authority; they have a saying: 'Prison is a place for heroes.'

Crete has been populated since Neolithic times, when settlers are thought to have come from Anatolia. The island is dotted with ancient Iron Age palaces, the biggest and most magnificent of which was excavated at Knossos by Sir Arthur Evans at the beginning of the twentieth century. Evans named the culture responsible for building the palaces 'Minoan', after the mythical King Minos, son of Zeus and the island's first ruler; Minos founded the Cretan navy and sacrificed boys and girls to the Minotaur. Minoans were farmers, and counted bull leaping among their sports. The civilisation was destroyed by a combination of invasion and the eruption of a volcano on Santorini, one of the most violent cataclysms in the history of the Western world. In Roman times the island's forests provided wood for the ships of the Mediterranean and when there were no more trees left, the people grew olives and reared sheep and goats on the denuded hillsides. No animal dangerous to man is to be found on Crete. One legend claims this as a legacy of Hercules, who wanted to make the birthplace of Zeus safe for humans.

For centuries Crete has been a stepping stone between Europe, Asia and Africa, and for nearly a thousand years has been fought over and occupied by Muslim pirates, Venetians and Turks. In the thirteenth century the island was taken over by the Venetians, whose harsh regime caused a revolution. Crete seized its independence and declared itself a republic; it took five years of armed struggle before the Venetians once again ruled the island. In the seventeenth century, the Turks took Crete away from the Venetians and it became part of the Ottoman Empire. There followed 200 years of conflict between the Christians and the Muslims. At the end of the nineteenth century, world powers intervened: the Turks were finally expelled and in 1897 Crete achieved (temporary) independence.

Any story about Crete will be dominated by a set of four silent, brooding characters, as dangerous as any islander – the mountains. They run the length of the land, crisscrossed by steep gorges watched over by birds of prey, eagles, falcons and kestrels. The highest peaks carry snow all the year round. On the lower slopes, in the warm, fertile valleys, rosemary, sage, oregano and thyme scent the hillsides growing among daisies, poppies, wild orchids and cyclamen, shaded by chestnuts, oaks, olives, pines, plane trees and tamarisks.

In the west are the White Mountains, containing some of the wildest terrain in Europe. The peaks rise to 8,000 feet and were a refuge to desperate men fleeing from the Turks with a price on their heads. To the east of the White Mountains a low rolling valley leads to the colossal heights of Mount Ida, whose summit reveals a panorama of the whole of the island. South-west of Ida stands Kedros in solemn isolation and to the east of Kedros towers the last of Crete's great mountain characters, Dikti.

The mountains hide a series of high upland plains, surrounded by hills and accessible only to shepherds on foot. Winter snows can make even these impossible to reach. For hundreds of years bandits and vendettas made moving around the mountains dangerous. The locals went armed and almost every man on the island possessed some sort of weapon, even if it was an ancient and unreliable gun inherited from a great-grandparent.

Nestling in the White Mountains is the plain of Omalos, the subject of a violent resistance song dating back to the battles against the Ottoman Empire.

> *When will we have a clear starry night?*
> *When February arrive?*
> *So I can take my rifle*
> *and my bandolier*
> *and descend to Omalos*
> *on the road to the Mousouro clan.*
> *I will then deprive mothers of their sons,*
> *I will deprive wives of their husbands,*
> *I will leave motherless babies behind,*
> *Babies that cry because they've lost their mothers,*
> *Babies that cry out for water in the night,*
> *Babies that cry out for milk at dawn,*
> *Babies that cry out for their mothers when the morning comes.*
> *Oh when will we have a clear starry night!*
> *Oh when will we have a clear starry night!*

To the south-west of the White Mountains, and protected by them, is Sfakia, one of the few places on the island never to have been occupied by a foreign power. Its people are renowned for their ferocious spirit and their hospitality. Sfakia was a centre of resistance against both the Greeks and the Turks. The legendary Cretan resistance fighter Daskaloyannis came from Sfakia. In 1771, after a long struggle, he was finally captured, and was then sentenced to be skinned alive inside the city of Heraklion. He is reported to have endured the ordeal in silence. Before the Second

World War it was possible to say: 'the men of Sfakia, those champions of the Cretan Revolution, are still a race apart'.

Mount Ida is the home of legend. Hidden below its peaks lies the great plateau of Nida and the cave of the God Zeus, a deep, mournful fissure approached up a steep path and across a frightening ledge. Tracks from Nida lead down to the town of Anogia, a village which for centuries has been a refuge for resistance fighters. South of Ida is another sheltered and remote fertile plain, the Amari valley. For a while in the Second World War the valley became such a place of refuge and safety to British agents that they gave it the name *Lotus Land*.

The invasion of the island in the Second World War was unlike anything that had been known before. By the end of 1940 Hitler's armies had swept across Europe and were about to enter the war in North Africa. General Franz Halder, chief of the German general staff, argued that: 'The mastery of the Eastern Mediterranean is dependent on the capture of Crete' and that 'this could best be achieved by an air landing.' On 28 April 1941, from his *Führer* headquarters, Hitler issued 'Directive No. 28', ordering the occupation of Crete, 'in order to have a base for conducting the air war against England in the Eastern Mediterranean'.

One man who tried to prepare the island for its next invasion was an Englishman, John Pendlebury. In 1929, at the age of twenty-five, Pendlebury was appointed curator of the archaeological site at Knossos, Crete, and director of excavations at Amarna, in Egypt. Winchester School and Cambridge University educated (Classics tripos with a distinction in Archaeology), Pendlebury was unconventional, sharp, possessed of a beguilingly playful nature, and passionate about Crete. Over six foot tall, he was a formidable athlete: he fenced, held international high-jump records and could clear hurdles 'with the speed of a cheetah'. His fitness levels were staggering: in one archaeological season alone on Crete he is said to have walked more than a thousand miles.

All who met John Pendlebury seemed to fall under his spell. 'He made a wonderfully buccaneerish and rakish impression, which may have been partly due to the glass eye,' wrote a future fellow Special Operations Executive agent, Patrick Leigh Fermor. (Pendlebury had lost the eye as the result of a childhood accident; during the war he would take out his prosthetic eye and leave it on his desk as a signal to his colleagues that he was away on a mission.) Manolaki Akoumianakis recalled that Pendlebury's 'companions were shepherds and mountain villagers. He knew all their dialects'; he could drink and walk the legs off any Cretan. Of hosting celebrations for the saint's day of Saint John, Pendlebury wrote: 'It was the best we have had up to date. I really felt the village father! – Pretty near 1000 people and dancing from 9-3! Total cost of making the whole village tight £7!' Pendlebury's home on Crete was the Villa Ariadne, a large, low, square building, constructed of yellow and brown stone which had for years been the centre of the archaeological work at Knossos.

When he was not moving around the island, Pendlebury would hang around the cafés and restaurants of Heraklion's Lion Square – a market area dominated by the Morosini Fountain, a series of huge white marble bowls supported by lions, and once home to the biggest slave market in the Eastern Mediterranean. Pendlebury would sit, eating sweet cakes and drinking coffee in the Patisserie Reginaki – known as 'High Life', or drinking wine at Maxim, a restaurant built into one of the Byzantine arches that surrounded the fountain. As he sat, he listened to the conversations going on around him. He became aware of a discreet net of Nazi sympathisers who were quietly gathering intelligence and names that would be useful after the German invasion.

One, an Austrian woman called Frau Myro Bauritz, taught foreign languages and freelanced as a commercial 'letter writer' for the Greek companies with contracts in France. When not teaching, Frau Bauritz was hard at work making lists of German-speaking students in the city. Jan Knoch was a German tourist

whose pleasure it was to wander about the island making draw-
ings. He based himself in Pitsidia near the south coast in an area
called the Mesara Plain. Knoch became quite well known to the
locals and had a favourite spot on a hill, from which he would
spend hours sketching the landscape. In front of him lay Timbaki,
destined to turn into the biggest German airfield on the island.
Knoch vanished just before the invasion, but reappeared in 1942
working as a Wehrmacht engineer with the rank of major. A third
spy was Hans Kruger, who also disappeared immediately before
the invasion. He taught languages at the exclusive Commercial
School in Heraklion. After the war his name was found on orders
discovered in the German Kommandantur.

   With the outbreak of war, Pendlebury, aged thirty-five, offered
his services to British Naval Intelligence. 'I know Crete and most
of the Aegean Islands intimately,' he wrote in his application; 'I
have many personal contacts all over the Aegean which should be
a good source of information, since, particularly in Crete, I am
known to a great part of the population.' The interviewing officer
concluded that he was 'tough and generally desirable'. A month
later, Pendlebury was an emergency intelligence officer, working
in a dingy basement at the War Office in London as part of Military
Intelligence (Research). His friend and fellow agent, Nick
Hammond, recalls him 'swooping onto the practical details of
planning with unbounded energy and enthusiasm. He talked to
me of swordsticks, daggers, pistols, maps; of Cretan *klephtes* from
Lasithi and Sfakia, of hideouts in the mountains and of coves and
caves on the south coast; of the power of personal contacts formed
by years of travel, of the geography of Crete, its mules and caïques,
and of the vulnerable points in its roads.' (Klephtes were thieves
living in the mountains. In hard times they would form gangs to
raid the fertile lowlands and coastal areas.) When Hammond and
Pendlebury talked on the phone they spoke in Greek – Pendlebury
in Cretan dialect and Hammond in the argot of northern Greece.
By June the following year, having undergone basic explosives

training, Pendlebury was back on Crete, living once more at the Villa Ariadne, and masquerading – though not at all convincingly – as the British vice consul.

The military situation in Greece and the Middle East soon deteriorated. In November 1940, Crete's locally raised defenders, the 5th Cretan Division – regarded as being the best marksmen in the Greek army – were sent from Chania to fight on the Albanian front, where they were deployed in atrocious conditions of cold and wet. Though woefully equipped, the division fought heroically, most notably at Mount Trebesina in early 1941, pushing Mussolini's forces back into Albanian territory. British and Commonwealth troops, including fifty Middle East Commando, were sent to Crete to fill the gap left by the division's departure.

Pendlebury feared that if the Axis powers captured Greece, his beloved Crete would be next to fall. His main priority, therefore – which he pursued with some urgency – was to organise a Cretan military force to replace the 5th Division. Pendlebury's official role within British military intelligence required him to liaise between the Allied forces on Crete and the Greek authorities. This gave him the chance to see how the commandos worked and to form ideas about organising the resistance. The commandos did not know that Pendlebury was working for military intelligence, but they were clearly impressed by the Englishman: 'From the first days of our landing, his knowledge of Crete and the Cretans was invaluable both from the point of view of the higher staff and our humbler pleasure in knowing where and how to buy the best wine and eggs . . . His good friends were everywhere and to go about with him was a rather Bacchanalian Progress of Cretan hospitality.' His job was to identify whether the allegiances of influential Cretans lay with Great Britain, Germany or Italy. He headed for the upland plains, especially those above Omalos, Anogia and Nida, where he concluded that 'Anglophily is rampant!' Pendlebury knew that if the Germans occupied the island these plains, as in conflicts past, could once again become places of refuge and resistance.

In the event of a German invasion, Pendlebury planned to make his hideout on the Nida plateau – 1,500 metres above sea level, forty miles south-west of Heraklion, and overlooked by the deep and forbidding cave among whose awesome stalagmites and stalactites legend had it that the Titan Rhea hid the infant Zeus. The plateau was inaccessible by road and could only be reached through the guerrilla strongholds of Anogia and Krousonas. Knowing that there was a chance that enemy aircraft might try to land on the plain, he organised for it to be strewn with massive boulders. He wrote home to his wife, Hilda: 'We shall take our weapons and go into the high pastures!' He knew the families who lived on the plains, the men who were to become the andartes, the resistance fighters, and he knew the leaders, the 'kapitans', of whom three were especially important.

The first was Kapitan Antonis Grigorakis – nicknamed Satanas, and known to SOE as Kapitan Satanas. He had been badly wounded in an uprising on the island five years earlier. Pendlebury described him as 'a very dignified old gentleman who looks like an Elizabethan Pirate. He got his nickname because it was thought that only Satan knew how many times he had been wounded or how many bullets were still inside him.' The second key figure was Kapitan Georgios Petrakoyiorgi, a tall, hatchet-faced businessman who owned an olive oil factory; he was assessed as a natural leader who knew what he wanted and exuded calm and confidence; Petrakoyiorgi was given the codename 'Selfridge' and he armed his men at his own expense. The third and most unpredictable of the kapitans was Manolis Bandouvas, a sheep farmer and vast bear of a man with a curling moustache and a reputation for self-importance. With 'his sad ox eyes and correspondingly deep-throated voice in which he was fond of uttering cataclysmic aphorisms such as "The struggle needs blood my lads",' Bandouvas could be very intimidating; he was given the codename 'Bo-Peep'. He did not like taking orders from the British.

The three kapitans formed the backbone of Pendlebury's emerging network. Proud, independent, highly influential characters, they all required careful handling; where they led, others followed. They were striking figures, as were their mountain men followers, wearing dark blue baggy breeches, knee-high boots, embroidered waistcoats and black headscarves; and always with a dagger thrust into a purple silk sash, tied at the waist like a cummerbund. They carried weapons as a matter of course. After the invasion the Germans referred to them as Pendlebury's thugs. Pendlebury's chief concern was to supply these men with weapons, ammunition and equipment.

Pendlebury dragooned other people to help him, many of whom never knew exactly what he was planning. One of these was bespectacled former Field Security officer Lance Corporal Ralph Stockbridge, a quiet man with a dry sense of humour, whose speciality was intelligence gathering. He knew the value of small fragments of information, meaningless or unimportant in themselves, but which could be built up, like pieces of a jigsaw, into a bigger and more valuable picture.

Throughout the early months of 1941, Pendlebury continued his reconnaissance of beaches and landing sites, seeking out potential members for the resistance, and haranguing the British authorities at GHQ Cairo for weapons. He had secret hiding places in Heraklion and near Suda Bay where he stashed flares, rifles, ammunition, detonators and medical supplies. He trained men in the use of firearms and explosives and taught them about organisation. In the cities he recruited agents, gave them cover stories and found places to hide their radios. He worked out what installations should be destroyed before they fell into German hands, including the Cable and Wireless office, the harbour, the power station and the telephone exchange. He arranged for three radio sets to be sent into the mountains, one to Mount Ida, one to Mount Dikti and the third to East Crete. In spite of this, GHQ Cairo ignored what he was doing and made no provision for radio communication with the island once it had fallen to the Germans.

2

Defenders of Crete

On 6 April, the Wehrmacht rolled through Greece. On the 18th, as Athens was placed under martial law, the country's new prime minister, Alexandros Koryzis, the former governor of the Bank of Greece, returned home from emergency meetings with the British and King George II of Greece and shot himself dead.

The British Army reeled back from the German military onslaught, fell apart and retreated to Crete, leaving behind much of its heavy equipment. Soon, thousands of Greek, British and Commonwealth troops were disembarking at Heraklion with their weapons but little else: 'Few of the men had overcoats. None had bedding. Most had lost their toilet kits. There were no mess facilities.'

In Albania, the commander of the 5th Cretan Division, General Georgios Papastergiou, who actually came from northern Greece, abandoned his men and arranged to meet his family in the Cretan capital, Chania, before travelling on to the comparative safety of Egypt. The general's desertion of his unit was met with fury on Crete, causing many to say: 'He returned without his children' – that is, the young men of the Cretan Division. Towards the end of April, Papastergiou turned up in Chania. He was met by riots and protests, during which he was murdered by an enraged citizen. (His name carries shame to this day, and attracts the Cretan condemnation: 'May his bones be blackened by the tars of hell, may the earth of his grave sit heavy on him!')

By the end of April, Hitler's intentions towards Crete were clear. The man tasked with organising the defence of the island (codenamed 'Operation Scorcher') was the commander of the New Zealander Division, Major General Bernard Freyberg VC. Freyberg was described by Wavell's ADC, Peter Coats, as 'a man of quickly changing moods, easily depressed and as easily elated'. Freyberg was fearless in battle and had been wounded almost as many times as Kapitan Satanas. 'Tiny' Freyberg was six-foot two, a qualified dentist, former prize-fighter, and a personal friend of Winston Churchill. The citation for his VC for actions on the Western front contained the sentence: 'The personality, valour and utter contempt of danger on the part of this single Officer enabled the lodgement in the most advanced objective of the Corps to be permanently held.'

Freyberg was part of the small, privileged circle of military and political leaders to be given access to Ultra intercepts. In 1941 this handed him the huge potential advantage of knowing before-hand German plans for an airborne invasion of Crete. He ignored them. Convinced – and possibly obsessed – with the idea that the main invasion would come from the sea, he deployed his forces accordingly, without realising that only one beach, in the north-west sector of the island, was suitable for assault ships and landing craft.

Apart from around 30,000 fighting men under his command, 'Creforce' was augmented, unofficially, by andartes, who were not given uniforms, exposing them to execution by the Nazis as *francs-tireurs* (unlawful combatants). What Freyberg did not realise was the extent to which other ordinary Cretans – women, children, old men, boys, shepherds from the hills – were prepared to take up arms against the invaders. One islander, Giorgios Tzitzikas, who was twenty-three in 1941, remembers: 'The population said, "Our sons are fighting in Albania", we had to take their place, and take their place they did.'

*

On the morning of 15 May 1941, German bombers appeared over the Cretan cities of Chania, Rethymnon and Heraklion. The bombing raids, softening-up attacks for the main assault, were repeated every morning from six o'clock for the next few days, and became known as the 'morning hate'. On the 16th, Bernard Freyberg signalled to Churchill: 'Have completed plans for the defence of Crete . . . everywhere all ranks are fit and morale is high . . . All defences have been extended, and positions wired as much as possible . . . I do not wish to appear over confident, but I feel that at least we will give an excellent account of ourselves. With the help of the Royal Navy I trust Crete will be held.' Churchill's response left no room for doubt as to the importance of Creforce's mission: 'Our success in "Scorcher" would of course affect whole world situation. May you have God's blessing in this memorable and fateful operation, which will react in every theatre of the war.'

In Suda Bay, a huge natural harbour, ship after ship was hit, disabled, or sunk. A gigantic pall of smoke hung over the port. The bombing of the island had a devastating effect on the Cretans, who watched as their towns were pounded to dust. But it also acted to rally them: 'There was fear and fear brought anger,' recalled resistance fighter Giorgios Tzitzikas: 'Let me tell you the iron that was coming down and the fire made the Cretan heart harder than German steel and the Cretan spirit hotter than the German fire. When they came . . . we, the Cretan people, were ready for them.'

3

Operation *Merkur*

On the same day that Bernard Freyberg sent his confident signal to Churchill, a German paratrooper, Jäger Martin Pöppel, and his comrades in the signals platoon, 1st Battalion, 1st *Fallschirmjäger* (Parachute) Regiment, disembarked from lorries which had carried them from their bases in Europe to the olive groves of southern Greece. For the first part of the journey many of the vehicles and troops were loaded onto trains. The men travelled incognito and in secrecy: before they embarked the paratroopers were ordered to remove their insignia and not to carry any personal papers. Battalion identification symbols were stripped from their vehicles. Once aboard the trains they were told not to sing *Fallschirmjäger* songs. The airfields strung along the Aegean coast-line which weeks earlier had been occupied by the RAF, now became crowded with Luftwaffe transport aircraft, spotter planes, bombers and fighters assembled ready for battle: *Unternehmen Merkur* (Operation Mercury), the conquest of Crete.

Pöppel and the rest of his unit quickly established themselves in the captured British tents that were to be their homes for the next few days. Lorries arrived from Athens laden with German beer, which the men kept cool in holes in the ground. They passed the time relaxing under the hot, Greek sun – smoking, eating, drinking, writing home to their loved ones. The Fallschirmjäger had been formed in 1936 by Hermann Göring. Their commander, Luftwaffe commander Kurt Student, was anxious to see his young paratroopers prove themselves in major combat. Pöppel and most of his comrades had volunteered for the elite division at the age of eighteen; most were fanatical Nazis with an unswerving faith in their Führer. Drop-out rates were high: only the toughest made it through the harsh twelve-week training process, which aimed at hardening them mentally and physically. For the first few weeks they learnt weapons and demolition training, plus simple tactical deployments, and punctuated by gruelling sixteen-mile route marches carrying full kit. The next month was dedicated to parachute training: falling and rolling, leapfrogging, as well as work on trampolines, jumping from towers and from dummy transport aircraft; the route marches were extended to thirty-five miles. Finally: intensive parachute training, with the standard RZ20 *Ruckenpackung Zwangauslösung* ('rucksack packed to open'), an awkward piece of equipment which was attached by a single line to the back of the body harness, forcing the paratrooper to launch himself from the aircraft in a spread-eagle dive. Clumsy as it was, the RZ20 parachute could open at just under two hundred feet, which meant the troops could jump from low altitude and spend less time dangling defenceless in the air. The Fallschirmjäger landed in a forward roll, their limbs and joints protected from fractures by elbow and knee pads.

Before being allowed to jump, the recruits were buckled into their parachutes and blown about on the ground by winds generated from howling, lorry-mounted aircraft engines. Once they had satisfied their instructors that they could land without injury and free themselves from the billowing canopies and entangling lines, they were ready to jump from an aircraft and earn the coveted 'Storming Eagle' jump badge (*Fallschirmjäger Adler*), an oval wreath of oak leaves, on which was mounted an eagle in symbolic attack mode, like a Stuka, its talons open, ready to grasp its unsuspecting prey.

All airborne troops were issued with a copy of 'The Parachutist's Ten Commandments', drafted by their spiritual leader and supreme commander general, Kurt Student, who would lead them in the invasion. One of the commandments exhorted: 'For you, combat shall be fulfilment.' Another: 'Together with your comrades you will triumph or die.' 'Calm and caution, vigour and determination, valour and a fanatical offensive spirit will make you superior in the attack . . . Never surrender! Your honour lies in victory or death.' In battle, this elite fighting unit would 'reserve chivalry for the honest foe'; 'armed irregulars' would 'deserve no quarter'.

On 19 May, the paratroopers received their final orders for Operation *Merkur*. Because the island was so small (an area of about 160 miles by thirty), the soldiers were confident that victory would be easy. Highly inaccurate German intelligence reports were also encouraging, telling them: 'There are no Greek troops in CRETE. The British troops are a permanent garrison. British troops which fled from the PELOPONNESE have been brought to ALEXANDRIA.' The Fallschirmjäger spent the rest of the day cleaning their weapons and equipment. Morale was high; Greek shoe-shine boys polished the soldiers' side-lacing jump boots, promising their customers an 'extra top-class Stuka shine'.

At airfields in Topolia, Aliartos Megara and Elefsina, Luftwaffe groundcrews opened the bomb-bay doors of Junkers 52 transport aircraft and heaved in huge aerial-delivery containers full of equipment and weapons, to be dropped with the paratroopers and their comrades in the assault glider units. The men were given strips of cloth to be laid out on the drop zones in prearranged patterns to coordinate air support and supply drops. The outside of each supply canister was painted with coloured stripes and dots to indicate its contents: K.98k rifles, MP38 and MP40 sub-machine guns, MG 34 light machine guns; 75mm recoilless wheel-mounted guns, dismantled and packed into two drop containers. Other containers carried specialised equipment, optical sights, communications equipment and ammunition. Once on the ground, unloading their combat kit from the containers was a paratrooper's top priority.

That evening the paratroopers finished the beer, and sang nostalgic songs of home to the music of a scratch band. For some of the men the jump on to Crete would be the first time they had parachuted into action. Jäger Pöppel, however, was an old hand, having already hurled himself out of aircraft into the battles of Holland and Norway.

In the dead of night, the men of the first wave were driven to the airfields. A lorry stopped by each plane; the troops climbed out and the vehicles went back to ferry more men. The paratroopers piled their parachutes and kit on to the ground, their blue-grey, steel parachute helmets balanced on top. They sat shivering in the cold, suddenly grateful for the uniforms that had originally been issued for the attack on Norway and icy conditions. Some chatted and smoked, others sat, silent. More lorries rolled on to the field, carrying aircrew who swung into the cockpits. Engines fired and propellers turned, blowing choking clouds of dust over the troops.

The order came to get ready. The troops clambered to their feet and pulled on their equipment, shrugging on pouches full of ammunition. Then they draped long cloth bandoliers with more ammunition round their necks, securing them to their belts by loops. Some of the paratroopers had more ammunition pouches strapped round their calves, secured with ties to the top of their jump boots. Everyone carried a special gravity knife in a compartment in the right-hand thigh pocket of their woollen jump trousers. The knife had a retractable blade which was released and locked by a catch on the top of the handle. Some men carried a second, folding knife, with a clip along the scabbard, secured in the top of one of their jump boots or belt. Other pockets were used to hold stick grenades.

They had enough iron rations for two days: processed cheese and meat, ersatz instant coffee, rusk-style biscuits or crackers, dextrose tablets to quench thirst and a small water bottle. To cook they carried the standard German Army folding tiny 'Esbit' stove and solid fuel tablets. Once all the equipment was buckled on, the paratroopers had to step into their jump smocks, long tunics designed to go over all the equipment and webbing and stop it from snagging the parachute lines. Each smock had a 9mm semi-automatic Luger pistol sewn into a pouch on the back and was fastened at the front with heavy-duty brass zips. Next the men struggled into their parachute harnesses, helping one another secure the straps. Finally, weighed down by their kit and ammunition, they put on their special rimless parachute helmets, padded with foam and secured with three leather straps at the side and back. Fully kitted up, each man carried around ninety pounds of equipment.

The first rays of dawn appeared on the horizon, revealing the huge number of transport aircraft waiting to take them to Crete: over 500 Junkers and 80 gliders for over 15,000 troops. When the airborne men had seized their objectives another 7,000 comrades would arrive by sea.

The order came to board. Each man held his parachute release cord, from which dangled a steel hook. To stop it snagging on the steps into the aircraft steps he looped the cord and gripped the end between his teeth, leaving his hands free to haul himself up into the fuselage.

The assault gliders carried nine men, plus the pilot, to be towed then dropped in a simultaneous glider-borne assault. The glider men sat in a line down the centre of the aircraft, with the last four men facing the rear ready to open the only door. Along the sides were breakaway panels that could be kicked clear to allow escape. The glider's wheels were jettisoned after takeoff. The troops sat and waited; the temperature inside the planes started to rise. The pilots began to check the magnetos, running up the engines in a deafening roar, making communication possible only by sign language. At last, each great, yellow-nosed Ju 52 shuddered, the engines revving hard in one unified sound. The planes moved forward, rumbling towards the end of the runway. As the aircraft accelerated, nothing could be seen through the portholes, only swirling dust which soon rose 3,000 feet into the air. One by one they lifted, the sweating paratroopers silent, listening to the heavy clunk of the undercarriage retracting. Feldwebel Wilhelm Plieschen took out his camera and photographed his friends as they removed their heavy, rimless parachute helmets and settled back against the plane's uncomfortable fuselage.

The aircraft banked, turning south. Suddenly, they broke out of the dust clouds into a dazzlingly clear sky: below was the Acropolis, topped by the beautiful structure of the Parthenon, and ahead, vivid blue sea. Aircraft and gliders stretched to the horizon, protected by fighters and fighter bombers: Stukas, Junkers 88s, Dorniers, Heinkels, Messerschmitt 109s and Messerschmitt 110s. In a leading glider sat Generalleutnant Wilhelm Süssmann, commander of 7 *Flieger* Division; with him were his divisional staff. The pilot of the tug, Sergeant Hausser, saw an aircraft flying across his path which he recognised as a He 111 bomber. The Heinkel's take-off from southern Greece had been delayed by engine trouble, and its pilot Oberfeldwebel Paul Gerfehr was racing to catch up, unaware that he was flying into the flight pattern of the glider-borne troops. Hausser did the only thing he could – he pushed his joystick forward and put his huge Ju 52 'Iron Annie' and the glider it was towing into a dive. At the same time Gerfehr pulled his stick back and began to climb. The two planes missed each other, Hausser's plane and its glider returned to level flight, but turbulence from the slipstream of the bomber made the tow-rope vibrate like a violin string, putting it under great strain. It snapped. The glider containing Süssmann and his divisional staff lurched and soared up, banking left, heading for the island of Aegina. Hausser watched in horror as the glider's starboard wing broke off, and the fuselage fell, tumbling over and over towards the ground, hitting the island in a puff of smoke. Süssmann and his staff were the first casualties of Operation Mercury.

Although Crete is not much more than a hundred miles from the Greek mainland, the flying time for the invaders was more than two hours, and many of the paratroopers fell asleep. They were woken by the shrill sounds of klaxons and the pilot's voice giving the 'Prepare to Jump' order. From the Plexiglas cockpits the aviators could see the mountains looming up from the sea. The soldiers leapt to their feet and hooked their static lines to the steel cables running the length of each aircraft. The planes descended to 200 feet, the load of paratroopers shuffled forward. At the door each man grabbed the bars on either side of the hatch and pulled himself forward and out of the aircraft, diving into space, spread-eagled and battered by the slipstream. Each plane emptied in just under ten seconds. The paratroopers tumbled in space, the roar of the Junkers' engines replaced by silence and the swish of their bodies falling through the air. The static cords jerked, opening the parachute packs, and deploying the shroud lines. Hundreds of canopies blossomed in the sky – white, yellow, red and green. The sickly smell of aviation fuel was replaced by the rich, luxurious scents of thyme, rosemary and pine as the chutes carrying men and equipment canisters floated down towards the scrubby fields and gentle olive groves of northern Crete.

On the terrace of his Italianate villa, high above Creforce head-quarters at Chania, Bernard Freyberg sat eating his breakfast. He watched as the sky above his head filled with aircraft, descending gliders and paratroopers. Then he looked at his watch, said 'They're dead on time,' and went on to finish his boiled eggs.

4

The Battle of Crete

At Maleme airfield, a key German objective on the north coast, gliders swooped through the thick dust cloud thrown up by the bombing earlier in the day. In one glider travelled Major Walter Koch and the battalion staff of 1 *Luftlandesturm* (Airborne Assault) Regiment. At seven minutes past seven his pilot began the descent, travelling at 240 feet per second, heading for the Tavronitis valley next to a ridge called Hill 107, looking out over Maleme airfield. Blinded by the sun, the pilot could not see the landing area, or accurately judge his height. When he finally saw the objective he realised he was still about 600 feet above the earth: much too high. He put the nose hard down and glided in, unable to slow down. All around the other pilots were doing the same. The speed and chaos made the gliders more widely dispersed than planned.

As Koch's transport landed, the barbed-wire-covered skid, designed to slow down the landing, tore off. The violence of the impact knocked him and his men to the floor of the fragile craft, tearing a hole in its side. Some men died on impact, others were injured; many had broken bones. Those who could scrambled out, running for the cover of the stunted gorse bushes that grew all around, or dived into the scrub, blinded by smoke, and immediately came under fire. Koch fell, shot in the head. All around more gliders were plummeting to earth, disappearing into the unexpectedly hilly landscape. Some crash-landed hard, splintering apart, throwing occupants on to the rocks. The air filled with the cries of dying and badly wounded men. To the west and east of Maleme hundreds of paratroopers floated down to earth; some hanging limp in the harnesses. Parachute canopies bobbed across the ground like jellyfish.

Later, Freyberg 'stood on a hill watching the attack over Maleme enthralled by the magnitude of the operation'. While watching the bombers he had 'suddenly became aware of a greater throbbing, or overtone, during the moments of comparative quiet'. Looking to sea he saw hundreds of planes, tier upon tier, coming toward him. They were huge, slow-moving troop carriers with more airborne troops. They circled counter-clockwise over Maleme airdrome and then, only 300 feet above the ground, as if by magic white specks suddenly appeared beneath the planes. 'Coloured clouds of parachutists floated slowly to earth.'

As far away as Paleochora, on the south coast, the church bells rang a warning, sounded by Father Stylianos, who set about raising a force to march north towards Kandanos. Another priest, Father Frantzeskakis, strode at the head of his band, rifle in hand. At the northern port of Heraklion all was calm. The bombing of the last few days had stopped. Private Reg Spurr was enjoying a beer in a taverna with men from the Royal Engineers and the Black Watch, oblivious to the fact that twenty-five miles to the west the invasion had started. Far off they heard a bugler sounding the alarm, followed by three 'G' notes, the signal for paratroopers.

A swarm of Ju 52s appeared low over Heraklion, and hundreds of parachutes flowered in the sky. Spurr and his mates dashed into the street; a dead paratrooper crashed to the ground, splayed like a doll in front of them; within seconds a Cretan was stripping the man of his weapons. Ahead three more paratroopers arrived, two hit the road, already dead; the third landed on a wall struggling to get out of the harness trailing behind him. Suddenly it looked as though an unseen hand was pulling on his lines from the other side of the wall. He lost his balance and disappeared. An agonised scream tore through the air. Spurr burst through a gate in the wall to find a middle-aged woman, in traditional Cretan dress, shouting angrily. In her hand was a vicious-looking carving knife; at her feet lay the dying parachutist, his throat cut wide open, blood pumping on to his chest. The woman slashed at the parachute cords, hacking open his smock, looking for weapons.

Spurr dashed off in search of his unit. He was soon surrounded by a crowd of running people. In the group were British, Greek and Cretan soldiers, civilian men, women and children. Most of them were armed with anything that could be used to inflict an injury, including hammers, saws and garden implements. Many of the women carried knives. The group ran to the West Gate out of Heraklion. Spurr found himself alongside a young Cretan couple: the woman brandished a large knife, and twisted to show him that she had a shotgun concealed in her skirts. The man motioned to the top of the massive arch that formed the gate shouting: 'We are going up there where the German parachutes are.' Spurr saw armed civilians and soldiers, all roaring at the paratroopers descending from the air. A Greek, Captain Kalaphotakis, appeared, trying to take charge. Spurr shouted to a British sergeant: 'By the look of this lot they don't need us do they?'

'No,' the NCO replied. 'I think we had better get back to our own mobs.'

The crowd started jeering at a bedraggled unit of confused paratroopers, doubling up the road towards the gate. The civilians opened fire, though some of the weapons were so old they would not work. A hail of bullets hit the German troops, who tumbled dead to the ground. Once more Reg Spurr tried to leave and get back to his unit. The shouting crowd surged forward, charging another unit of invaders. Small-arms fire crackled, echoing off the buildings; bullets ricocheted everywhere. The people gave a loud cheer. Smoke and the smell of cordite drifted through the air.

More soldiers lay dead and bleeding round the gate. The defenders reloaded their weapons.

That afternoon Spurr passed the site of a skirmish and found six or seven Germans lying dead in a dried-up creek. Close by were some houses where Spurr found two civilians, one, an old man slumped on his knees, his head forward and his hands clasped behind him. He had been shot in the back of the head and his corpse riddled with bullets. Next to him was a woman, still alive, writhing in agony. She was pregnant and had been bayoneted several times in the stomach. She died before Spurr could help her. He stumbled out of the house and vomited.

The casualties on both sides mounted very quickly. The 7th British General Hospital, situated between the sea and the Maleme Road, was right in the path of shellfire and bombs. Staff tried to move the sick and wounded to the safety of caves on the beaches. They established three caves for the casualties and a fourth for the exhausted medical teams. Soon the caves were overflowing with injured Allied soldiers. As the hours wore on a new category of wounded man began to appear: German parachutists.

Later in the day the German 10th Parachute Company landed in the vicinity of the hospital. Lieutenant Colonel Plimmer, a New Zealander and the commanding officer of a field ambulance company, was forced at gunpoint to surrender. As he climbed from his slit trench with his arms above his head he was shot dead. Twenty-six miles away to the west of Chania, at the small, almost derelict port of Kissamos Kasteli, lay an unfinished airstrip guarded by the 1st Greek Regiment under the command of Colonel Papadimitrakopoulos and a British major, T. G. Bedding, a former PT instructor. The regiment had been flung together using a thousand volunteers from the town and the surrounding villages. They were badly equipped and had only 600 rifles and two ancient machine guns, together with about 1,800 rounds of ammunition some of which was the wrong calibre. For three weeks they had been trained by a handful of New Zealand officers and NCOs who had managed to scrounge two Bren guns and a few more boxes of ammunition. Kissamos Kasteli was not very high on General Freyberg's list of battle priorities.

The battalion fought on with anything it could lay its hands on: ancient shotguns, old flintlocks, axes, knives, even nail bombs improvised from plastic explosives. One of the villagers, Dr Stylianos Koundouros, found his father digging up an old Turkish rifle, hidden during an arms requisition years before; he made his father hand it over, and then ran off to join the regiment, heading for the noise of battle, the rifle in one hand, his medical kit in the other. 'The Germans had never seen something like this in Europe,' recalled George Bikoyiannakis, from the village of Galatas near Chania. 'These people were fighting with farming tools. Even broomsticks. They would tie kitchen knives to them and use them as spears.'

The rag-tag force took on a formation of seventy-two Fallschirmjäger, mostly teenagers, under the command of Oberleutnant Peter Muerbe. Apart from Muerbe himself, and a couple of senior NCOs, none of the youths had seen combat. They were armed with rifles, Schmeisser sub-machine guns, long-barrelled Mausers (some equipped with telescopic sights), heavy machine guns, mortars and thousands of rounds of ammunition. It was planned to drop more supplies to them later in the morning and prearranged recognition signals had already been set up. The paratroopers had been told 'only a token show of resistance is to be expected from irregulars among the inhabitants . . . they have no heavy equipment'.

At 08:14 hours, the first parachutists flung themselves out of the Junkers, arms outstretched in the starfish position. They dropped in two groups; many were hit and died before they reached the ground. The survivors were hunted through the vine and almond groves by Cretans who had grown up among the culverts, stone walls and gulleys that surrounded the town; every rock and bush was a familiar landmark. The hidden areas of dead ground quickly became killing zones. The defenders crawled on their stomachs, creeping behind the parachutists and slaughtering them. The villagers took the arms and ammunition from the dead soldiers. Bewildered young Germans heard the sound of their own weapons being fired against them and returned fire in panic, killing their own comrades.

Just over an hour later the surviving invaders of Kissamos Kasteli had been surrounded and trapped in a group of farm buildings. Major Bedding ordered his men to mount a siege. He knew that the Germans would soon run out of ammunition and water. The temperature was climbing towards fifty degrees. With nothing to fire and nothing to drink, the elite troops would have to surrender. Inside one of the stone buildings, in a hot, dark room, were four terrified civilians, members of the Vlahakis family: old Spiro the father, his elderly wife and their two grandchildren. Spiro's son was outside fighting. By now the German commander, Muerbe, was dead and Gefreiter Walter Schuster had taken command.

Without warning, one of his men fired at the cowering civilians. The noise was deafening; ejected rounds sprayed onto the floor, and the Cretans were blown back, dead, their bodies slamming against the wall. Schuster asked the soldier what he thought he was doing: the paratrooper shrugged and said they would have died anyway in the crossfire.

Colonel Papadimitrakopoulos and his men mounted a reckless charge across open ground shouting '*Aera!*' ('Like the Wind') – the battlecry of the Evzones, the elite troops who had fought for Greece since the middle of the nineteenth century. (When the Germans had marched into Athens in mid-April, it had been an Evzone who had been forced at gunpoint to take down the national flag flying over the Acropolis and replace it with the German swastika. The Evzone did what he was told took, but refused to hand over the Greek flag. Instead he calmly wrapped it round him, before throwing himself off the ancient building, dying a martyr's death on the yellow stone a hundred feet below.)

Many Cretans now fell in Colonel Papadimitrakopoulos's charge, cut down by automatic fire. The fighters who reached the building smashed their way in through the door and windows, struggling with the enemy in hand-to-hand combat. When it ended, only eighteen of the seventy-two who had jumped that day were still alive. The survivors stumbled into the blazing light, their hands above their heads. A Cretan with a badly wounded arm lunged at one of the soldiers with a bayonet, plunging it in and killing him. Bedding stopped any more revenge attacks and put the survivors in the town jail for their own safety.

At Maleme, the young Mihalis Doulakis watched his father beat to death with his walking stick a young Fallschirmjäger; the soldier had become hopelessly tangled in the lines of his parachute, unable to get at his emergency gravity knife in his breast pocket to cut the rigging. Similar scenes to those Colonel Bedding witnessed in the battle for Kissamos Kasteli were repeated all over the island. A song from the old days once again became popular:

Where is February's starry sky
That I may take my gun, my beautiful rifle and bandolier,
Go down to Maleme's airfield,
To capture and kill the Germans.

Cretans staked out wells, waiting for the soldiers, who they knew would be desperate for water; it was a trick their grandparents had learnt in the uprising against the Turks. It was a tactic that Pendlebury had urged the Creforce commanders to adopt, explaining the need for snipers to cover water sources and wells. A few days before the invasion, Pendlebury had used a captured German topographical map to identify a spring just outside the gates of Heraklion: 'All the German soldiers who land to the west of Heraklion will need water and will be drawn by that spring,' he told Satanas. 'Therefore we must fortify that point. One can see it exactly opposite the Venetian walls so we can hit them from there.'

The 14th Infantry Brigade manning the garrison at Heraklion was commanded by Brigadier Brian Herbert Chappel, a regular army officer from Bedfordshire. Chappel had set up his headquarters in a cave among the West Wadi, an outcrop of rocks to the east, between the town and the airfield. One of the many visitors to the cave was John Pendlebury, come to badger him for arms. Patrick Leigh Fermor was working at Chappel's brigade headquarters, employed, in his own words, as a 'junior intelligence dogsbody'. He remembers John Pendlebury arriving at headquarters one day with Kapitan Satanas: 'I was enormously impressed by that splendid great figure with his rifle,' he recalled of Pendlebury. 'He had a Cretan guerrilla with him festooned with bandoliers . . . the great thing was that [John's] presence filled everyone with life and optimism and a feeling of fun'. The kapitans were chronically short of weapons, and it made Pendlebury 'angry to think that the British garrison had 400 unissued Lee Enfield rifles lying in the ancient Venetian galley sheds alongside Heraklion harbour, which could be used to arm and defend'.

Chappel agreed to release some weapons to Satanas, who had been charged with distributing them. He took them to his home village of Krousonas and gave them to a sergeant of the gendarmerie, saying: 'You will give one to each man and keep a note for me and a register.' Each man received a rifle and about one hundred rounds of ammunition and Satanas and Pendlebury had a record of where the guns went.

At Rethymnon, a town about halfway between Heraklion and Chania, twenty-three-year-old Giorgios Tzitzikas had been sent by his commanding officer to carry a message to garrison headquarters that the Germans were descending on the villages of Pervolia, Misiria and Pigi, just to the east of the town. At headquarters he found chaos: frightened officers were trying to hide, terrified of being bombed. He delivered his message and, as he started back, realised that the headquarters was next door to a building where new gendarmerie recruits were billeted. The barracks was deserted; Tzitzikas went inside, hoping to find weapons. On the upper floor in the sleeping quarters he found two Mannlicher rifles, ammunition pouches and bayonets. Seizing them he ran outside into a disorganised crowd of gendarmes, soldiers, and civilians shouting, 'To Pervolia, to Pervolia, save our town, lads', and handed one of the Mannlichers to a comrade. On the way a gendarme captain tried to take the rifle away from him, saying he had stolen it. Tzitzikas pointed the gun at the captain, saying: 'I'll kill you if you take another step, because I took it from where the gendarmes had abandoned it, and now I'm going to use it.'

Very soon Tzitzikas was in action, fighting to stop the paratroopers entering Heraklion. Late in the day he charged a German machine-gun post which was dominating a gorge and which had inflicted terrible losses on the Cretan fighters. As he ran, Tzitzikas tripped on a wire and crashed to the ground, breaking the stock of his weapon. He recovered and crept to the machine-gun post where he shot the gunner in the back. The soldier toppled onto the gun and his comrades fled. Tzitzikas, now alone, heard people shouting: 'Greeks, Greeks' as a rallying cry; then a woman's voice: 'Greeks, Greeks! I've got a gun, come and get it.' Tzitzikas moved off in the direction of the noise to rejoin the fighting: civilian men and women, of all ages, killing the enemy with anything they could lay their hands on.

Late on that first afternoon came the second wave of Fallschirmjäger, including Martin Pöppel and his comrades. Pöppel himself landed in an olive grove and, apart from getting caught in a tree, arrived almost unopposed. The temperature on the ground was soaring; many of the men took off their jump smocks and hid them in the undergrowth, disobeying the regulations that said the men should take off their smocks, unbuckle their equipment, put the smocks back on and put the equipment on over their uniforms. They formed up and set off for the airfield. The savage fighting continued into the evening. When the Allied forces began to run out of ammunition the local militia came to their aid, flushing out pockets of the enemy all over Heraklion.

Thousands of documents were retrieved from dead paratroopers and taken to the Allied intelligence officers. Geoffrey Cox, an intelligence officer and former war correspondent during the Spanish Civil War, ended the day with two sackfuls of captured papers in his dugout. Before going to sleep he decided to see what they contained: among the paybooks, codebooks, aerial photographs and other military papers, he found a bloodstained carbon copy of a typescript. Cox read the document by torchlight and, with the help of a German dictionary, concluded that it was the operation order for 3rd Fallschirmjäger. At the bottom of the order was an instruction that it should be burnt once read and was not to be carried into action. Cox took it immediately to General Freyberg, who asked him to read the report out loud.

Freyberg sat listening behind a wooden trestle table; in front of him was a hand grenade with which he planned to stall any sudden attack. What Cox read were not only the orders for the 3rd Fallschirmjäger, but a summary of the whole invasion plan for Crete, detailing the attacks on four strongpoints: the port of Chania, the airfield at Maleme, and the towns of Rethymnon and Heraklion. It also revealed the Germans' intelligence regarding the size of Allied forces on the island as being inaccurate, putting them at only 5,000, when in fact there were more than 22,000.

When Cox had finished, Freyberg sent a signal to Wavell in Cairo. 'Today has been a hard one. We have been hard pressed. So far, I believe, we hold aerodromes at Rethymnon, Heraklion and Maleme and the two harbours. The margin by which we hold them is a bare one, and it would be wrong of me to paint an optimistic picture. Fighting has been heavy and we have killed large numbers of Germans. Communications are most difficult . . . [I have seen] a German operation order with most ambitious objectives, most of which failed.'

The German invaders had not succeeded in taking any of their first-day objectives; huge numbers of dead and wounded paratroopers lay all over the drop zones – nearly 2,000 killed after less than twenty-four hours. The enemy seemed to be clinging on by their fingertips. Creforce and the Cretans had all but won the battle.

5

The Next Nine Days

On the evening of 20 May 1941, in his headquarters on the second floor of the Hotel Grande Bretagne, Athens, Generalleutnant Kurt Student took stock. On one wall of the apartment was pinned a large map dotted with paper flags marking the positions of Axis and Allied units; in the centre of the room was a large, brilliantly lit table on which stood field telephones, a tangle of wires, stacks of paper, two black files and an ashtray full of cigarette stubs. Assessing the situation with Student were his ADC, Major Reinhardt, Generalmajor Julius 'Papa' Ringel of the 5th Mountain (*Gebirgsjäger*) Division and Generalleutnant Alexander Löhr. As commander of *Luftflotte* 4, Löhr had been responsible for bombing operations on the Eastern front, including the fire-bombing of Belgrade, which killed thousands of civilians and turned the Yugoslav capital into a blazing marker for subsequent raids. It was to the highly decorated Löhr that Hitler had handed overall responsibility for the Luftwaffe element of Operation *Merkur*.

The atmosphere in the room was tense. A large number of senior commanders lay dead or dying on Crete. The elite assault regiment had been all but wiped out; aerial reconnaissance reported that the surviving invaders appeared to be scattered and disorganised. Ringel's mountain troops were still on the Greek mainland and could not join the fighting until an airfield had been secured for them to land their transport planes.

In Germany, Hitler had forbidden his propaganda minister

Joseph Goebbels to report on *Merkur* until the outcome was absolutely certain. Just before midnight the corrected casualty reports for 1st and 3rd Fallschirmjäger came in: they were catastrophic. General Löhr thought the invasion had been a fiasco and believed the operation should be aborted; Reinhardt asked his chief if he could start organising the withdrawal. In spite of the pressure to halt the battle, the highly ambitious Student wanted to continue. They should concentrate on securing the large coastal airfield at Maleme; he ordered Ringel to ready his mountain troops to be airlifted on to Crete at first light the next day.

Maleme was overlooked by the high ground known as Hill 107, which was the key to the airfield's defences. Hill 107 was defended by the New Zealand 22nd Infantry Battalion. During the first day of the battle, the Wehrmacht had disrupted the battalion's communications and cut off the western elements from their comrades to the east of the ridge. Thinking the men in the west had been overrun, the battalion commander withdrew in the night to regroup. At the same time soldiers on the airfield itself heard German voices and, thinking they were surrounded, they too withdrew. At dawn the soldiers on the west of Hill 107 also withdrew. Maleme was now undefended.

Very early in the morning of the 21st, the second day of the battle, a Junkers 52, piloted by Hauptmann Kleye, flew onto the western edge of the airfield. The German troops on the newly captured Hill 107 watched as the aircraft's wheels touched the ground. Shells exploded near the plane; it taxied to a halt, swung round, then the engines roared as Kleye revved them hard and lumbered back into the sky. Kleye had been sent by Student to discover the extent of the airfield's defences. He radioed to his general that a landing and disembarkation was possible, but only if executed with maximum speed.

At about the same time Freyberg received the following Ultra decrypt:

<u>Personal for General Freyberg Most Immediate</u>

On continuation of attack Colorado [Crete] reliably reported that among operations planned for Twenty-first May is air landing two mountain battalions and attack Chania. Landing from echelon of small ships depending on situation at sea.

Freyberg seriously misinterpreted the signal, and then sent one of his own:

Reliable information. Early seaborne attack in area Chania likely. New Zealand Division remains responsible coast from West to Kladiso River. Welch Battalion forthwith to stiffen existing (sea) defences from Kladiso to Halepa.

Later that day hundreds of Junkers aircraft appeared over Maleme airfield, carrying 8,500 men of the 5th *Gebirgsjäger* (Mountain Division) and their commanding officer Colonel Ramcke. The pilots began the descent, braving the shells that were exploding on the runway. Nearly twenty aircraft were hit, crashing on to the airfield in flames. Soldiers scrambled from the ones that managed to land, hidden by the swirling red dust thrown up from the propellers. They were badly shaken by the battering their transports had taken, but they now had a foothold and used it to keep the runway open. More and more Junkers landed, weaving between the burning wreckage that littered the runway. An Allied artillery commander with a view of the airfield reported that the German troops 'needed seventy seconds to land, clear the men and gear and take off'.

Cox reported the prevailing belief at headquarters that a seaborne invasion was imminent and that the airborne invasion was only a preliminary diversion. Freyberg had five battalions with which to counter-attack Maleme but he kept almost all of them watching the coast for a German armada. Throughout the rest of the morning the men of the Sherwood Rangers looked on in tortured frustration as, one after another, Junkers transport aircraft passed them, landed and unloaded men and materiel; they were forbidden to traverse their guns because coastal artillery was only to be used against the naval invasion.

In Heraklion, a group of German paratroopers penetrated the city's West Gate, dividing into two attacking forces – one moving down Kalokerino Street towards Lion Square and the centre of the town, the other probing to the north, parallel to the sea, heading towards the harbour. There was prolonged opposition from armed civilians and retired soldiers; one, Colonel Tzoulakis, used his rifle to pin down a group of paratroopers near a burning mattress shop. He lost his life to machine-gun fire.

Near the harbour some civilians, including a boy scout, fired from the roof of the Ionian Bank at paratroopers in the building opposite, which caught fire. The soldiers surrendered and as they came forward, throwing down their weapons and manhandling a small air-portable field gun, a group of British soldiers from the Yorks and Lancasters appeared and started firing at the civilians on the roof, mistaking them for the enemy. The civilians shouted, pointing at the paratroopers who quickly gave themselves up to the soldiers and were marched off to a temporary POW compound near Liberty Square.

A fierce firefight in the tiny Barrel Makers Square saw another group of paratroopers overwhelmed and killed, their bodies left where they fell. Near Lion Square a popular policeman, well known in the city for his daily walks with his pet dog, was seen firing a Steyr sub-machine gun at fighter aircraft strafing the city at roof height. He too died, blown up in the bombing; only his leg, still with a boot on, was ever found.

Kapitan Satanas was in Heraklion with Pendlebury, desperate to get hold of his troop of one hundred armed guerrillas waiting ready at his home village of Krousonas. The two men thought

that this small force might be able to launch flank attacks on the
growing force of paratroopers collecting to the west of the city.
They split up, Pendlebury and his driver taking the shorter,
quicker route – a distance of about ten miles – on roads that went
dangerously close to enemy positions; Satanas headed south
through Knossos, a longer but safer route. After they parted
company Pendlebury went back for a final time to his office near
Lion Square to get a message to his Cretan fighters that they must
somehow take and occupy the ridge overlooking Heraklion airfield
to the east of the city. Then he set off, heading straight towards
the Germans.

A few miles south of the city, the Villa Ariadne's caretaker,
Manolaki Akoumianakis, received Pendlebury's message stressing
the importance of holding the ridge. Manolaki's son Micky was
missing, thought to have been killed fighting on the mainland.
The old man vowed vengeance on the boy's life; hours later
Manolaki himself was dead, killed in an attack trying to hold the
ridge. His body, still clutching his straw hat, was found by his
daughter Philia. He would not be buried for another month – the
time it took for his son Micky to return safely to the island.

The battle lines in Heraklion continued to shift back and forth
throughout the next day. The Germans took the port and city
centre, but were then pushed out on the west side. There was
more fierce fighting round the West Gate and at one point the
townspeople saw a white flag and thought the Germans wanted to
surrender. They were wrong; the white flag party was carrying an
ultimatum: surrender or be carpet-bombed. The Cretans refused
to give in. The Fallschirmjäger commanding officer, Major
Schultz, who had led the first successful penetration of Heraklion's
city walls, ordered his soldiers to withdraw to clear the way for the
Luftwaffe to carry out the bombardment. It was Friday 23 May.
The bombers droned over Heraklion and the ground shook under
the endless detonation of high explosive. Terrified civilians and
defenders fled to the south of the city towards Knossos. Fire, flame

and smoke engulfed everything; the day became known as Black Friday.

By the third day of the battle, the invading troops had established a strong foothold around Heraklion airfield. As they moved through the olive groves along the coast and south into the hills they passed the corpses of their comrades who had dropped and died on the first day, the bodies bloated and stinking in the sun. Many appeared to have died from a single bullet to the head, as if they had been executed after landing: the pockets of their jumpsuits had been ripped open, their equipment and clothing had been looted and their high-laced paratrooper jump boots were missing.

Along the coast, on 24 May, the Luftwaffe began to bomb the port of Chania. All day the bombers came, flattening the town. The bombing terrorised the civilian population and Allied soldiers alike. Refugees fleeing the city were machine-gunned by German fighter and bomber crews. From the surrounding villages survivors watched as their town was destroyed. The sun set on a beautiful Mediterranean evening, the sky still bright blue and the sea glittering. Geoffrey Cox stood with a brother officer looking down on the city over which hovered a tall cloud of smoke and dust; beneath it 'tongues of red and yellow flame [were] writhing like giant boa constrictors'. The bombers left the harbour intact, knowing that after the battle they would need its services. Freyberg abandoned his headquarters near the town, leaving a muddle of telephones manned by an exhausted duty officer sitting at the foot of an olive tree. The British Army was falling apart.

On Tuesday 27 May, Freyberg received permission to withdraw. He drove by car to Sfakia, the tiny port on the south coast of the island. The same day Brigadier Chappel, commander of 14th Brigade and the Heraklion sector, was told that Royal Navy warships would arrive around midnight to take off 4,000 of his men. There was only enough room on board to evacuate the British and Commonwealth troops in the town; the Cretans and Greek regular troops who had fought for Heraklion were to be abandoned.

Before Chappel left he was visited by Kapitan Satanas. The imposing white-haired warrior, in a colourful waistcoat, jackboots, and a rifle slung across his back, stood in front of the khaki-clad brigadier. Satanas put his hands on Chappel's shoulders and said: 'My son, we know you are going away tonight. Never mind! You will come back when the right time comes. But leave us as many guns as you can to carry on the fight till then.' Chappel agreed and ordered his men to hand over as many arms as they could collect.

After dark the troops trailed down to Heraklion harbour, where the cruisers HMS *Orion*, *Ajax* and *Dido* awaited them. The men were ordered not to smoke and not to carry objects such as mess tins that might clatter together. In shuffling silence they slunk past the airfield and haunts where they had enjoyed the hospitality of the locals. One soldier from the Black Watch remembers: 'Nobody could get out of his mind the people who had welcomed their Scottish comrades so warmly, who had fought beside them so bravely and who were now being abandoned on tiptoe at midnight, and without warning, to the vengeful enemy.'

For Captain P. A. Tomlinson, an Australian medical officer, the overriding image as they pulled out of Heraklion was 'one large stench of decomposing dead, debris from destroyed dwelling places, roads were wet and running with burst water pipes, hungry dogs were scavenging among the dead. There was a stench of sulphur, smouldering fires and pollution of sewers. Conditions were set for a major epidemic.'

The troops embarked in the dead of night, without the Germans realising that they had left. Major Burckhardt of the *Luftwaffejäger* Brigade had fought a hard battle and endured many casualties: 'I never expected such bitter fighting and we began to despair of ever gaining our objective or indeed of surviving at all . . . I had 80 men left of my 800, no food, little ammunition and was no nearer success.' The next day, Burckhardt 'received the biggest surprise of an astonishing battle, they had all gone in the night'. Brigadier Chappel left with a heavy heart, knowing that the 'Greeks and the Cretans, after the gallant performance will be treated hard and will feel that we have left them in the lurch'.

The remaining troops in the north of the island, apart from small pockets of rearguard fighters, had to make their way south, across the White Mountains. The swarms of men heading south from Suda Bay looked like crowds leaving a football match. Some were in organised groups, others just individual soldiers trudging on up the steep sides of the mountain; all were short of food and water. They moved in the darkness, which gave them respite from the merciless attentions of the dive-bombers. During the night an enemy aircraft dropped an orange flare, casting a hideous light over the olive trees and farm houses, forcing the soldiers to scatter. Makeshift dressing stations were set up along the route, trucks hastily converted into ambulances, crude white crosses of torn cloth stretched across grey blankets.

By dawn the lines of retreating men stretched up the steep mountain side to the horizon. 'The daylight gave faces and uniforms and bodies to the dark shapes of the night, revealing them as walking wounded with bloody bandages, one man with a bandaged stump of an amputated hand; as sailors of [a] boat in Suda; as airmen; as Cypriot muleteers; as detachments marching under officers or NCOs; as other men straggling in ragged lines or small groups,' remembered one survivor. 'Every few yards a figure lay on the roadside in the sleep of the utterly exhausted.' Every ridge promised to be the summit and beyond every ridge, another ridge, another tortuous climb. Some men broke down in the embrace of the White Mountains and sat by the road shouting hysterically about dive-bombers.

Eventually the fleeing soldiers reached the top and were rewarded with the sight of the Askifou Plain, 'set up like an oasis on the gaunt White Mountains'. Ahead were fields and white houses, the track led round the western edge to another ridge, the last one before the steep descent to Sfakia and rescue.

By the end of May, 16,000 Allied soldiers had been taken off Crete, in what veterans later called 'the forgotten Dunkirk'. There were about 30,000 British and Commonwealth troops on Crete when the invaders descended from the sky; by the end of the battle, over 4,000 of them were dead; 17,000 were prisoners of war, including 3,000 wounded.

John Pendlebury never made it to the rendezvous with the andartes at Krousonas. His precise movements after he left Heraklion are unclear. Not long into his journey, near German positions at Kaminia, he became involved with a company of Greeks who had been dive-bombed and who were under attack from paratroopers. Eyewitness Polybios Markatatos described what happened next: 'Presently four parachutists appeared at close quarters and there was a hand-to-hand struggle in which the unknown soldier [Pendlebury] killed three with his revolver and I the fourth. Immediately afterwards he told me to direct covering fire towards the road.' Markatatos recalled that Pendlebury went ahead and, whilst kneeling, taking cover at the corner of a cottage, was wounded in his right breast. 'It was impossible to move the man and we were in a desperate position, so I went on firing at the Germans until my ammunition was exhausted, when we were taken prisoner.' Pendlebury was left in the house of one of his 'followers', Giorgios Drosoulakis, whose wife Aristea took him in and laid him on a bed. All that could be made out in the Englishman's delirious mutterings were 'John, John' and what sounded like 'Bleberry'. Later another German patrol arrived with a doctor, who gave Pendlebury an injection and dressed his wounds; the doctor left, promising to return, but did not reappear.

The next day the battle resumed in earnest: more paratroopers descended, some of whom set up a field gun at positions close to the Drosoulakis house. Pendlebury remained inside for two days, before the paratroopers discovered him: a badly wounded man in a Greek shirt, who wore no uniform, had no dog tags and would not answer their questions. Eventually they took him outside, propped him up against a door and shouted a question at him. Three times Pendlebury was heard to say 'No'. The soldiers lost their patience and shot him dead. Crete's most devoted British friend fell to the ground.

John Pendlebury died somewhere in the first few days of the battle. He had done his best to prepare the islanders for occupation and in the end had given his life for them. The legend of this brave man lived on through the war and even the mention of his name came to torment the Germans. Nick Hammond later wrote of his friend: 'It had always been his intention to stay in Crete and lead the resistance, he never talked as if any other course was possible . . . he felt himself a Cretan and in Crete he would stay until victory was won.'

6

The Occupation Begins

By 1 June, Crete was in German hands. The invading troops had paid dearly for their victory. Crete became known as the graveyard of the Fallschirmjäger: the German 11th Airborne Corps committed more than 24,000 troops to the battle and lost almost a fifth of that number, and a huge amount of materiel – 370 aircraft destroyed or damaged, including 143 Junkers 52s.

In July, Generalleutnant Student, whose brainchild Operation *Merkur* was, stood in front of his Führer to receive a Knight's Cross of the Iron Cross. Hitler later told Student: 'We shall never do another airborne operation. Crete proved that the days of the airborne corps are over. Airborne forces are a weapon of surprise. In the meantime the surprise factor has exhausted itself.' Student wrote: 'Those who fought on Crete have to be proud, attackers and defenders alike. The name of the island is connected with bitter memories. I admit I was wrong in several considerations when I proposed this attack. The result was, not only did I lose many paratroopers, whom I considered my children, but that the paratrooper formation which I created disappeared.'

The fog of war cleared, quiet settled over the island and the long night of occupation began. German soldiers had landed expecting that they would be welcomed with open arms and were outraged that the civilian population met them with force and violence. The Wehrmacht had a clear view of what was acceptable soldier-like behaviour and, for them, the Cretans had breached it. They were war criminals who had committed atrocities for which they must be punished.

The thirst for revenge was born even before the battle for Crete ended. On the morning of 23 May, General Papa Ringel, commander of 5th Gebirgsjäger, issued the following notice to his men:

> The murder of a German Airman on 22 May has proved that the Greek population, in civil or German uniforms, is taking part in the fighting. They are shooting or stabbing wounded to death and removing rings from them and also mutilating and robbing corpses. Any Greek civilian taken with a firearm in his hands is to be shot immediately, as is anyone caught attacking the wounded . . .
>
> Hostages (men between 18 and 55) are to be taken from the villages at once, and the civilians are to be informed that if acts of hostility against the German army take place these will be shot immediately. The villagers in the area are to be informed that 10 Greeks will die for every German.

On 31 May, General Student, with the approval of Göring, issued an order calling for immediate reprisals:

> It is certain the civilian population including men, women and boys have taken part in the fighting, committed sabotage, mutilated and killed wounded soldiers. It is therefore high time to combat all cases of this kind, to undertake reprisals and punitive expeditions which must be carried out with exemplary terror.
>
> The harshest measures must be taken and I order the following: shooting for all cases of proven cruelty, and I wish this to be done by the same units who have suffered such atrocities. The following reprisals will be taken:

1. Shooting.
2. Fines.
3. Total destruction of villages by burning.
4. Extermination of the male population of the entire region.

My authority will be necessary for measures under 3 and 4. All these measures must, however, be taken rapidly and omitting all formalities. In view of the circumstances the troops have a right to this and there is no need for military tribunals to judge beasts and murderers.

The victors needed no second bidding. On 2 June, twenty-five-year-old Oberleutnant Horst Trebes, who had grown up in the Hitler Youth, visited Wehrmacht photographer Franz-Peter Weixler telling him to expect to see 'something interesting' that afternoon. He was going to lead a punitive expedition to Kondomari, where the mutilated bodies of some German paratroopers had been found. Weixler immediately protested, saying that it would be no better than murder. Weixler later claimed that he asked to speak to a senior officer, to stop the cull, but was refused. He went back to Trebes and found him briefing the troops, telling them that the job was to be done with great speed: 'In reprisal for our comrades who had been murdered.'

The expedition set off, four lorries of members of 111 Battalion *Luftlandesturme* Regiment, commanded by Trebes. With him were two lieutenants, an interpreter, about twenty-five paratroopers and Weixler. En route they stopped by the corpses of more comrades. One lay on the ground, his feet caught in the canopy of his parachute; another lay on his stomach, his parachute dangling on its lines above his body. Both men had died as they hit the ground, their bodies bloated; their faces black, crawling with flies; rotting and unrecognisable. Trebes made another speech about the Greek barbarians who had dared mutilate the men.

The lorries ground into Kondomari, disgorging angry

paratroopers who stormed into the houses. The terrified inhabitants were forced out at gunpoint, by soldiers screaming and shov-
ing them along the unmade up road towards the centre of the
village. A woman asked one of the soldiers what they were doing;
he ignored her, motioning her to join the others. Behind her a
tough-looking elderly man in black pantaloons and pale jumper
limped along, leaning on his stick. The houses and streets emptied,
the grassy square filled. Some sat down, others stood, talking in
low voices, eyeing the soldiers disbelievingly. A group of villagers
stood round Oberleutnant Trebes listening while a German interpreter told them of their crimes. Some of the soldiers retrieved a
Fallschirmjäger smock with a tear in it which appeared to have
been made by a knife; Trebes ordered them to blow up the house
where it was found. One villager came forward and confessed to
the killing; another, a young man, began to argue with the
interpreter.

Then the women were separated from the men, who sat on the
edge of the road, waiting. For a while nothing happened, then the
men were told to stand and were marched towards some trees,
among the olive groves; behind the trees was a high dry stone
wall, cutting off any chance of escape. There was no question of a
trial. The soldiers bearing rifles and automatic weapons formed a
ragged line, some kneeling some standing. The Cretan men
huddled round and to the side of a gnarled old tree. Weixler again
implored Trebes to call off the executions and return to base with
the man who had confessed. Trebes refused and told the women
that when the men had been shot, they would have two hours to
bury them. Somehow Weixler helped a few of the villagers to
escape. He photographed the entire proceedings with his 35mm
Leica. The surviving images have an aura of unreality. Clean-
shaven young men in crisp white Greek shirts, black waistcoats,
modern pullovers; some seemingly calm, others with arms crossed,
wearing wry half-smiles; the stern, the moustachioed, the bespectacled; middle-aged men in straw summer hats; elderly men in

traditional Cretan dress. Trebes shouted an order the Cretans could not understand; the soldiers raised their weapons. Another order and the quiet of the afternoon was broken by the crash of small-arms fire. Some men fell at once; others instinctively turned their backs, arms raised against the fusillade of bullets; some fell mid-flight, metres from their compatriots; none escaped. The men were reduced to a mass of corpses, huddled into each other and the ground, bodies twisted and misshapen.

The executions took about fifteen seconds. Dust hovered over the scene, kicked up by the bullets. The soldiers stopped firing, the dust slowly settled and the distraught wailing of the women filled the air, growing louder and more agonised as they tried to understand what the soldiers had just done to them. In the moments that followed Weixler photographed the bodies. He asked Trebes if he knew what he had done. The young Nazi replied that he had merely carried out Göring's orders. The soldiers cleared their weapons and returned to the vehicles.

Next, it was the turn of Kandanos, where, during the invasion, a small detachment of German motorcycle troops, armed with MG34 sidecar-mounted machine guns, had tried to move through the village on their way south to secure the port of Paleochora. The villagers barred the way at Floria and the next day ambushed troops of the 5th Gebirgsjäger at Kandanos Gorge. Outnumbered and heavily outgunned, the villagers fought for two days before retreating to the mountains.

On 3 June soldiers from the 11th Battalion, 1st *Luftlande* Assault division, stormed into Kandanos, executed about 180 of men, women and children, slaughtered the livestock and burned down the houses. Other villages in the area, including Floria and Kakopetro, met the same fate. Kandanos was declared a 'dead zone' into which Cretans were forbidden to enter. Signs were put up on all the roads into the village saying: 'Here stood Kandanos, destroyed in retaliation for the bestial ambush murder of a paratrooper platoon and a half-platoon of military engineers by armed men and women. Never to be rebuilt again.'

A few days later Göring awarded young Trebes the Knight's Cross for 'bravery on Crete'. Weixler was court-martialled for taking photographs and helping some of the Kondomari villagers to escape.

7

Fortress Crete

In June 1940, General Student left for mainland Europe and was replaced with General Andrae, a senior commander in the Luftwaffe and former head of the state police in Germany. Chania was chosen as the headquarters of '*Festung Kreta*' — Fortress Crete — with a divisional commander in Archanes, south of Heraklion, who was given the Villa Ariadne, sometime home of John Pendlebury. Control of the island was shared with their Axis partners, the Italians. The Germans held the most strategically important regions in the west — Chania, Rethymnon and Heraklion — while the Italians, under General Angelo Carta, were given command of the more minor eastern provinces of Sitia and Lasithi. All towns were heavily garrisoned and supported by a system of outposts. The Germans used two security forces: the *Feldgendarmerie*, military police, and the *Geheime Feldpolizei*, the field secret police. Later they were able to call upon the *Jagdkommando* Schubert — a paramilitary force set up by a German of Greek origin, Friedrich 'Fritz' Schubert, nicknamed 'The Turk'. He recruited violent men — criminals and murderers — to terrorise the islanders using torture, rape, beatings and burning.

In the towns and cities the regime began to establish itself with increasing efficiency. In Heraklion, on the first day of peace, engineers retrieved a huge electric motor that had been used in the harbour and used it to pump the town's water supplies. The streets were cleared of barricades, and the detritus of battle was gathered up. Hundreds of parachutes were retrieved and piled into the water of the Morozoni Fountain in Lion Square where they were washed by local women for reuse. Frau Bauritz presented herself to the German intelligence service and gave them her lists of German-speaking students. These young people were rounded up and pressed into service as translators. Frau Bauritz herself was recruited as a translator at the Kreiskommandantur, the German headquarters in the centre of the town.

While control of the towns and more accessible villages was comparatively simple, the wild mountains, populated by warriors whose ancestors had fought invaders for over three hundred years, were another matter. It was here that the resistance was born and operated. If the Cretans themselves found the mountains danger-ous, even the toughest Axis paratroopers and Alpine soldiers would find them terrifying. For many months after the German invasion they avoided going near them, and when eventually they had to take the fight to the guerrillas, lodged in mountain eyries, they went in force, finding safety in numbers, brute force and firepower.

Although most of the Allied troops left behind became prison-ers of war, about a thousand remained in hiding after the German victory. Most lived in the mountain areas and were looked after by the Cretans, despite the risks: anyone caught harbouring fugitives could expect the destruction of their houses and execution. In the high villages, it was possible for stranded Allied soldiers to move about, in uniform, carrying weapons. British soldiers could be seen sitting in cafés, smoking cigarettes and chatting up the girls, while their Cretan hosts plotted the overthrow of the Nazis. Acts of defiance surfaced at all levels: when the Germans issued new ID cards to the Cretan population, 'the village policeman provided blank passes to British soldiers on the run, and even affixed their signature too'.

General Andrae, Commander of Crete, ordered leaflets to be dropped over the mountains proclaiming:

SOLDIERS
OF THE
ROYAL BRITISH ARMY, NAVY, AIR FORCE!
- - - - - - -
There are MANY OF YOU STILL HIDING in the
mountains, valleys and villages.
You have to PRESENT yourself AT ONCE TO THE
GERMAN TROOPS.
Every OPPOSITION will be completely USELESS!
Every ATTEMPT TO FLEE will be in VAIN.
The COMMING WINTER will force you to leave the
mountains.
Only soldiers, who PRESENT themselves AT ONCE
will be sure of a HONOURABLE AND SOLDIERLIKE
CAPTIVITY OF WAR. On the contrary who is met in
civil-clothes will be treated as a spy.
                    THE COMMANDER OF KRETA

Escaping soldiers tried to make their way south where they hoped
to find some sort of vessel to take them to Egypt. Many were led
back across the mountains by Cretan guides to the region on the
south coast by the Monastery of St John the Theologian at Preveli,
where the men were hidden and, at night, flashed torch signals
from the beach, hoping they might be spotted by Allied craft
patrolling the coast. After a few weeks, with no sign of a submarine or motor launch, the Cretans decided it was too risky to go on
using the monastery and sent the men back into the protection of
the surrounding villages.

An engineer from Rethymnon, Dimitri Bernidakis, devised a
new signalling system for the stranded soldiers: a red light to flash
the message in Morse and a green light as a reference point. Both
lights were set up in an open-fronted hut where they could be seen
from the sea but not from the land. The signal the troops flashed
was: 'SOS we are British. Don't answer. We are on the beach waiting for you. Take the green light as a guide. German coastguards
1000 metres either side.' For nearly two months the message
winked into the darkness, with no success. In the meantime some
soldiers and Greek civilians managed to escape – in caïques, fishing boats, small abandoned naval craft – anything that seemed

seaworthy. The lucky ones who made it to Egypt were sent to be debriefed by British intelligence officers at GHQ in Cairo, where it was decided to send a reconnaissance party to Crete to explore the possibility of rescuing more Allied soldiers. Former merchant seaman Commander Francis Pool, RNR, was sent to the island in command of HM Submarine *Thrasher*. Before the war 'Skipper' Pool had been in charge of the Imperial Airways flying-boat operation based at the former leper colony on the island of Spinalonga in north-eastern Crete, and the re-fuelling station at Elunda Bay; he knew the waters around Crete and spoke fluent Greek.

For fifteen nights *Thrasher* patrolled the south coast looking for any signs of life. At 22:00 hours on 26 July 1941, off the beach at Preveli, the crew spotted the green light and flashing red Morse signal. Pool was put ashore with his Cretan guide, Stratis Liparakis. Hours later the submarine commander was face to face with the abbot of Preveli monastery, Agathangelos Lagouvardos, an immense, heavily bearded, twenty-five-stone man in long black robes. They discussed how many soldiers there were in hiding, and how many Pool could take back with him. Just before dawn the next morning, *Thrasher* touched bottom off a small harbour at Limni. With the help of two commandos and a couple of naval officers, 78 Allied soldiers were guided down the beach and put on board the submarine, crammed in alongside the crew.

Thrasher departed for Alexandria and Pool stayed behind on the island to continue gathering information. It became clear that the number of Allied soldiers requiring rescue was greater than anyone had thought. In the forests near St Apostoli Amariou, Pool and Lagouvardos established temporary headquarters. The two men set about meeting influential Cretans, including the kapitans who had been working with archaeologist John Pendlebury, and a key figure in the andartes, Colonel Andreas Papadakis. Papadakis had appointed himself head of AEAK, 'the Supreme Committee of Cretan Struggle', which he and six other patriots had formed in the ruins of Chania two weeks after the German invasion. AEAK's aims were to organise an intelligence network and carry out acts of sabotage against the occupying forces. They counted among their number the chief of police in Rethymnon.

Colonel Papadakis was one of the many Cretans who offered sanctuary to stranded Allied soldiers. Among those sheltering in the colonel's grand house, above the village of Kali Sykia, was an escapee from Galatas POW camp named Jack Smith-Hughes. Smith-Hughes a rotund, Greek-speaking British Army subaltern, had been a barrister before the war and was in charge of the Royal Army Service Corps field bakery in Chania. After making his way across the White Mountains in May, he became one of the thousands left behind on the beaches at Sfakia.

Smith-Hughes suggested that Papadakis accompany them to Egypt, to liaise with SOE Cairo about how the resistance on Crete should be organised and encouraged. On 9 August, Smith-Hughes, Pool, Abbot Lagouvardos and Colonel Papadakis met to discuss the possibilities. A translator, Manolis Vassilakis, minuted the meeting.

Papadakis asked Commander Pool if he had come to do more than rescue marooned British soldiers. Pool said that the main purpose of his expedition was to look at organising the Cretan resistance; he hoped Papadakis would accompany him to Cairo. Papadakis, who could be difficult, said he was not sure and would have to talk to his comrades. Then Pool asked if Papadakis had ever met Kapitan Satanas and if the kapitan could supply a radio to communicate with Cairo. Finally Pool asked who was going to be in overall charge of the resistance; he wondered about Nikolaos Plastiras, the much-admired war hero and republican who was living in exile in France.

The men talked on in the shade of an oak tree. When they finished, Commander Pool and Colonel Papadakis signed and approved the minutes. The men split up, having agreed to meet again on 19 August when the next British vessel was due to arrive and take Pool back to Alexandria. The link between Crete and the

free world, broken on 20 May, had been restored, although weak
and uncertain.

News of the Allied submarine rescues spread amongst the people
of Crete and the work of gathering up the remaining stragglers
began, fuelled by the rumour that the British might be back in a
few months to liberate the island. The Cretan guerrilla leaders set
about devising techniques for leading bands of soldiers across the
mountains and the use of wireless sets to coordinate operations.

Soon runners became an important link in the chain, both for
the resistance cells and future SOE operations. One of these, a
young man called Giorgios Psychoundakis, became a part of the
escape network, leading soldiers along routes from his village of
Asi Gonia, handing them on in relays to other guerrillas who
protected them and saw them safely on their way. Psychoundakis
had a lively sense of humour and a winning personality. A former
shepherd boy, he had an intimate knowledge of the west part of
the island and of travelling across mountains and open ground
by night. Patrick Leigh Fermor, who came to know him well,
recalled: 'When the moon rose he got up and threw a last swig
of raki, a fierce and addictive clear spirit tasting of aniseed down
his throat with the words, "Another drop of petrol for the
engine," and loped towards the gap in the bushes with the
furtiveness of a stage Mohican or Groucho Marx. He turned
round when he was on all fours at the exit, rolled his eyes, raised
a forefinger portentously, whispered, "the Intelligence Service",
and scuttled through like a rabbit. A few minutes later we could
see his small figure a mile away moving across the next moonlit
fold of the foothills of the White Mountains, bound for another
fifty-mile journey.'

Psychoundakis's description of a journey from Vourvouré to the
village of Platanos in the Amari valley gives some idea of the
physical demands of the work. The outward journey took four
nights. On the third night an exhausted Psychoundakis arrived at

the house of Niko Souris, a Greek from Alexandria who was working for the British, rounding up stragglers. They talked for a bit
and then Psychoundakis went to bed, 'Tired to my bones'. The
next day the two men set off at dawn and a strange thing happened,
Giorgios could not recognise Niko as the man he had talked to the
night before: 'I gazed and gazed at him all the way but utterly
failed to find even the faintest similarity . . . I understood that my
great weariness the night before must have made me see him
otherwise, and today, when I had recovered a little, I saw him as
he really was.' When he finally reached his destination he sat
down to rest but when it came to setting off on the return leg,
'We found walking afterwards all the harder . . . Finding two bits
of wood we broke them and used them as walking sticks to hobble
along . . . This was my first long march and it was a more exhausting one than any other I made. It was not really so long compared
with others I undertook . . . but I was not used to it yet.'

It was not long before the Wehrmacht tried to penetrate the
escape network. Hauptmann Paul Schmidt, head of counter-espionage, devised a ruse which he hoped would lure the locals into
revealing the points on the coast from where the rescuers were
operating. He sent officers disguised as British soldiers into the
hills asking to be taken to the submarines. Most of the mountain
people realised what was happening and pretended not to know
anything about the wandering British or the rescue missions; one
or two unfortunates fell for the trick and were arrested and shot.
In the region of Asi Gonia, a key safe haven, the German spies
appeared, dressed in British uniforms, and were immediately
rumbled, villagers and andartes shouting and threatening them;
some were thrashed 'like donkeys' and led off, bound with ropes,
to be handed in to the island authorities as 'escaping POWs'.

The behaviour of the villagers and appearance of andartes in Asi
Gonia attracted the attention of the Germans, as had Colonel
Papadakis's expeditions in broad daylight to Preveli monastery,
which some had warned were foolhardy. On 25 August 1941,

German troops arrived in force and surrounded the monastery, which they plundered and wrecked. They took away all foodstuffs, including livestock, and set up strongpoints in the area and at the nearby harbour of Limni. Preveli became redundant as a hiding place, and the British no longer had a safe harbour from which to retrieve their soldiers.

The Cretans set about devising new rendezvous points on the south-west coast. The rallying point in the mountains was the beautiful village of Yerakari in the Amari valley, situated in the foothills of Mount Kedros and Mount Ida, a place where the inhabitants were loyal to the resistance cause. Escaping soldiers were led from village to village, all converging on Yerakari. The Germans eventually declared the south coast of the island a forbidden zone. In another attempt to stop the British troops escaping, the authorities confiscated fishing boats; even so a small trickle of caïques made it to mainland Greece carrying soldiers and olive oil; they returned with cigarettes and Cretan 5th Division soldiers who had been marooned after the Greek surrender.

The summer of 1941 had been particularly hot and dry, and was followed by a long hard winter. Conditions for ordinary Cretans deteriorated very quickly. Giorgios Psychoundakis returned home from shepherding Allied soldiers to discover that his father's entire flock of sixty sheep had been stolen: a terrible blow. A flock of sheep could mean life and death to a family, especially when the occupying forces were requisitioning foodstuffs. There was nothing Psychoundakis could do: under the Germans the Cretan state, always prone to lawlessness, had ceased to exist. The philosophical Giorgios left his revenge in God's hands.

By the winter of 1941/42, food was becoming scarce all over Crete and even basic supplies, such as shoe leather, ran out. Soon old car tyres were being cut up for footwear: a skilled man could get a dozen pairs out of a single tyre. In the mountain areas, the people fell back on subsistence living – grass soup, wild herbs, snails. In the towns, the population was on the verge of starvation.

On the Greek mainland the situation was worse: it was estimated that in Athens, by Christmas 1941, a thousand civilians a day were dying of starvation. The Greeks call this period 'The Great Famine'. In February 1942, Hermann Göring wrote in his diary: 'The inhabitants of occupied areas have their fill of material worries. Hunger and cold are the order of the day. People who have been this hard hit by fate, generally speaking, do not make revolutions.'

8

Ungentlemanly Warfare

British wartime policy in Crete was dominated by political as well as military objectives. In 1943, John Melior Stevens, in charge of the Greek desk at SOE Cairo, stated in a report: 'As I understand it, the aims of the British Government in Greece are twofold: first to obtain the greatest military effort in the fight the Axis, and, second, to have in post-war Greece a stable government friendly to Great Britain, if possible a constitutional Monarchy.' Stevens was right, Churchill wanted Greece to remain a monarchy and did not want the communists to gain political power. The resistance movement on Crete, therefore, needed to be directed by the British. Special Operations Executive officers were briefed to prevent any communist-inspired groups from getting a foothold on the island and to disrupt the use of Crete as a staging post in the supply chain to the Axis armies in North Africa.

SOE was a shadowy affair. Few of the officers working in the field can have had a clear idea of the structure of the organisation in which they served, and neither were they meant to. The organisation had its roots in the pre-war intelligence services. In July 1939, Neville Chamberlain signed a document that was to become SOE's founding charter. 'A new organisation shall be established forthwith to coordinate all action, by way of subversion and sabotage against the enemy overseas,' the paper stated. 'This organisation will be known as the Special Operations Executive . . . It will be important that the general plan for irregular offensive operations should be in step with the general strategic conduct of the war.' A Foreign Office paper defined the methods of SOE as including 'Industrial and military sabotage, labour agitation and strikes, continuous propaganda, terrorist attacks against traitors and German leaders, boycotts and riots . . . We need absolute secrecy, a certain fanatical enthusiasm, willingness to work with people of different nationalities and complete political reliability'. Churchill described the organisation as being 'The ministry of ungentlemanly warfare'.

In the early years of the war in the Middle East SOE was still finding its way. Agents going into the field were largely untrained amateurs, making things up as they went along. One Agent remembered that the course placed emphasis on unarmed combat and the use of explosives for sabotage, which one officer said 'anyone with an ounce of schoolboy left in him is bound to enjoy'.

Another said that in his training, 'I was initiated into the mysteries of plastic light explosive, slow burning fuses, detonators and primer cord, and was given detailed instruction in the most effective method of blowing up a railway line. The knowledge that no railway existed on Crete did not dampen my immediate ardour and each morning I happily destroyed an increasingly longer stretch of the metals laid for us to practise on in the desert round our camp. These daily explosions in the sand represented all the training I received before being recalled to Cairo.'

SOE's Cairo headquarters and SOE's main headquarters, at Baker Street, London, retained separate identities (until they were forced together in the autumn of 1942, and even then Cairo was seen as enjoying far too much freedom). Eventually SOE Cairo set up schools in Egypt, with a parachute school at Kabrit north of Suez, and operations in Albania, Greece, Crete and Yugoslavia were handled by a section known as Force 133.

In Cairo there were two clandestine intelligence forces: SOE and the Inter-Services Liaison Department (ISLD), a cover name for MI6. Both were based in a large, grey, pillared block called Rustom Buildings (known to local taxi drivers as 'the secret building'). ISLD was concerned with intelligence gathering; there would always be a certain wariness at what was seen as the gung-ho approach of many of their colleagues in Force 133 SOE. The two organisations sometimes acted in unison and sometimes in competition. 'Nobody who did not experience it,' wrote one British colonel, 'can possibly imagine the atmosphere of jealousy, suspicion, and intrigue which embittered the relations between secret and semi-secret departments in Cairo during the summer of 1941, or for that matter for the next two years . . .' Ralph Stockbridge wrote that SOE was 'basically a bunch of adventurers, while ISLD was a very mixed bag. SOE personnel were always treated as officers and gentlemen, not as agents.'

In Zamalek, an expensive and glamorous part of Cairo, close to the exclusive Algezira Sporting Club, a group of SOE agents congregated in a house they named Tara, after the legendary seat of the High Kings of Ireland.

Tara was first acquired by a young SOE recruit, Billy Moss, who thought it would be more fun to live there than in the official SOE hostel at Heliopolis, known as 'Hangover Hall'. Moss was recruited to Force 133 SOE in September 1943 at the age of twenty-three. He was born in Japan to a Russian émigrée mother and her wealthy English businessman husband. He had the sort of 'exotic' background that appealed to some SOE Cairo recruiters; a certain worldliness, a strong sense of adventure, and very useful linguistic skills. Moss was a tall, handsome, 'devilishly languid man. An adventurer with a literary bent and an attractive air of unaffected self deprecation.' At the outbreak of war he joined the Coldstream Guards as an ensign and saw action fighting with Montgomery's 8th Army in North Africa.

'I found Tara, a whole villa, by chance,' Moss recalled; I 'was very careful who to have in it'. The house was grand, and came with its own cook and several other servants, including a butler called Abbas. At its centre was a vast ballroom, with floor-to-ceiling windows and a sprung parquet dancefloor over which hung two huge crystal chandeliers. Moss moved in with Pixie, his

Alsatian puppy, and began to look for kindred spirits within Force 133 to join him.

An early housemate was the Polish Countess Zofia Roza Maria Jadwiga Elzbieta Katarzyna Aniela Tarnowska, or Sophie, and soon nicknamed by Moss 'Kitten'; they would marry in 1945. The countess was reckless and headstrong. When her mother sent her to a convent she rebelled, stood on a pudding to prove it was inedible and ran away, refusing to return. She and her first husband, Andrew Tarnowski, had a son who died, aged two, in July 1939, the same day that she gave birth to their second son, Jan. When war broke out Sophie declared that she would never abandon Poland and burnt her passport; but when the German army flooded across the Polish frontier she fled with her son and husband, leaving behind an aristocratic world of riches and privilege. The journey was the start of a series of adventures that two years later took them to Cairo. On the way, Sophie's son died and her marriage to Andrew broke down. She used her connections with the British governor in Cairo to help her found the Polish branch of the International Red Cross and spent her days nursing badly injured soldiers and airmen and her nights with Cairo's high society. When Moss met Sophie, he realised she was perfect for Tara and persuaded her to move in. Sophie arrived equipped with a swimming costume, a uniform, an evening dress and two mongooses (both named Kurka) which shared her bed. Sophie's initial impressions of her future husband were: 'extremely good looking, he danced well, he was amusing. He was a very good companion.' Sophie's reputation was protected by a fictitious chaperone, Madame Khayatt, who suffered from 'distressingly poor health' and was never seen.

Another recruit to the household was Xan (Alexander Wallace) Fielding, an athletic, boyish-looking young man. Like Moss, Fielding was ex-Charterhouse. Like many Force 133 SOE agents, he was also a classicist and a linguist.

They soon welcomed the handsome name-dropping buccaneer,

Patrick Leigh Fermor, fresh from his exploits with Cretan andartes. Since his earliest years, Leigh Fermor had seemed 'impervious to all forms of external discipline': he had even been expelled from his school in Cambridge as a young boy on the grounds that he was too dangerous a mixture of 'sophistication and recklessness'. There is a legend about him at school that he used to creep into the gym, climb up the exercise ropes and walk backwards and forwards, like an acrobat, along the narrow beam from which they hung.

In 1933, two months after his eighteenth birthday, and the year in which Hitler proclaimed the 'Thousand Year Reich', Leigh Fermor took off across Europe, intent on walking to Constantinople. With him he carried the *Oxford Book of English Verse* and a copy of Horace's *Odes*. Leigh Fermor's considerable charm and resourcefulness attracted invitations from members of the European establishment and aristocracy: his itinerary was studded with châteaux, palazzi and Schlösser where he was a welcome and entertaining guest. In 1935 he reached Greece and became involved in a campaign by Royalist forces in Macedonia to stop a Republican revolution.

Other Tara habitués included two Force 133 agents operating in Albania: Lieutenant Colonel 'Billy' McLean was a doyen of White's and had fought as a guerrilla leader with Orde Wingate's Gideon Force in Abyssinia; by the time he was twenty-four he been promoted lieutenant colonel. The other was David Crespigny Smiley, whose father was a baronet and whose mother was the daughter of Sir Claude Champignon de Crespigny, a balloonist, sportsman and adventurer. After the war Smiley came to hold the record for most falls in the Cresta Run. He described the days spent at Tara as the happiest time of his life. 'I loved it. I really loved it. We were all such good friends. I don't ever remember an angry or a cross word. We all got on frightfully well.'

Tara became the hottest social spot in Cairo, its guests including diplomats, writers, war correspondents and royalty; King Farouk of

Egypt turned up at the house one night with a case of champagne. The inhabitants of Tara awarded each other nicknames and had a bronze plaque made which they screwed to the front door of the villa. It declared that the house was lived in by, amongst others, Princess Dnieper-Petrovsk (Sophie Tarnowska); Sir Eustace Rapier (McLean); the Marquis of Whipstock (Smiley); the Hon. Rupert Sabretache (Rowland Winn); Lord Hugh Devildrive (Xan Fielding); Lord Rakehell (Leigh Fermor) and Mr Jack Jargon (Moss).

Life at Tara was high-octane and not for the faint-hearted. During the days the group could be found sleeping off hangovers, sunbathing on the roof, or 'hustling things at the neighbours'. Moss wrote in his diary that the entertainments at Tara included mock bull-fights in the ballroom, one of which ended with a sofa being set alight and thrown blazing through a window. (Leigh Fermor was notorious for falling asleep with a lighted cigarette in his hand and waking up to find his surroundings on fire.) Another night a Polish officer was encouraged to shoot out the lights. For their first Christmas together in December 1943, Leigh Fermor cooked turkey stuffed with amphetamines (Benzedrine tablets). Sophie, who acted as hostess, remembered that in Poland they had made liqueurs by adding soft fruit to vodka. She tried to recreate this by adding prunes to raw alcohol in the bath. The result was not a success. After two days the mixture was tasted and found to be disgusting. The two agents who tried it passed out and Sophie complained that they should have left it for at least three weeks before trying it.

On the eve of an agent's deployment, 'there would be a big party and a car would call and those who were going to be dropped into enemy territory left just like that. Without a goodbye, without anything,' recalled Sophie Tarnowska. 'We never allowed ourselves to be anxious about them. We believed that to be anxious was to accept the possibility of something dreadful happening to them.'

It was men like these who were to dominate the work of SOE all over the Middle East, in the Balkans, Greece, and on the island of Crete.

9

The Cretan Resistance is Born

For Colonel Michail Filippakis the fall of Crete was especially bitter. He had fought in the defence of Heraklion and at the end of the battle had been a member of the party escorting the mayor of the town to make his formal surrender to the Germans. The ceremony took place in Lion Square. After nine days of fighting the colonel was exhausted and needed a shave. In spite of this he wore an immaculate uniform, with a shining Sam Browne belt across his chest. Next to him stood the mayor, nervous but smart in a white blazer and straw hat. In front of them stood a German Fallschirmjäger officer wearing a gleaming new jump smock, and camouflaged helmet, his parachutist's belt tight round his waist emphasising his athletic physique. Over the German's shoulders Colonel Filippakis could see armed guards and the streets to the square blocked off by military vehicles mounted with heavy machine guns.

The colonel had not only lost his command, his home in the city had been destroyed in the bombing. After the surrender he had no choice but to head south to the mountains just above the south coast and the village where he had been born, Achendrias. The house he owned there was small and primitive; he was nearly penniless.

When he heard that a band of civilians were trying to escape on a boat that had lain abandoned for more than four years he warned them that they would die. Either the boat – which was little more than a wreck – would sink or it would be spotted and strafed by the Luftwaffe. The men ignored him. They cut down a telegraph pole to make a mast and tore open two mattresses to get at the cotton stuffing which they used to caulk the rotten wood of the hull.

Filippakis was impressed and thought they might possibly get through. He wrote a message to GHQ Middle East, put it in a bottle and gave it to the escapers. The message said that he was going to light a signal fire on a nearby beach at Maridaki. He proposed to do this in exactly one month's time. The men and the bottle set off on a clear bright day, in the makeshift vessel which was named *Argos*.

A month later the colonel kept his word. He and his son went to the beach, collected firewood, and lit a fire. Most of the wood was damp and there was no flame, only a lot of choking smoke. With watering eyes father and son stared into the dark, and to their horror saw a red flashing light which they thought was coming from a German patrol boat. Trapped, they hid behind a few rocks.

The light vanished and they heard the sound of oars. Slowly a small rubber dinghy rowed by two men appeared off the beach. The sailors revealed themselves to be Royal Navy officers; the *Argos* had made it to Egypt; the fugitives had been picked up half dead by a destroyer patrolling ten miles off the Egyptian coast at Mersah Matruh. In the dinghy were stores, including aspirin, bandages, coffee and corned beef for the colonel's village. Filippakis was told to expect some British officers to appear in another month's time and to prepare a hiding place for them. Then the sailors pushed off, rowing the dinghy back to the submarine *Torbay*, from which it had come.

The next month, at night, Colonel Filippakis heard a knock on his door. When he opened it he found himself staring into the faces of two British SOE officers: Jack Smith-Hughes of SOE and Ralph Stockbridge of ISLD. They had brought with them a heavy portable radio, spare batteries and a charging machine. Filippakis welcomed them in. The Cretan arms of SOE and ISLD were in business.

After his escape to Egypt, Smith-Hughes had written a report describing his contact with Colonel Papadakis and the AEAK organisation. Smith-Hughes volunteered to return Crete and help forge links with the colonel and his associates. His offer was accepted, he was rapidly put through Force 133 training and sent with Stockbridge on the *Torbay*.

In addition to developing contacts with resistance leaders, Smith-Hughes's orders were to send military intelligence back to GHQ, and to carry on rounding up British and Commonwealth stragglers. He was given the codename Yanni and dressed in Cretan baggy trousers, high boots, a black shirt and a black-fringed turban, though his bulky frame and pinkish complexion made it difficult for him to look like anything other than an Englishman. Eventually he was persuaded to wear long trousers, like a city dweller. Colonel Papadakis assigned Psychoundakis as Smith-Hughes's runner. After ten weeks Smith-Hughes completed his mission and was recalled to Cairo in December, where he took over the running of SOE's Crete desk.

A few weeks later another SOE officer, Xan Fielding, code-name Aleko, disembarked from the *Torbay*. Other agents followed, including classicist Tom Dunbabin and Patrick Leigh Fermor. Dunbabin hailed from Tasmania and, like John Pendlebury, was a distinguished archaeologist. A fellow of All Souls College Oxford, and former deputy director of the British School in Athens, he could not drive, did not shoot, box, ski or even ride a bike. He was, though, very tough. One night Dunbabin was sleeping with some guerrilla fighters in the mountains, his head resting against a rock as a pillow. A young fighter, a boy of about fourteen, offered Dunbabin a pillow made from the soft packing used in parachute containers. Dunbabin turned down the offer, throwing the pillow away and declaring: 'We are at war!'

Cairo put great store by Dunbabin, rarely acting without asking his opinion, sometimes bringing him back to the Egyptian capital to do so.

In May 1942 it was decided to send parties of commandos drawn from the Special Boat Service and the Special Air Service to attack the airfields on western Crete. Crete had become an important transit camp and supply point for North Africa. Rommel's army and the Germans were winning the war in the desert; the Afrika Korps had routed the Allies and it seemed to be only a matter of time before Rommel took Cairo.

Tom Dunbabin provided the commando parties with local guides: Giorgios Psarakis, Kimonas Zografakis and Kostas Mavrantonakis. The raiders ran into considerable difficulties and with mixed outcomes: one group managed to destroy five aircraft and 200 tons of stores and fuel at Kasteli airfield, while another destroyed or badly damaged twenty Junkers 88 bombers; ten German soldiers were killed in the raids. In reprisals, fifty Cretan civilians – including Jews, a seventy-year-old priest, and a former governor general of the island – were rounded up and executed.

By the summer of 1942 the small group of SOE and ISLD officers on Crete were working closely with andartes, and strengthening the structure of the Cretan resistance. Manolis Paterakis, a slightly built man with a large nose and chin, who in profile looked like Mr Punch, became Patrick Leigh Fermor's right-hand man. His job was to act as the Englishman's guide and liaison officer. He was a brave fighter and former gendarme. Leigh Fermor described him as 'a good egg, wiry as an Indian, crack shot, granite, with a sense of conviviality, irony, stoicism and humour'. Paterakis was the second-born of six boys and had fought against the Germans in the battle for Crete. After the German victory he fled to the mountains and joined a guerrilla group, becoming a senior member of the Cretan resistance.

Yerakari remained an important centre of the resistance, a staging post on the route across the mountains that the British came to call the 'High Spy Route'. The Amari valley – Lotus Land – was a welcome place of refuge to many British agents. The people were so hospitable, wrote Dunbabin, that they 'plucked you by the sleeve as you walked down the narrow street, to come in and drink a glass of wine with them'. John Houseman, who would soon join Tom Dunbabin in Amari, remembered: 'It was rather tiring, to be continually rather afraid of traitors and German patrols, but always without fail, if I went to a village or town, I was offered food, drink and company fit for any "King of the Mountains" as we were so often called.'

Dunbabin succeeded in setting up an extremely efficient intelligence-gathering network. Like Stockbridge he believed in the power of good intelligence and thought it more important than sabotage or other forms of direct action. His radio was kept in a mountain hideout three hours' walk away from another powerful resistance stronghold in Anogia. Messengers came from all over the island with information about Wehrmacht troop movements, shipping in the harbours and anything else that might help GHQ Middle East piece together what the Axis powers were up to. Dunbabin had spies everywhere, even in the Heraklion Kommandantur – where a female agent, Kyveli Sergiou, smuggled confidential military documents to the surgery of Dr Yiamalakis to be photographed and the negatives sent to Dunbabin to be passed on to Cairo.

'Our work consisted chiefly of keeping our finger on the pulse by organising and using a most efficient spy service which covered the whole of the island,' John Houseman wrote later. 'Sabotage was virtually impossible, not because of the difficulty, but because of the small value and the disastrous atrocities which the Germans carried out after the act . . . The danger was not for us personally, for we could always run away, but the danger was with a few families who put us up and offered us their all, for they, if betrayed, had to suffer the loss of their lives and all their belongings and perhaps the burning of the whole village.'

As the resistance became more organised, Colonel Papadakis became more difficult to control. He began to refuse to cooperate with any Cretans who were not part of AEAK (Supreme Committee of Cretan Struggle). On 12 February 1942, in the presence of Xan Fielding, Papadakis and three others held a meeting of the committee of the AEAK. The members drew up a memorandum to be transmitted by Fielding to SOE Cairo. The committee argued that it was the only appropriate organisation for GHQ to deal with. They asked for more agents to be sent to the island, and demanded that they, the committee, should have complete freedom of action and 'must enjoy the absolute trust from General Headquarters'. It also demanded that GHQ did not interfere with the internal workings of AEAK and that it should have the final say in choosing people to work with.

In Cairo, Jack Smith-Hughes wrote a response to Papadakis and sent it to Crete with two Greek SOE recruits: Second Lieutenant Evangelos Vandoulas (nickname Vangelis, codename 'Rich') and Private Apostolos Evangelou (nickname Manolis, codename 'Poor'). The letter stated that it was the Allied intention to liberate Crete as soon as possible and apologised that the British had not already done so. It told him that Vangelis Vandoulas was to be the liaison officer between AEAK and Cairo and that 'he is also authorised by our general to contact every person he judges he has to'.

After delivering the letter the Greek agents rendezvoused with Xan Fielding at the home of Vandoulas's family in Vaphé. When they arrived in the village Vandoulas's father and mother were ecstatic to see their son, who had been away in Egypt for nearly a year. Cousins, uncles and nephews arrived to see the returned hero and vast quantities of retsina and raki were consumed before Vandoulas was left alone with Fielding to talk about the letter and Papadakis. Vandoulas did not mince his words: 'The man's dangerous; I hadn't been with him more than five minutes before he started ranting about his committee and telling me I was under his orders. I told him I was under orders from Cairo and he didn't like that at all. Frankly I don't see how we are going to work with him and his mad ideas.'

Fielding's relationship with Papadakis deteriorated. He found the colonel high-handed: requisitioning supplies dropped by parachute and insisting that they were his to dispose of as he saw fit. He used his own men to collect the drops and would often claim that the supplies had been stolen. When runner Giorgios Psychoundakis complained to Papadakis that his clothes and foot-wear were so worn out that he was practically naked, Papadakis refused to help him and Fielding had to intervene. He argued with the colonel for two hours. Later he admitted to Psychoundakis that he too could not work with the man, even if he was the leader of the resistance on the island. Papadakis accused Dunbabin and Fielding of treachery, saying they were planning to give themselves up to the Germans, that they were going to do this because the Allies in North Africa were on the point of collapse and the Russians were about to surrender.

SOE Cairo needed to take control and get Papadakis out of Crete. After many attempts to persuade him, he eventually agreed to be evacuated off the island in order to get his family to safety. When, on 5 August, the submarine to transport them to Alexandria did not turn up, Papadakis suspected a trap; he threatened to kill Fielding if the submarine did not appear. While the British and the Cretans were arguing on the beach, the Royal Hellenic Navy submarine *Papanikolis* was sailing up and down the coast trying to locate the rendezvous beach. On its first attempt it surfaced close to a fishing boat and almost sank it, causing further delays. The party waited on the beach for three more days; all the while Papadakis's henchmen watched Fielding and kept their Marlin sub-machine guns trained on him. After several frustrating nights the rendezvous point was located and the submarine surfaced off Rodakino beach. On board was Smith-Hughes, who had come along to mollify Papadakis. At last, the colonel who had proved so troublesome to the British was taken off Crete. In Heraklion, Andreas Polentas, took over Papadakis's command.

The SOE and ISLD did not have many radios on the island, but a river of information flowed from them transmitted in Morse code. Spies who had been innocent civilians before the arrival of the Germans collected valuable intelligence about the comings and goings of ships in the harbour, of aircraft from the airfields, troop movements and map references for the position of German military supplies. One SOE agent wrote: 'The information coming out of Crete at that time was of the utmost importance . . . because the Germans were using the island as their main base for the supplies of their forces in North Africa and information concerning their movements was used prior to the Battle of Alamein.'

Agents came and went, delivered by motor launch or submarine. Ralph Stockbridge was taken off the island shortly before Colonel Papadakis. He took with him a young Greek, Lefteris Kalitsounakis, Papadakis's nephew, who had been forced to work for the colonel as almost a slave. Kalitsounakis was persuaded to join ISLD and the men returned to Crete a few weeks later, with Kalitsounakis as Stockbridge's assistant. With them was a third ISLD agent, John Stanley. Their submarine was to be met on the north coast by Patrick Leigh Fermor. Unfortunately Leigh Fermor had drunk a great deal of wine and raki that day and was nowhere to be found. The three men made it by dinghy to what they thought was the right beach. Kalitsounakis went ahead and immediately ran into a barbed-wire fence. They were in a minefield. Kalitsounakis's training in Cairo had included a course on explosives. He knew that a recently exploded mine leaves a smell like almonds, and he could smell almonds. He guessed that some of the minefield must have been detonated by wandering sheep. Very carefully he retraced his path, found the others and told them to walk only in his footsteps. This they did, and managed to unload the supplies from the dinghy. Sometime later they found Leigh Fermor in a deep, raki-induced sleep.

There were other dangers. No one was aware that the Germans had managed to insert a double agent into their midst, a man called Giorgios Komnas, who was a clerk in the Kommandantur at Heraklion. He had provided SOE with some very detailed information about Wehrmacht forces, which he claimed had been taken from ration returns. SOE intelligence officers in Cairo found that some things did not tally. In one report Komnas described in detail an SS battalion based at Prama, commanded by Major von Teitzen. There were no SS battalions on the island.

Cairo sent a signal expressing its concerns to Leigh Fermor, who sent a letter by runner to Andreas Polentas, the man who had taken over from Papadakis. It read:

Headquarters have a strong base to believe that the numbers concerning troops etc., incoming and outgoing with planes or ships, i.e.: The information we have sent recently, are heavily exaggerated. This, if true, can be attributed to two reasons:

a) the agent who sent this information had made a big mistake or

b) had taken these figures from somebody who had deliberately given an exaggerated idea of the forces the enemy has sent to Libya.

Headquarters has asked us to clear this up as soon as possible.

Polentas refused to believe that Komnas was a double agent. He knew that the Germans used certain tactics to fool Allied intelligence and spies. One ploy was to move troops on to air transports off ships in the day and disembark them at night, then take them by lorry to another part of the island. Polentas put the discrepancy in numbers down to ruses such as this. He then did a very rash thing. He was due to meet Vangelis Vandoulas in a cafe in Chania. He took Komnas with him and introduced him to the agent saying, 'My dear Vangelis, it is my pleasure to introduce you to my friend Giorgios Komnas. Dear Giorgios this is my cousin Vangelis Vandoulas. I have already spoken to you about him when he arrived from down there.'

Vandoulas was horrified, 'down there' meant from Egypt. This was a very serious breach of security. Vandoulas stood up shook hands with Komnas, bought him a drink and then apologised and left saying that he had an urgent appointment. He went back to his hotel, found his radio operator, Apostolos, and together they left the city, heading for his home village of Vaphé where he met Leigh Fermor.

Vandoulas told Leigh Fermor what had happened. As they talked a messenger came from Polentas with a warning from Komnas that the *Geheime Feldpolizei* chief in Chania had heard that the RAF had recently made a big supply drop in the area and was ordering a large-scale search. Leigh Fermor immediately moved his headquarters. Vandoulas and his radio operator stayed on in the village.

Early on the morning of 14 November 1942, Vandoulas and Apostolos were having breakfast and getting ready for the 08:00 hours transmission to SOE Cairo when they heard a prolonged whistle: the villagers' signal that German soldiers were in the area. Vandoulas ran out of the house to be confronted by the sight of a German patrol about fifty metres away, talking to a villager, demanding that he identify Vandoulas's house. They stopped Vandoulas and asked him the same question, without realising who they were talking to. Vandoulas said that he thought the man they were looking for was the villager they could see running down the road. Vandoulas then bolted and managed to disappear into the hills.

His radio operator was less fortunate. Apostolos was stuffing signal papers into his pockets and heading for the back door where he was arrested by Germans who had now surrounded the building. Meanwhile Vandoulas's sister Elpida, managed to hide the radio set and other equipment in the attic. Apostolos was marched off for interrogation to Chania. Once the soldiers had gone Elpida took the radio, batteries, signal books and a sub-machine gun to a hiding place in the mountains.

From the moment that Komnas had been introduced to Vandoulas in the cafe in Chania the whole thing had been a plot. Once he knew who Vandoulas was, Komnas had reported this information to the secret police. The messenger sent to Polentas with the warning of the raid was a trick to win the trust of Vandoulas and the others in the resistance. The trick worked, Andreas Polentas, one of the most senior men in the resistance, was arrested and taken to Agyia jail with Apostolos.

At first the prisoners pretended that they did not know each other. They were interrogated for hours and deprived of food. Apostolos's cover story was that he was a black-marketeer going about his business and that Vaphé was one of his regular business haunts. After a few days Polentas and Apostolos were tortured, stripped and kept in unlit cells. The forms of torture became progressively more savage, but neither man broke. In the end they were shot. Apostolos had been a schoolmaster before the war, Polentas a lawyer.

A 'National Revolutionary Court Martial of Crete' was convened in secret to try Komnas, in absentia, for his treachery. One of the witnesses, Gregory Morakis, testified that: 'When I was first summoned to watch Giorgios Komnas I was not the least sure about his treacherous actions, since up to that time he appeared to be an Anglophile. During the course of time I was able to discover that he was working for the German occupation forces and in more particular for the German counter-espionage unit. He thought I was pro-German and thus unveiled to me his secrets, giving orders and information concerning the discovery of the radio and cooperating with the British Intelligence Service.' In his testimony Morakis says that he tried to warn Polentas of the danger and had also warned Leigh Fermor, but nobody would believe him. The court found Komnas guilty and, in 'Verdict No. 1 of the National Revolutionary Court Martial of Crete' ordered that he be captured and executed, and that if possible he should first be interrogated. The verdict was transmitted to Xan Fielding, who asked that Komnas be delivered to his organisation.

In the event Komnas stayed in Chania under the protection of the Germans. He was moved to a safe house surrounded by German billets. Nonetheless, an andartes operation was mounted to execute him. On the night of 22/23 September three men entered the building, one to carry out the sentence and the others to act as bodyguards. The executioner was armed with a knife and had vowed to scrawl the words 'Traitor!' on the walls in Komnas's blood. In the frenzy of the attack he stabbed his victim over and over again. Blood pumped from the writhing body, covering the floor and the bed he was lying on. The executioner had not expected this, or the smell it caused, and began to retch, unable to carry out his promise. He tried to scrub the sticky red blood off his hands with whatever he could find and then fled with his comrades. The Germans found Komnas's body the next day. Almost every piece of cloth in the room, the bedclothes, the curtains, even the tablecloth, was smeared with his blood. He had been stabbed seventeen times, Cretan justice had been done.

10

A Terrible Tragedy

In November 1942, General Bruno Bräuer took over from General Andrae as commander of Fortress Crete. He was forty-nine years old, short, with a slight stammer, and famous among his men for his gleaming gold cigarette case. As a young major he had commanded the elite General Göring Regiment, and on 11 June 1938 became the first German paratrooper to jump from a plane. At the start of the war he was commander of the 1st Fallschirmjäger Regiment and had been part of the forces that stormed through Poland, France and the Low Countries. In Holland he captured Dordrecht Bridge in very heavy fighting and acquired a reputation for extreme bravery.

Had Operation *Seelöwe* (Sealion), the invasion of England, happened Bräuer and his men would have been in the vanguard. His orders were to parachute into Kent, near the village of Paddlesworth, and take the seaside town of Sandgate. But *Seelöwe* was cancelled and on 20 May 1941 Bräuer jumped with elements of 1st and 2nd Fallschirmjäger over the area east of Heraklion with orders to take the airfield. He and his men fought for eight days and achieved nothing. When the Allies in Heraklion heard that German forces from Maleme airport were heading for the town they withdrew to the harbour to await evacuation, thereby handing Bräuer his objective.

Bräuer's initial approach to the command of Crete differed to that of his predecessors, Student and Andrae. He made little of the stories of mutilation that had so enraged Kurt Student and tried to educate his officers about the 'warrior spirit of the Cretans'. Bräuer wrote a report explaining why, in his view, the people had risen up with such ferocity. It was called the 'Memorandum by the German High Command concerning the attitude of the civilian population in Crete towards the German armed forces and the reaction of these'. In it he concluded that many of the reports of atrocities were caused by the general chaos and excitement accompanying the invasion and that it was even possible that some of the reports were imaginary. He pointed out that legitimate troops had been forced to fight in civilian clothes because the speed of the mobilisation had meant that proper uniforms had not been issued. Bräuer explained that the Cretans had spent hundreds of years fighting invaders – Arabs, Venetians, Turks – and had a tradition that every islander is a soldier. Bräuer also concluded that some of the blame could be assigned to 'Captain John Pendlebury, who, disguised as a vice consul appealed to the population to fight', and in whose house were found arms and maps.

Bräuer went to some lengths to try to woo the people under his dominion. He opened the forbidden zone south of Mesara, and sent his ADC on a tour of the Mesara Plain with the unenviable task of making speeches, explaining that the new *Festungskommmandant* was a passionate lover of all things Greek and that his dearest wish was to help and succour the island population.

Leigh Fermor suggested that SOE counter Bräuer's advances and designed a leaflet showing a steel-helmeted German covered in blood and wading among corpses in Cretan dress, against a background of mountains of commandeered wheat and oil jars. The soldier can see that an Allied invasion is coming over the horizon and holds his hands out saying: 'You know I love CRETE and the CRETAN people. Please don't kill me when the bloodthirsty English come!'

Bräuer was under no misapprehension about the loyalty of his subjects: 'Nearly the whole population remains hostile towards the forces of occupation and is still pro-British,' stated one Wehrmacht report. The same report revealed the poor quality of German information regarding British agents on Crete: 'A reconquest of the island by the British is expected in the near future. Account must be taken of the assistance which the civilian population is giving to the two British organisations whose activity on the island has been ascertained, i.e. The espionage organisation of Captain Huse [he meant Smith-Hughes] and the sabotage organisation of Captain Jellicoe.' German intelligence was working in a fog.

Bräuer declared that if the Allies invaded he and his men would fight to the last man and the last round. In the south he tripled the garrison at Askifou to defend the passes against a landing at the bay of Sfakia and in the north he improved the defences at Suda Bay. His men sweated across country on training exercises, working alongside tanks and artillery. They practised street-fighting, scrambling about on exercise in the ruins of villages around Heraklion. Bridges were prepared for demolition; ammunition stocks were built up and underground command bunkers constructed.

Much of the building work was done by forced labour. Leaflets were distributed describing what would be required and detailing the punishments for non-compliance. The area commander for Rethymnon issued the following orders:

1. The Provision of workers for the German Forces.

2. In accordance with the orders of the 'Commandant of the Fortress CRETE', 2.6.41, all inhabitants are liable to compulsory service. All distribution of available labour will be made by the Area Commander and no other arrangements will be valid.

3. The Area Commander will requisition labour by the issue of a requisition form. The whole community are responsible for ensuring that the workers requested are punctually provided.

In exceptional cases individuals will be requisitioned by name and the community as a whole is responsible for their appearance.

4. Requirements of labour in individual parishes are relatively so small that sufficient workers will be left available for agricultural work. It is the duty of the parishes to work out for themselves a fair system of detailing the necessary workers. All able-bodied men between the ages of 16 and 60 are liable for duty. Women and children are liable on special requisition. Workers on Labour Service may not leave their work without express permission nor may they change their occupation unless a substitute is actually available.

5. Workers who refuse to present themselves are to be reported by name to the Area Commander with details of their family and economic status. This does not however relieve the parish of the duty to provide the requested number of workers.

6. The following officials are exempt from Labour Service:-
   State officials.
   Mayors or village headmen and their secretaries.
   Those providing work on essential public services provided this is noted on the back of the Identity card by the Area HQ or a special pass can be produced.
No other exceptions are permitted. Those who are already working on behalf of the German forces or who are in possession of a Green card may not be called upon for work in the parish authorities . . .

7. Refusal to work will be regarded as sabotage and be punished accordingly. The individuals may be punished by reduction of wages, imprisonment, imprisonment in a concentration camp or in severe cases, by court martial. In addition the parish will be subjected to a forced levy in kind of oil and grain etc., and this levy will increase with every day that the refusal of the individual to work continues . . .

A day's hard labour was rewarded with 700 drachma, enough to buy two eggs. The price offered for a requisitioned cow, 120 drachma, was not enough to buy three cigarettes. A British officer in Cairo wrote that the Germans 'know the Cretans hate them and are living for the moment to dig up their rifles and say it with bullets'; the invaders were 'hurt and puzzled at not being loved, and are constantly asking why'.

By the summer of 1943 the war had turned in favour of the Allies. America had joined the struggle and Hitler's armies in the east were defeated at Stalingrad. Huge amounts of equipment began to pour across the Atlantic and a joint Commonwealth–American force invaded French North Africa in Operation Torch. In May, nearly a quarter of a million German and Italian troops surrendered in North Africa. By June, Operation Husky, the plan to invade Sicily, was well under way. Valuable intelligence for Torch and Husky had been painstakingly gathered on Crete and transmitted to the Allies via ISLD radios under the command of Ralph Stockbridge. But the anticipated liberation of Crete did not come. Britain, meanwhile, was keeping a close eye on how the post-war order might look in the Mediterranean.

In July, Leigh Fermor wrote an overview for SOE Cairo, describing the situation on the island from the British point of view. In his 'Report No. 3', typed on thin blue airmail paper, he described living 'in the remote mountains . . . hiding like a lizard among the rocks. This area, though useless for [Communist] party ends, is of great military importance; [here] they are still talking in bated breath of the mass executions [last year] . . . the bulk of the villagers live in a state of terror and abject unresisting peonage to the handfuls of Huns scattered along the coast.'

He described the nature of the resistance organisation on Crete. It was in central and western Crete that the British held most influence and many of these areas had been renamed by SOE agents, their codenames reflecting literary and fantasy schoolboy-ish imaginings: the guerrilla centre at Anogia was called 'Camelot',

while the White Mountains were 'Lost Horizon'; the Amari province retained the name 'Lotus Land'; Heraklion was 'Babylon' and
the Mesara Plain near the secret landing places was 'Badlands'.
Similar codenames were given to the main Cretan guerrilla leaders: one, Periklis Vandoulakis, who had tried to save Polentas
from the *Geheime Feldpolizei*, was 'Orestes'. The left-wing General
Mandakas was called 'Trotsky' and the communists in general
became 'Lollards'.

Leigh Fermor believed that when the Allies arrived, the Cretans
'will follow those officers who showed courage and initiative
during the invasion two years ago and won't give a damn for the
rest . . . If it's a choice between a mediocre officer and a BO-PEEP,
the villagers will follow BO-PEEP every time.' Bo-Peep, the hot-
headed – others described him as 'thug-like' – Manolis Bandouvas,
was a kapitan Leigh Fermor admired to the point of hero worship,
describing him as a 'brave and patriotic man and a born leader. Of
his many faults the only one I would mention here was his sacrifice of truth to his own purposes. We were always on excellent
terms.'

There were concerns that Bandouvas, the other kapitans and
the guerrillas who followed them were being wooed by the
communists, who had called a pan-Cretan conference, to which
the SOE was not invited. One of the two resolutions that the
conference passed said: 'That Greece denounces the King and
Tsouderos Government and refuses to admit the intervention of
Britain after the liberation to restore the monarchy and a Fascist
regime.'

Leigh Fermor always claimed to the Cretans that his stance was
strictly non-political, writing: 'Russia is our ally, Stalin and
Churchill work together in complete harmony. If the communists
wish, we can go for the same here in miniature. Meanwhile, internal Greek politics are no concern of mine, my mission is strictly
military.' This was not altogether true. The SOE went to some
lengths to undermine the communists. Leigh Fermor was worried

that Tom Dunbabin wanted to recruit well-educated men, including doctors, lawyers and other professional men, while the communists on the other hand were targeting 'vital and fighting elements'.

In another of his reports Leigh Fermor described a very personal tragedy. On 5 May 1943 he had accidentally shot and killed his closest Cretan friend, Yanni Tzangarakis, codenamed 'Sancho'. According to Leigh Fermor's account:

> We were sitting round the fire in Siff's sheepfold at Camelot [Anogia] about ten people in all when news came that 300 Germans had arrived and were on their way to where we were. I told everyone to get packed up and take as many rifles as could go round most of the company, including three shepherd lads, cousins of Siff's had been amusing themselves by doing Greek and British arms drill with my rifle and practising loading and unloading . . . all the rifles were lying on their sides newly oiled with their bolts open except mine, and I drew the bolt backwards and forwards easing the springs to see if it was working smoothly after being oiled. Without realising it I had put a round in the chamber. I pressed the trigger and hit Sancho who was sitting by the fire . . . through the left hip . . . I am sorry at letting the firm down like this. It's all a very unhappy business . . .

Any trained soldier given a weapon which has been handled by someone else will normally check to see what state it is in. He will especially want to know if it is loaded. An eye witness says that Leigh Fermor picked up a loaded, cocked weapon, with the safety catch off, and accidently fired it. This is called an 'accidental discharge' and is one of the worst sins a soldier can commit. Had Leigh Fermor done what he claimed, 'eased the springs' to check that the rifle was working, he would have pulled open the bolt, revealing the round in the breech and ejecting it, sending it spinning into space and clattering to the ground. This would have caused him to look down into the magazine to check if there were any other bullets in it before closing the bolt, an action which chambers another round and cocks the weapon. Leigh Fermor's rifle was a 7.92 Mauser; the rounds are over three inches long and made of a brass or steel cartridge holding a copper or lead bullet. The bright yellow or silver of the metal casing is in strong contrast to the deep black 'bluing' of the oiled breech and impossible to miss.

However, none of this happened. Leigh Fermor changed the facts and did so for a good reason: he wanted to protect the person who had really loaded the gun, a child whose kapitan father had recently been executed by the Germans.

Among the ten or so people at the hut were Andreas Papadakis's nephew Lefteris Kalitsounakis, who worked for ISLD, and Manolis Paterakis's cousin, Giorgios Tzitzikas. Earlier in the day, which was very wet and cold, some shepherds, who helped guard the SOE radio, had approached the British asking to be paid for the work. To their fury they were refused, and they went away into the rain. A short while later Yanni appeared escorting a criminal cousin, who had murdered his young nephew and become a liability. If he was sent to trial there was a danger that the Germans would offer him a pardon in return for betraying the guerrillas. The resistance had two options: execute the cousin or send him to the authorities in Egypt, where he would be out of harm's way. It was decided to get him off the island. He had brought great shame on his family. Some thought that Yanni should have executed him on the way to the sheepfold.

The two men sat down next to the warmth of the fire in the hut, trying to dry off. There were some boys from nearby Anogia at the sheepfold and one of them, the boy whose father had been executed, began playing with the rifles, which included Leigh Fermor's captured German Mauser. The gun could be loaded by hand or with a five-round clip and the youngster tried both methods. After a while he got bored and left the rifle loaded, with the safety catch off.

Several of the disgruntled shepherds appeared with the urgent news that 300 German soldiers had appeared and were searching all the houses in the area. They warned that it was only a matter of minutes before they arrived. Leigh Fermor, who was very excitable, ordered everyone in the hideout to pack up and leave. He grasped the Mauser, swinging it round with his finger on the trigger, and the weapon fired. The bullet left the barrel travelling at 2,700 feet per second, it could smash through thirty three inches of dry pine at 100 yards. It hit Yanni in his left hip at point-blank range and his body absorbed the round's colossal force. The deafening noise of the gun firing was followed by a stunned silence. The stench of burnt cordite hung in the air. Everyone stared at Yanni, who was lying on his side by the fire, moaning. Leigh Fermor went slowly over to him, pulled back his friend's soaking wet cloak to reveal that the round had entered his left hip, making a clean wound with hardly any blood. Then, as somebody fetched a field dressing, they cut open his britches and discovered that the bullet had caused terrible damage on its route round Yanni's frame. The Cretan was deep in shock and seemed to be feeling little pain. He murmured, although no one but Leigh Fermor could hear what he was saying. There was no doctor near and no hospital. Within a few minutes Yanni Tzangarakis was dead. His murdering cousin slept through the whole incident. Yanni's body lay in the open until dawn, when they carried him to a nearby ilex grove and buried him.

The tragedy was that the panic-stricken flight from the sheepfold had been in vain. There were no German soldiers: it had been a false alarm raised by the shepherds to get SOE out of the hut and out of the area. The tale that Leigh Fermor later concocted was to protect the youth who had played with his gun. If the true story came out the boy would be punished and the feeling was that he had suffered enough with the death of his father. Yanni was not only a close friend, said Leigh Fermor later, but also 'the best and hardest worker we have ever had'.

The Italians Change Sides

By the summer of 1943 the importance of Crete to both sides in the conflict had shifted again: the war had turned decidedly in the Allies' favour. The second battle of Alamein brought defeat to Rommel and the ejection of the Italo-German army from North Africa. The Soviet victory at Stalingrad in May brought defeats to the Wehrmacht on two fronts – shattering Hitler's strategic visions for the war and forcing the Axis on to the defensive in the East and in the Mediterranean.

The Allies landed on Sicily on 9 July, the start of Operation Husky – the invasion of Italy by land and air. On 24 July the Grand Fascist Council of Italy, meeting for the first time, passed a vote of no-confidence in Mussolini, and invited the exiled King Victor Emmanuel III to reclaim his constitutional powers. *Il Duce* was arrested by the Carabinieri and whisked out of the public eye. He was replaced by Marshal Pietro Badoglio, who started armistice negotiations with the Allies. The alliance between the Italians and the Germans was on the verge of collapse.

The Italian forces occupying Crete, led by General Angelo Carta, were in a difficult position. If there was an armistice they would have to support it. If the Allies invaded Crete General Carta and his men would be caught between the Germans and the Cretan resistance. Carta decided that he needed to get in touch with the guerrillas and SOE as soon as possible and ordered his head of counter-espionage, Captain Franco Tavana, chief of the Deuxième Bureau Siena Division, to contact the British through Mihalis Akoumianakis (codename 'Minoan Micky'), the head of counter-intelligence for the local elements of Force 133. The first meeting took place at the clinic of a doctor who was a member of the National Organisation of Crete (EOK) which, with the encouragement of the SOE, had evolved from the Supreme Committee of Cretan Struggle (AEAK) founded just after the invasion by Colonel Papadakis and other patriots. Captain Tavana and Micky talked for five hours. General Carta's message was simple: he wanted the Greeks to consider the Italians as allies against the Germans. He proposed that, should the Germans enter Lasithi in the east, his Italian troops would fight them and hold them up for at least two days to establish a bridgehead for the Allies at the Straits of Selinari, between Heraklion and Lasithi. Carta wanted a quick answer. A message about the proposed landing site was sent via Akoumianakis's radio to SOE Cairo, who responded: 'Proposal for the creation of a bridgehead to support a landing is under consideration.'

Micky asked Leigh Fermor to come to Heraklion for a conference with Tavana. He and Micky cycled into Heraklion to the surgery of a dentist Dr Stavrianidis, a member of the resistance. Leigh Fermor had been living rough and had not had a bath for six months; his clothes were filthy. Stavrianidis told his housekeeper to run the agent a bath and to take his clothes and wash them. Franco Tavana arrived, a slim young man wearing a polo shirt and corduroy shorts; Leigh Fermor was dressed in his host's scarlet silk pyjamas. The Italian and the Englishman spoke in French. Tavana 'struck me and all our friends in Heraklion as an admirable man', recalled Leigh Fermor: 'highly strung, courageous, hated Germans, polished, well educated, a lawyer, unhappily married with an eye for the girls . . .' The Italian was in an agitated state and at one point seemed close to tears, declaring: '*Mon cher ami, permettez moi de vous appeler ami* – My dear friend, allow me to call you friend.' He went on to explain that he was 'bound by honour to remain faithful to the alliance with Germany until they make an unfriendly movement'.

On 1 August a signal arrived at SOE in London. It was an 'unparaphrased version of a most secret cypher telegram' which had originated from Leigh Fermor. Its importance was indicated by the people who were to read it: the Chiefs of Staff, General Eisenhower and General Alexander.

1) We have received information from Crete that Tavana . . . has contacted British officers and reported that Germans propose disarm Italians. Many large Italian Units have been ordered by Germans to move to Chania and Retimo and senior Italian officers have been ordered to report to Archanes but have not complied as they fear a trap. Carta will refuse to hand over arms and is prepared actively to assist British landing. British officer has requested supplies of demolition materials to destroy bridges and impede German troop movements and considers that Cretans are sympathetic towards Italians.

2) In view of present situation we consider that only direct support we can give is from the air.

3) We have accordingly instructed agents to act as follows:-
    (a) Urge Italians to resist disarmament at all costs.
    (b) Inform them to expect support from the air.
    (c) Tell Italians to give targets and bomb lines at once.

4) We have also instructed Political Warfare Executive to conduct propaganda action as follows.

    (a) By broadcasting to Cretans in name Commander in Chief instructing them not to rise prematurely but to avoid impeding Italians in any action they may take against Germans.
    (b) By leaflets to Italian troops in Crete urging them to resist German attempts to disarmament and informing them that

if Germans succeed they will be transported to Germany to work for Germans.

(c) By leaflets to Italians in Rhodes on lines of (b) above and in addition informing them of German actions in Crete and inciting them to make active efforts themselves to disarm Germans.

Leigh Fermor's signal ended with the words 'I am moving to Heraklion perhaps Lasithi August first in Italian car and uniform sent by Italian staff to Gerakari – RPT Gerakari – on own responsibility.'

Leigh Fermor did not know that General Carta had also opened negotiations with the formidable Kapitan Bandouvas, Bo-Peep, now leader of the largest guerrilla force on the island. Bandouvas's headquarters were on a mountain plateau overlooking the province of Viannos. Men were arriving every day from all over the island including shepherds, mountain villagers, priests, students, army officers, two heavily armed monks, escaped British soldiers and a handful of communists. The camp was self-sufficient and boasted rows of huts for accommodation, a baker, a cobbler and an armourer. Bandouvas had 120 men under his direct command and claimed that he could summon over 2,000 more if there was a call to arms.

Carta told Bandouvas that the Italians would collaborate and had already instructed some Italian units to surrender their weapons and ammunition to him. Bandouvas thought that the hour of liberation was at hand. His view was confirmed when Leigh Fermor too promised to supply him with arms and ammunition. On 20 August, a huge drop of arms, ammunition, clothing and other equipment floated from the sky in silver containers. It took a whole day to unpack and distribute the drop. As well as rifles, Bren guns, Sten guns, grenades and quantities of .303 ammunition, some of the containers were packed with British uniforms, enough for Bandouvas to dress his men up as regular British soldiers.

On 8 September the Italian government signed an armistice
with the Allies. Bräuer sent German troops into the Lasithi province and redeployed some Italian troops to new locations, trying
to break up the Italians' military cohesion. General Bräuer's
number two, the brutal General Friedrich-Wilhelm Müller, sent
out a 'General Order to all Italian Troops in Crete'. It began 'The
Commander of Fortress Crete has charged me with the defence of
the province of Lasithi'. He went on to describe what that meant.
The Italians could do one of two things: they could remain loyal
to 'Mussolini's new government' and carry on fighting under the
command of the German military authorities; or they could hand
over their weapons and work on alongside the Germans in non-
combatant roles.

The Italians were left in no doubt as to what would happen if
they stopped collaborating with their former allies: 'Whosoever . . .
sells or destroys arms of the Italian forces, or whosoever deserts
from his unit, will be considered a *franc-tireur* and as such shot.'

When General Carta forwarded this order to his men he wrote:
'The above is a natural consequence of the situation resulting in the
armistice. We are in a besieged fortress. It is therefore essential to
follow the orders of the German Command with a sense of realism.'

Bandouvas took the war into his own hands. Thinking that the
Allies were only days away from storming ashore and liberating
his homeland, he led his newly equipped force on a premature
attack which started with the killing of two German soldiers
collecting potatoes in a field near Kato Simi. Bandouvas broadcast
a call to arms, mobilising the whole province of Heraklion. On
the 11th he set an ambush near the village. A German unit was
caught unawares and in a fight that went on into the afternoon
more than 400 enemy soldiers were killed; many more were
wounded and twelve were taken hostage.

Retribution was swift. Under the orders of General Müller,
2,000 troops of the 65th *Luftlande* (Infantry Division) poured into
the area on 12 September. Their orders were to: 'Destroy Viannos

and promptly execute all males beyond the age of 16 as well as everyone who was arrested in the countryside, irrespective of age or gender.'

At first the troops persuaded the villagers that they meant no harm and coaxed some who had fled into the mountains to return. The next day, the 13th, the soldiers went berserk. For two days they murdered, raped and tortured villagers. Then they blew up the buildings and set them alight with flame throwers. No one was spared, not children, women or the infirm. A German daily report stated: 440 enemy dead, 200 taken hostage and that fresh action was being taken against newly reported enemy concentrations in the area. The survivors were not allowed back into the ruins, nor were they allowed to bury their dead.

The reprisals so terrified the people in the villages surrounding Bandouvas's headquarters that they refused to continue helping him. Bandouvas sent a message which asked: 'When are the British landing to help us fight the Germans?' He realised that the British were not going to land after all. He was now wanted by the Germans, and the Cretans were angry with him for the havoc that he had brought down on them. Bandouvas asked Tom Dunbabin to evacuate him and the remains of his group to Alexandria, something that Dunbabin was only too happy to do.

Leigh Fermor saw that the situation with the Italians was spinning out of control. It was decided to get General Carta off the island as soon as possible. Carta agreed, and, led by Leigh Fermor and the Cretan officer Manolis Paterakis, the party set off across the mountains with several of the Italian's senior staff. The trek took three days and nights. On the first morning they were woken by a German reconnaissance aircraft. The plane circled the olive groves dropping leaflets with a message in Greek which read:

The Italian General Carta, together with some officers of his staff have fled to the mountains, probably with the intention of escaping from the island. FOR HIS CAPTURE DEAD OR

ALIVE IS OFFERED A REWARD OF:
THIRTY MILLION DRACHMA

Carta's response to the dropped message was: '*Ah! Ah! Trente pièces d'argent! C'est toujours un contrat de Judas!*' He folded the leaflet into his pocket, vowing to reply.

Eventually the fugitive party found their way to a huge cave by the sea where Tom Dunbabin, Bandouvas and forty of his guerrillas were waiting to depart. Bandouvas argued that he and his men should be evacuated first.

In the dark they heard the noise of a motor launch, about a hundred yards off the beach. It was commanded by a Conradian figure, the white-bearded Captain Bob Young. Since the fall of Crete he had put ashore and taken off many SOE operatives in his 112-foot motor launch; on its forward deck was mounted a Hotchkiss 3-pounder gun. Calm and unflappable, Young stood on the armour-plated bridge peering through his binoculars, looking for the line of white surf that would tell him he was near the shore and for the Morse code signal flashed by torch that would tell him he was off the right beach.

As soon as the recognition signals were seen, a rubber dinghy splashed into the sea, men clambered aboard and rowed towards the land, paying out a line as they went. A storm was brewing, sending up a swell. Leigh Fermor stood watching on the sand holding a large leather briefcase in his hands which, without Carta's permission, Franco Tavana had given him. It contained comprehensive details of the defences of Crete. Leigh Fermor was anxious to get aboard, hand them personally to Captain Young, and return to the beach. The wind blew harder, drenching the fugitive party in spray as the dinghy bucked though the waves. Once on board Leigh Fermor went below to hand over the documents. On shore the noise of the sea drowned out the voice of Bandouvas, who was shouting, arguing that he should have been the first to go aboard.

The sea was now very rough and Young decided that it was too risky to hang about so close to shore. He ordered his crew to weigh anchor and head for home. Leigh Fermor came back on deck and realised what was happening. He was being taken to Cairo. Bandouvas stood on the beach, humiliated by his rejection in favour of the Italian general, watching the wake of the launch as it powered south towards the horizon.

It took another month before the another launch appeared to take Bo-Peep to Egypt. When General Bräuer realised that the kapitan had gone he had thousands of leaflets printed and distributed:

17.11.43
APPEAL

The gang leader Bandouvas has abandoned the island altogether with his bodyguard. Thus has Crete been delivered from this paid subject who has caused so much harm to the peaceful population. If so many women have to be widowed and children orphaned, then this criminal is to blame.

The struggle against the remains of his band continues with inexorable harshness. I extend my hand once more to the peaceful population for the re-establishment of an ordered life, guaranteeing the safety of the individual and property.

The first measures have been taken. The forbidden zones in the gang territories have been abolished. The situation of the poorer population will improve through generous social security measures. I appeal to the wealthy population of Crete for the execution of the latter aim, so that it should contribute to this work of active solidarity through voluntary contributions. Contributions in money and in produce may be handed in to the Prefectures.

Furthermore the peaceful population is called upon to support the German Army's struggle against Bolshevism, that international enemy of civilisation, family, religion and peaceful life, by every means.

The German army is the friend of the Cretan people. It will not again allow this beautiful island to become a theatre of war or a place of activity by gangs, the enemy of the people.

He who helps the army in this struggle is welcome.

The Commander of Fortress Crete

Few Cretans were deceived.

12

Operation Abduction

In Cairo, Leigh Fermor put his enforced leave to good use. It occurred to him that the Carta Affair might serve as a blueprint for the abduction of a senior Nazi officer – perhaps the hated Müller himself. Leigh Fermor's plan was simple. He wanted to drop a small abduction team by parachute onto Mount Dikti, kidnap Müller from his headquarters and whisk him to the coast for a rendezvous with the Royal Navy and a boat to Alexandria. The Angelo Carta incident had shown that, with the help of the guerrillas, they would find it comparatively easy to evade German search parties.

The plan was put to Jack Smith-Hughes, now twenty-four and a major, who liked the idea and sent it on to Brigadier Barker-Benfield, overall commander of SOE in the Middle East. Barker-Benfield gave it his full approval. The only dissenting voice in Cairo came from Bickham Sweet-Escott, a senior executive of the Special Operations Committee. He argued strongly against the idea, saying that the risks of reprisal were not worth the capture of even an enemy general. 'I made myself extremely unpopular by recommending as strongly as I could that we should not [go ahead] . . . the price would certainly be heavy in Cretan lives. The sacrifice might possibly have been worthwhile in the black winter of 1941 . . . the result of carrying it out in 1944 when everyone knew victory was merely a matter of months would, I thought, hardly justify the cost.' His was a lone voice and he lost the argument. The operation was given an official thumbs up.

*

On Crete, Tom Dunbabin was surprised when, out of the blue, an order arrived from SOE Cairo marked 'URGENT': 'Find and identify drop zone for four man parachute team under Paddy aim abduct Müller.' Dunbabin received it while interrogating one Anastasios Symionidis – alias Kazakis – a German counter-intelligence agent and traitor who had been trapped and captured the previous day. Dunbabin had been trying to sieze Kazakis for nearly a year. The interrogation ended and Dunbabin ordered Symionidis's execution.

Dunbabin then turned his attentions to the problem of the parachute mission, which he had himself suggested in a report to Cairo earlier in the year, writing: 'It should be easy to kidnap Müller, one of our agents is on good terms with his chauffeur and he might be abducted on the road. Alternatively it sounds easy to break into the Villa Ariadne with a force of about twenty.'

Dunbabin sent word to the recently arrived Sandy Rendel, recently arrived from Cairo, telling him to prepare a landing site on the Omalos plateau, high up on Mount Dikti. At SOE Cairo, Leigh Fermor, now promoted major, looked for a second in command. He told his new friend Billy Moss about the plan and it dawned on him that this likeable young SOE officer, with whom he now shared the social whirl of Tara, was the obvious choice.

Next, Leigh Fermor and his liaison officer Manolis Paterakis were sent to Ramat David in Palestine for ten days' intensive parachute training. On the course they met Giorgios Tyrakis, a tough, round-faced man of twenty-six, who wore his beret tipped to the back of his head. He had been fighting in Albania when Greece surrendered but had managed to get back to Crete in time to fight the German paratroopers. After the battle he helped evacuate scattered Allied stragglers and joined the intelligence network. An SOE wireless set was hidden in his village and he and others volunteered to defend it. Giorgios had been evacuated from the island for rest and recuperation and to train as a parachutist. Leigh Fermor asked him to become part of the kidnap team.

On the course they had to jump from the back of lorries travelling at thirty miles an hour, before graduating to aircraft and the real thing. After completing six jumps, four from a Hudson and two night-time jumps from a Dakota, they were entitled to wear parachute wings, which they wore, SAS style, above the left-hand pocket of their battledress. Moss was spared the training: at six foot he was considered too tall. Moss was delighted that his first jump would be untrained and that some people called him daring or brave. He confides in his diary that the truth of the matter is that he did not want to damage himself and that life in Tara was too enjoyable to have to go on a parachute course in Haifa. Moss's most enjoyable moments at Tara were spent in the close company of Kitten – Sophie Tarnowska.

Much time was spent going over the details of the plan. Leigh Fermor was a close friend of the well-connected and spirited Annette Crean, who worked for Force 133 at Rustom Buildings. 'In our flat we had an open fire,' recalled Crean. 'I often worried there could be concealed a microphone in the chimney that went direct to the enemy, so many secret plans were made round that fire. Paddy Leigh Fermor used to be a visitor . . . he was very keen to kidnap a particularly brutal German General [Müller] . . . and the arguments for and against this were discussed. He wanted to take Billy Moss with him, a tall, good-looking Guards officer who I felt sure would give the game away . . .'

They were not short of advice from their SOE comrades at Tara. One evening, Smiley, recently back from covert operations in Albania, sat in the bathroom with Moss and Leigh Fermor discussing the mission. Smiley began to lecture them on how to set up the perfect ambush. His audience of two listened in rapt attention. The three men sat nearly naked in the bathroom, draw-ing diagrams and maps with their fingers on the steamy tiles. Smiley advised them where the best place might be to stop the general's car and what sort of back-up team they might need. Smiley knew what he was talking about and the two adventurers hung on his every word.

While the team prepared, Müller, the 'Butcher of Crete', was replaced by the more moderate forty-nine-year-old General Heinrich Kreipe. Leigh Fermor knew nothing about the potential new occupant of the Villa Ariadne, but he was not going to be cheated of his chance for excitement. He persuaded everybody that the capture of any senior German officer from his own head-quarters would be a valuable blow against enemy morale, and a demonstration of Force 133's capabilities.

The final preparations for the mission were to draw stores, to be packed into canisters and dropped by parachute at the same time as the kidnap team. Marlin sub-machine guns, automatics, revolvers and ammunition began to fill up the cupboards at Tara along with less orthodox devices such as explosive-filled fake cow pats, and gelignited goats' drop-pings (Leigh Fermor claimed these had been devised by the famous magician Jasper Maskelyne). In mid-January, they received the go-ahead but bad weather then closed in and all covert flights over the Balkans were cancelled. When at last the news came that they were off the next night, the two agents flew into a frenzy of packing and tidying up their affairs. They even managed to cram in a last lunch with three young women who, given a few more minutes, might have swept them off to bed. Then back to Tara to finish the chaos of their packing. Guns and £4,000-worth of silver sovereigns were bundled into a sack and in the evening a tearful party was thrown to see them off.

The last hours at Tara had a profound effect on Moss, and the memory of it stayed with him for many years. Sitting around a small, red-laquer table they drank and sang, their faces lit by candlelight. The night dragged on as the two agents waited to leave on the first leg of their adventure. Just before the sun rose, Billy McLean appeared, a shy naked figure. He wanted to present them with the complete works of Shakespeare and the *Oxford Book of English Verse*, which he thought had brought him luck in Albania and he hoped the books would work the same magic for them.

On the way to the airfield they picked up Manolis Paterakis and Giorgios Tyrakis, who sat in the back of the car 'looking picturesquely guerrilla-ish singing huskily and out of tune, and Paddy still a little drunk, joining in at the top of his voice'.

The trip took them via Italy and involved several changes of planes. They were delayed several times. On one occasion the four of them sat in a military canteen waiting for yet another cancelled aeroplane. They were a strange bunch: two British officers and two Greek guerrillas, all dressed up like something out of a novel by Ernest Hemingway. They were heavily armed with Marlin submachine guns propped up against the table, revolvers at their waists, explosives and God knows what in the satchels – and at their feet, a sack containing thousands of pounds in gold sovereigns.

Moss declared: 'I can't imagine having to do this excursion with anyone but Paddy, he is absolutely ideal and a perfect companion . . . the only trouble is that we are both horribly lazy, and so nothing gets done, but we both "muddle through" somehow'.

When at last they took off they were accompanied not only by McLean's two books but by the canisters, the contents of which weighed nearly 500lbs and read like something out of an adventure comic. Apart from some German uniforms and other disguise materials, they were to take maps, pistols, bombs, coshes, commando daggers, knuckledusters, telescopic sites, silencers, sub-machine guns, wire cutters, signal flares, gags, chloroform, rope ladders, gold sovereigns, special silent footwear, gelignite, gun cotton, Benzedrine tablets, field dressings, morphine, knock-out drops and suicide pills.

13

The Best Laid Plans . . .

At about four o'clock in the afternoon on 5 February 1944, Sandy
Rendel sat in a cave. His radio operator George Dilley was squat-
ting in front of his set, 'knees bent, back hunched and earphones
on his head like an eastern priest bowing forward to conduct some
mysterious ritual'. Dilley was concentrating on the encrypted
Morse being transmitted from SOE Cairo. Leigh Fermor and the
others were to arrive that evening, parachuting onto the Omalos
plateau between Kritsa and Lasithi. Rendel and Dilley were the
only ones who knew that the reason for the mission was to kidnap
the divisional commander. Later that afternoon they set off with a
band of Cretan andartes to prepare the landing site.

At an airfield near Brindisi, on the southern tip of Italy,
Paterakis, Leigh Fermor, Tyrakis and Moss clambered into a
Handley Page Halifax bomber, especially adapted for the SOE,
with a hole cut in the belly of the fuselage to allow parachutists to
drop through. The plane lumbered into the sky, piloted by Cyril
Fortune, who had been told that the codename for that evening's
flight was *Whimsical.* As Fortune set course the abduction team
did what men often do before enterprises of great stress and
danger: they slept.

On the Omalos plateau, where it was now dark, the guerrillas
gathered wood for the three marker fires – which identified the
drop zone. To the edge of the landing site was a small hut in
which one of the guerrillas, Christo, discovered a couple of Cretans.
The men claimed to be hunting for hares but Christo believed

them to be collaborators. Some of the guerrillas wanted to execute them on the spot. Rendel, worrying that this might trigger a Cretan vendetta, persuaded his men to lock the collaborators in the hut until the drop had taken place; the prisoners were warned of the terrible things that would happen to them and their families if they talked to the Germans. Rendel knew that within twenty-four hours everybody in the locality would know about the arrival of the parachutists, by which time, even if the prisoners talked, Leigh Fermor and his team would have vanished into the night, making any information useless.

In the freezing interior of the Halifax, just around midnight, the RAF parachute dispatcher took the cover off the jump hatch. The drop zone was very small, forcing them to parachute in four separate passes, rather than all together in a stick. Leigh Fermor was the first to go. He slid into position and sat on the edge of the hatch, his legs dangling into the slipstream of the bomber, his static line attached to the wire that ran the length of the aircraft and which would automatically open his parachute. On the plateau, Rendel and the reception committee crouched in the snow. The thick clouds scudding across the sky acted like a switch, turning the light of the moon on and off. Over the whistling of the wind they heard the noise of engines: the plane was dead on time. The signal fires were lit, illuminating the crouching figures. The aircraft circled low, moonlight glinting on the Perspex canopy of the cockpit.

To Rendel's disgust, the pilot fired a pink flare. This was not part of the plan. The flare looked 'filthily artificial in the middle of the wild dark scene, like the last dismal dropping of a spent firework over a seaside pier at home'. Peering over the edge of the jump hatch, Leigh Fermor could see the white mountain tops, the reception party's fires, and the snow reflecting the lurid pink of the flare. He tensed and looked at the dispatcher, waiting for the signal to jump. 'GO!' Leigh Fermor tumbled into the freezing, roaring, 200 mph slipstream of the Halifax. With a tug on his shoulders, his chute opened and he drifted down, the noise of the plane's engines fading until suddenly there was calm.

Rendel saw what looked like a little puff of smoke leaving the aircraft. The parachute unfurled and the smoke turned into a white canopy, below which dangled a tiny vulnerable-looking marionette. For a second he felt sorry for the little figure floating in the darkness, then he reminded himself that Leigh Fermor was not a man who needed sympathy. The figure got closer and Rendel prepared to stride up and greet him with a Dr Livingstone-style 'Major Leigh Fermor I presume . . .?' Leigh Fermor took the initiative and shouted: 'Is it all right down there?'

'Yes,' shouted Rendel.

The ground rushed up and Leigh Fermor made a perfect landing, rolling on his side and releasing the chute which collapsed on to some of the andartes. The whole party broke into uproar, cheering and clapping, pulling Leigh Fermor to his feet, almost preventing him flashing the 'safe landing' code to the aircraft. One of the guerrillas shouted in delight: 'It's Captain *Livermore.*' Leigh Fermor's first request was for water: they had none with them. Overhead the plane banked and began its second run. The wind got up and huge clouds obscured the moon, mist rolled across the plateau. In seconds visibility dropped to zero. The plane circled for forty minutes. The ground party could hear the engines, sometimes loud and near, at other times distant, but not once were they able to see the aircraft itself.

The cloud cover became more and more dense, shrouding the plateau in darkness. The signal fires died, and after nearly an hour the noise of the engines faded away, never to return. Billy Moss, Giorgios Tyrakis and Manolis Paterakis and all the canisters of supplies were on their way back to Brindisi.

Rendel, Leigh Fermor and the guerrillas set off for their hideout. It was a relief to Rendel to have someone to talk to. Leigh Fermor would break off from talking tactics to start a vigorous discussion with Rendel about the relative merits of Stephen

Spender and Louis MacNeice. Both men were close friends of Annette Crean. Soon after his arrival, Leigh Fermor wrote a letter to Annette from his new 'manorial home':

> Dear Annette,
> Well, here we are at the old home, at least I am at the moment but the second we left the car a horrid cloud appeared that stopped Billy Manolis and Giorgios from jumping . . .
>   It's great fun being back and of course life is just one big whisker, as usual it's very cold and snowy and rather beautiful. Wish you were here. Must stop now as a runner is champing in the snow by the box hedge in the front drive. So God bless you and my love to Nina and all the girls and boys.
>   Love Paddy.
>
> P.S. Sandy is proving wonderful company and we laugh the whole time.

At the top of the letter Leigh Fermor drew a map of Crete with an 'x' showing his location, accompanied by cartoons of German and British officers.

Rendel wrote a letter of his own to Annette:

> It is absolutely grand to have Paddy with us . . . we have been talking everything from Bloomsbury to Bayswater and Chaucer to Noël Coward – a change from sheep stealing (which however is a romantic and enthralling subject too – carried out with a fine code of honour. You steal sheep in proportion to the nearness or distance of the relationship to the owner . . .)

Like many British officers, Rendel did not understand fully the subtleties of sheep stealing on Crete, which could be far from romantic or enthralling. It was a crime that could cause enormous disruption, often ending in death.

Rendel admired the relationship Leigh Fermor had with the guerrillas. One minute he could be in deep discussion about Cretan jackboots, talking knowledgeably about what sort of patch to put on the heel or toe, the next he would be singing Cretan songs with the gusto and accent of a local. One evening two ex-gendarmes appeared dressed in German uniforms and escorting a man they said was a traitor. They had trapped him by pretending to be military police and had 'arrested' him for black-marketeering. Fooled by the uniforms, the man pulled out papers and said that he was an informer working for them. The papers ordered German troops to cooperate with him and also authorised him to carry a firearm. Too late he realised his mistake, he had confessed his guilt to his own countrymen.

The former gendarmes wanted to interrogate him, which Rendel and Leigh Fermor knew meant torture him; instead they persuaded the policemen to take the man away and shoot him. They sent two others as witnesses to make sure that he was shot quickly and 'humanely'. The prisoner was a Muslim and asked to be allowed to kneel facing east for his execution. He was shot in the head over a hole at the end of a low cave. His body fell into the void and was never retrieved. In a report to SOE Cairo Leigh Fermor described the man's death as 'good riddance'.

For the next two months there were many attempts to parachute in the rest of the team. Twice a week Rendel and the others went to the Omalos plateau to wait for an aircraft. Once the plane arrived too late, just after the reception committee had extinguished the fires and were about to move off. The men on the ground raced about trying to relight the fires, an impossible task. The pilot could not see the prearranged flare pattern and flew off.

They had another problem. The pink flare dropped from the RAF Halifax the night Leigh Fermor arrived had aroused the suspicion of the Germans. Hundreds of reinforcements had been moved on to the mountain, 300 onto the plain of Lasithi on the opposite side to the hideout and another 500 on the side where the SOE man were hiding. The troops searched and surrounded Tapes, a village on the route to the rendezvous point and where many of the men who were helping organise the landing zone lived. The garrison at the neighbouring village of Kritsa had been increased, and patrols sent out over the plateau itself.

One evening the guerrillas heard shooting and feared the worst. The shots turned out to have come from two German patrols who had run into each other in the darkness and opened fire; two soldiers died and several more were wounded. At dawn the guerrillas had the 'grim pleasure' of seeing the invaders carrying their injured and dead comrades down the mountain.

After several frustrating weeks the group began to get nervous, telling Rendel that it was only a matter of time before the Germans found the hideout. The problem was solved when they received a signal from Cairo saying that the air drop had been cancelled and the rest of the kidnap team was going to be sent in by motor launch. They packed up the cave, hid the radio and moved out.

They soon ran into a patrol of twenty-five Germans, who clearly knew there were guerrillas and possible SOE agents in the area. The soldiers were frightened and made a great deal of noise, crashing into trees and calling to each other in loud voices, not wanting to walk into a firefight. Rendel considered opening fire but decided that this might result in executions and the destruction of one of the neighbouring villages. The party hid until the German patrol detonated three smoke bombs, signalling that they were pulling out. They were nearly discovered several more times on the way to the new hideout, at one point passing within seventy feet of a German ambush, the noise of their passing muffled by the noise of the wind.

Eventually they set up a new headquarters in the Viannos valley, above the village of Malle, one of the villages that had been destroyed by Müller. The hideout was a hollow in the mountain-side surrounded by rocks, which made it impossible for the men to be seen from any direction.

Leigh Fermor found the waiting taxing. On 30 March he sent a long signal to the Cretan desk at SOE Cairo:

My Operation

This has had many discouraging setbacks in its early stages, both in our lateness in arriving in Crete and the frequent absence of the quarry. But if Bill and the equipment and the other lads arrive tonight it looks as if our chances are as good as ever. Though it looks as if the original Quarry has been replaced so intend to try and get him as soon as possible.

The necessity of my presence in the drop ground excluded my making recces in the snatch area, so don't expect results at once. I am going to try and pull it off however.

DROPS

The failure of the RAF to drop the rest of the party during the three [good moon periods] seems quite extraordinary as many of the nights were perfect. I would be glad to understand what kept them back on several perfect nights when their impending arrival [was suddenly cancelled] and why on another perfect night they arrived two hours after moonset, circled for half an hour and then retired. Drops must take place as soon as possible after moonrise leaving a suitable gap for the local population or wandering Huns to clear off. This is in order to leave a good number of night hours for the collection and doing the job of work and my own drop was as near perfect as it could be. Although the weather conditions were the worst we [had experienced]. If fault there is, and to my mind there is, it should be there. The office, laying on late schedules etc backed us up very well for which many thanks. Unfortunately the results seem to prove that until the technique of timing the sorties is improved

Feb. and March are not suitable for this sort of infiltration into Crete.

Two months had passed since Leigh Fermor parachuted on to the Omalos Plain. March turned into April and spring arrived. As the weather grew warmer the valley round the hideout filled with wild orchids and mountain lilies. Goats roamed the hillsides, the tinkling of their neck bells mingling with the lazy humming of bees. To the west the peaks of Mount Dikti sparkled white with snow. Below the snow line were belts of pine forest and below that the cultivated valley stretched away, terraces of vineyards and olive groves nestling next to strips of young corn. Patches of almond blossom dotted the lower slopes of the hills and far in the distance the deep quiet blue of the Mediterranean. From time to time Allied aircraft appeared, flying over the burnt and charred villages.

After the tension and excitement of waiting for the drop onto the mountain plain, the days at Malle passed in a warm peaceful spring dream. The only near-mishap came one night when Rendel, relishing the silence, was quietly eating raisins given to him earlier in the day by an old lady, who had thrust them into his breast pocket. He lay chewing quietly, gazing at the sky and the stars, feeling 'sweet and good'. Half asleep, he sensed that some of the raisins were rather rubbery; a split second later he remembered that his breast pocket was where he kept his suicide pills. He spat them out across the room and, in front of his puzzled companions, began to swill water round his mouth. He did not have enough Greek to explain his curious behaviour.

At last a signal arrived giving the time and date of the rendezvous. Leigh Fermor suggested that on the way they visit the nearby 'Monastery of the Twelve Apostles', where the Archimandrite, or abbot, was a good friend of the resistance and allowed them to use his church as a hideout. The young cleric was described by Leigh Fermor as being 'alert, courageous and amusing'. The three-hour walk took them across a plain studded with young cypress trees and through vineyards and olive groves until they saw the little monastery before them, surrounded by its own fields. Apart from a theological student and a timid nun called Anna, the abbot seemed to live alone and insisted they dine with him. While Anna cooked their food, the group drank raki and were taken into the abbot's bedroom and shown a trapdoor concealed beneath a bed. It led to a cellar where they could hide if an enemy patrol suddenly appeared.

The evening was spent regaling the abbot with news of the war, drinking, smoking and singing, the trapdoor kept open, just in case. The scene was illuminated by the flickering light of a kerosene lamp. Eventually they fell asleep in the hot, smoke-filled room, their snores echoing off the walls.

The next day Rendel sat on the veranda overlooking the monastery orchard, enjoying a glass of sweetened, boiled goat's milk. A line of washing flapped in the wind, left out from the night before. Without warning two German soldiers appeared in the orchard. The washing line hid Rendel, who crept inside and warned the others to hide in the cellar. The theological student bundled their rucksacks down after them, and slid the bed back into place.

Above them the soldiers stamped into the room. The abbot offered them the hospitality of the monastery, apologising for its rough-and-ready state but assuring them that if they cared to sit down he would have a delicious omelette prepared from the freshest eggs. Could he persuade them to take a glass of raki with him?

The Germans sat complaining that the room stank of cigarettes. The abbot sent the theological student to the outside entrance of the cellar to fetch the wine. The SOE party waited, a dozen enemy soldiers only inches above their heads. The smell of cooked food drifted through the gaps in the floorboards and they could even see the studs on the soldiers' boots. Every now and then someone above shifted their feet or banged a piece of equipment on the floor, sending small spirals of gritty dust and cobwebs on to the hidden men.

Eventually the patrol stood up and thanked the abbot in solemn, halting Greek. The NCO handed the abbot a 'certificate' saying that certain elements of the German army had been received and entertained in a friendly and hospitable manner, implying that the man was a good friend of the occupying forces and should receive decent treatment.

Through a crack in the outside door Rendel watched the patrol move through the orchard, two of them carrying a heavy machine gun. They vanished and the abduction team emerged from hiding. On the back of the certificate they left their own commendation, praising the Archimandrite for hiding them and possibly saving their lives.

Several days later, on the night of 4 April 1944 Rendel and a crowd of people waited on a beach near Tsoutsouros on the south coast of the island to rendezvous with a Royal Navy motor launch. Among them were members of the resistance who needed to be evacuated as their lives were in immediate danger; and others who were being sent to Egypt for parachute training. One of the former group was a brave woman named Antonia Mathioudaki, who had been working as a typist and interpreter at the German headquarters in Chania, where she had access to secret documents. Through her brother she kept a stream of information flowing to Tom Dunbabin's radio near Anogia. Eventually she was discovered and forced into hiding. If captured she faced torture, deportation to a concentration camp or execution. Dunbabin, now in charge of Force 133 SOE operations on the island, decided that for her own safety Antonia must leave Crete. There were also four German prisoners of war, captured a few days earlier in the area between Heraklion and Chania. They had been taken from wireless station to wireless station and each time had seen British officers and NCOs all wearing local disguise. Rendel imagined that the prisoners must think every other Cretan was an infiltrated

Allied agent; in their four days of captivity they had met almost every SOE operative on the island.

This time the captain of the motor launch was New Zealander Brian Coleman, by now an old hand at secret rendezvous. A half-moon hovered in the sky over the dead calm sea. Standing with Captain Coleman on the bridge of the motor launch were Giorgios Tyrakis and Manolis Paterakis, anxious to set foot again on their home soil; next to them was Billy Moss who had christened the pair 'Man Thursday' and 'Man Friday'. They were two miles off the coast, the mountains of Crete towered in the distance and even at that distance they could smell the wild thyme scenting the warm night air.

The party on the foredeck included the heroic Kapitan Yannis Katsias, a guerrilla fighter who had been active in the Rethymnon area of north-west Crete; he was accompanied by two of his men.

As they neared the coast the Cretans began to speculate in loud voices about where, exactly, they were. Coleman ordered them to pipe down. Silence fell, broken only by the low pounding of the powerful engines. Coleman headed east, running parallel to the coast, trying to spot the flashing torch. He knew that there were German guardposts three-quarters of a mile to the west of the landing beach and a mile to the east.

Coleman sent a seaman forward to watch for rocks. In the bows a sailor swung a leaded line, calling back the depth soundings in a low voice. Everyone else was silent. Then on the bridge a lookout called, 'Flashing light sir! . . . And another.' Through his binoculars Coleman saw the irregular flashing; Moss described it as 'a sudden prick in a huge mountainous back cloth'. Coleman ordered the engines to half speed and asked the radio operator to come to the bridge, wanting to be sure that this was not a trap. The radio operator stared through his binoculars, silently mouthing the Morse code that flashed from the shore. After a moment he turned to Coleman. 'That's them alright, signal's correct.'

The launch nosed towards the shore and Coleman could make out the blurry shapes of men and women on the beach, surrounded by the rocks of a small cove. The Cretans on the deck heaved their packs on to their backs and swung their Marlin sub-machine guns on to their shoulders, talking excitedly. Paterakis and Tyrakis hummed a Cretan song. When they were fifty yards offshore a dinghy was lowered, attached to a line that had been made fast to the launch. The sailors rowed towards the beach with short rapid strokes against the soft swell of the sea. Another dinghy was lowered and made fast to the tow line. Soon it was loaded with guns, ammunition and kitbags; then the shore party clambered down a rope ladder, jumped aboard, and the dinghy was pulled towards the beach.

By now some of the reception committee were up to their waists in the sea, pulling on the line and shouting *'Trava, Trava!'* 'Pull, Pull!' The dinghy ground on to the sand of the beach, bobbing in the swell. Billy Moss was not prepared for his first island encounter with the Cretans. When he jumped off the dinghy and splashed through the surf to the shore he fell into the arms of what he thought was a group of over-made-up actors from *The Pirates of Penzance*. Men with heavy moustaches, turbaned heads; black, threadbare patched clothes; high boots; others in bare feet. The air was fetid with the smell of unwashed bodies and clothing. A filthy, unshaven Cretan dressed in rags came up to him and said, in an educated English voice, 'Hello Billy. You don't know me. Paddy will be along in a minute.' It was Sandy Rendel, who explained to the young captain: 'I haven't washed for six months, a man of the people, that's me.'

The young man Moss met next looked like an English public schoolboy. He grabbed Moss's gun and said: 'Paddy with Germans.' Then to Moss's horror he began to fiddle with the sub-machine gun: 'Tommy gun! Boom-boom', then he pointed along the beach saying, 'Here come Paddy.'

Moss was excited to see his friend. ('I saw Paddy and ran towards

On 20 May 1941 the Germans invaded Crete with the largest airborne force in history. They behaved with a ferocity not seen since they marched into Poland in 1939.

BUNDESARCHIV

Civilians quickly joined in the fighting. Many paratroopers met death still tangled in their harnesses.

GETTY IMAGES

After the first day the Germans took control of the battlefield.

The British withdrawal rapidly turned to chaos. The Commonwealth troops left behind to become prisoners of war numbered close to 17,000.

After the battle the Germans took revenge, hunting down the civilian men, women and even children who had fought against them.

Kandanos and Kondomari were the first places to suffer reprisals. The villagers were rounded up.

The men were separated from their families and shot. As the people buried their dead, engineers moved in and destroyed the villages with high explosives.

The Cretans and their island were badly battered in the fighting. Some people lost everything.

Colonel Michail Filippakis (*above, left*) helped the straw-hatted mayor of Heraklion surrender. Then he made his way to his village near the south coast from where he carried on the fight living as a poor civilian (*right*). Filippakis was one of the first to make contact with the SOE in Cairo, sowing the seeds of the resistance.

The resistance grew. People of all ages joined the fight. The Germans executed ten islanders for every soldier killed.

Throughout the occupation civilians, including women and children, were used as poorly paid forced labour.

Mrs Hariklia Dramoudanis's husband was a guerrilla leader, a kapitan. He was captured and executed, forcing her to flee with her family into hiding in the mountains.

In the winter of 1943 British SOE agent Patrick Leigh Fermor came up with a plan to capture a German general and smuggle him off the island.

Leigh Fermor chose a young Coldstream Guards officer, William 'Billy' Stanley Moss, as his second in command.

In Cairo, Moss (*right*) and Leigh Fermor shared a house with other SOE agents and the glamorous Countess Sophie Tarnowska (*left*), who Moss was to marry. They nicknamed the house Tara and it became the unofficial headquarters for planning the kidnap.

Guerrilla fighters, the andartes, were a vital part of the scheme. They were organised into bands led by kapitans. This photograph shows members of the Veisakis family under Kapitan Petrakoyiorgi. The father, Emmanouil 'Manoussomanolis', stands on the right and his three sons are (*left to right*) Dimitris, Costas and Manoussos.

Two leaders who helped with the kidnap: Kapitan Petrakoyiorgi (*left*), in peacetime a successful businessman; and Kapitan Mihali Xylouris (*right, seated right*) who sheltered the abduction team at his secret hideout on Mount Ida.

Three key kidnappers: Manolis Paterakis (*right*), Leigh Fermor's right hand man; Giorgios Tyrakis (*left*), recruited from a parachute training course in Cairo; and Antonios Papaleonidas (*centre*), a stevedore from Heraklion.

The twelve-man kidnap team was supported by a bodyguard of men under the command of Kapitan Boutzalis. On 21 May both units reached the final hiding place, about one mile from 'Point A', the kidnap junction.

Micky Akoumianakis (*right*), head of SOE counter intelligence, took a disguised Leigh Fermor (*left*) to a safe house in Heraklion to plan the escape route.

At the last minute Kapitan Boutzalis's (*left*) men were stood down – their presence was arousing suspicion in the area.

Two uniforms were stolen to disguise Leigh Fermor (*right*) and Moss as military policemen.

A reconstruction of the moonlit kidnap staged by Leigh Fermor in 1947. On the back of the photograph he wrote: 'The car is in the exact position of the General's when the coup took place.'

Moss drove the captured
general into Heraklion,
through twenty-two
German control points and
past the Kreiskommandantur,
the German headquarters
for the province.

When the soldiers on guard
at the road blocks saw the
pennants on the car's wings
they immediately waved it
through. The kidnappers
kept the flags as souvenirs.

The heavily guarded West
Gate was the last major
obstacle out of the city;
ahead lay the road to the
mountains. This photograph
was taken in 1942 before the
barriers went up.

On the first leg of the escape route the kidnappers climbed high above the snowline. For the next twenty days the captured General Kreipe (*second from front*), dressed in the clothes he had chosen for a day in his office and an evening playing bridge, was forced to tackle some of the most gruelling terrain in Europe.

The radio they had been counting on failed. SOE in Cairo had no idea that the kidnap had succeeded or even where the kidnappers were. Communication on the island was only possible through the heroic efforts of runners like Giorgios Psychoundakis.

Radio contact was restored with the help of British SOE agent Dennis Ciclitira who helped organise a boat and accompanied the team to Egypt.

The General was flown to London for interrogation and then transferred to Canada to be interned with other high-ranking Nazis. He was released in 1947.

In 1945 peace returned to the island. Mrs Hariklia Dramoudanis, whose husband and son were murdered by the Germans and who fled into the mountains to protect her family, died many years after the war. She remains a symbol of the unbreakable Cretan spirit.

him, I can't describe how wonderful it was to see the old son of a gun again.')

In contrast to the filthy appearance of Rendel, apart from his moustache Leigh Fermor was clean-shaven with neat hair flattened under a turban, although he too looked as though he was in a comic opera. His clothes included a bolero, a maroon cummerbund which held to his waist an ivory-handled pistol and dagger. His corduroy breeches were tucked into long black riding boots. He told Moss that 'Xan [Fielding] and I like the locals to think of us as sort of dukes'.

Moss had made similar mistakes of identity on the boat. He had thought that Yannis Katsias and his henchmen were sheep-stealers. In fact they came from Sfakia, a part of the island which for hundreds of years had produced the fiercest guerrilla fighters and where sheep stealing set off family vendettas that went on for years and could only be stopped by revenge killing. Katsias's family were in the middle of one such feud. He had to keep moving to avoid becoming a victim himself.

Part of the disguise Moss had brought with him included a Swiss skiing sweater. He began to wonder whether he had made the right choice.

Leigh Fermor took immediate command of the beach party. 'I saw him go off,' said Moss, 'And watched him as he gave orders, commanded men to do this and that . . . He seemed to have the whole situation at his fingertips and was capable of coping with anything.'

The equipment from the motor launch now lay on the beach, including each man's kitbag. The men piled it all onto the backs of mules – explosives, weapons, ammunition. When the job was at last done, Leigh Fermor produced gold coins to reward the members of the reception committee who had been especially recruited for the job. Every night for the past two weeks they had moved through the forbidden zone to the beach, hoping for the arrival of the launch. Now it was here their job was done and they could stand down, freed from the stress and the danger. After embraces and bristly kisses the reception committee disappeared into the darkness.

It was about midnight when they moved off, first up the steep, rocky gulley of the cove, after which they faced a hard climb to the top of the scarp. They trudged uphill through reddish rocky terrain, slippery underfoot and dotted with scrubby bushes. It took them over half an hour of breathless, sweaty scrambling to reach the top of the scarp face. Below them the sea appeared to get wider and wider as they gained height and could see more of the horizon. The moon hung behind them, its light glittering on the sea, showing the way home to Africa. Moss thought it was like looking through the wrong end of a pair of binoculars. He asked Rendel if all the hills in Crete were like this: Rendel's reply was to laugh. Moss thought that 'Crete appeared to be one big rock. I was sweating Cairo from every pore and hating it.' Once out of the gulley, they saw the impassive, craggy hills of the Asterousia Mountains, rising above them in silent challenge.

The team were heading for Kastamonitsa in the vicinity of Archanes, a town about fifteen miles south of Heraklion and where General Kreipe had his headquarters, and also not far from the Villa Ariadne. Kastamonitsa was the home of Kimonas Zografakis, a shepherd and trusted resistance fighter. Kimonas and his family had promised to provide a base where the abductors could hide and from which they could operate. It was Kimonas who helped guide the commando raiding party that had attacked the airfield at Kasteli. Only a few months earlier, Kimonas's elder brother had been arrested and executed.

At the top of the slope the men paused to get their breath back. After a few minutes they set off again. The going was easier, although still slippery from the chippings of rock underfoot.

The party had to cross a ridge which forced the men into silhouette against the moonlit sky. In the distance, in full view, was a manned German outpost. The previous month a group of guerrillas, returning through the area after acting as reception committee to another motor-launch landing, had been ambushed and their leader, Mihalis Eftaminitis, killed.

They ran bent double, hugging the skyline, heaving on the plodding mules. An Alsatian dog belonging to the German patrol loped by, inexplicably ignoring the men who were intent on bringing chaos to its masters.

After four hours' hard walking they reached the place where they were to hide for the rest of the night and all of the following day. The mules were unloaded and led off to a hiding place about an hour away. The men needed to sleep. They were young fit men but had found the route exhausting, as did the donkeys, stumbling under the heavy loads of equipment. They settled in the bed of a dried-up river, surrounded on three sides by rock and made invisible by trees and thickets of scrub. Leigh Fermor still had the fleece-lined suit in which he had parachuted onto the Omalos plateau; it made a perfect bed, blanket and mattress all in one. Silence fell and a slight drizzle began to fall.

They awoke the next morning to the bleating of two goats being slaughtered for breakfast. This was Moss's first experience of Cretan hospitality; one goat would have been enough, the second was in celebration of the arrival of the abduction team. Before breakfast the men washed in a nearby spring of freezing cold mountain water.

While the goats were being cooked some of Sandy Rendel's team arrived to escort him back to his headquarters on the Lasithi plateau, about a three-day trek away. They brought with them a water bottle full of raki which they drank from empty bully beef tins. For an hors d'oeuvre the shepherds plucked from the white-hot ashes of the fire the entrails, genitals, eyeballs, livers and kidneys. Moss had some American army 'K' rations in his rucksack which were added to the feast.

It had taken them a long time to reach the first hideout and they knew that at the present rate it would take them another two days to get to Kastamonitsa. Before he left, Rendel advised them to break the next night's march at Skinias, where a shepherd was expecting them and would be offended if the team did not accept his hospitality.

The party which had landed on the beach began to break up. Kapitan Yannis Katsias headed off with his fighters for a destination to the west, travelling with only their sub-machine guns and what they could carry on their backs. Rendel planned to set off back to his headquarters that evening. This would leave only the abduction team, Leigh Fermor, Billy Moss, Paterakis, Tyrakis, Zahari, Zografakis and Antonios Papaleonidas, a stevedore from Heraklion. The ISLD agent John Stanley had joined them for part of the journey. The British officers passed the morning drinking, smoking and talking about old friends in Cairo and the goings on at Tara. Moss had brought with him cigars, two bottles of whisky and some kümmel, which they drank along with more raki and the local wine served for their lunch. Moss remembers that 'At lunch time we ate very little and drank a great deal.' John Stanley passed out.

By now Moss had changed into his 'disguise' of ski jersey and trousers; next to Rendel and Leigh Fermor he felt he looked like 'an Englishman down on his luck'. To Moss, Rendel looked more Cretan than the Cretans: he drank wine from the bottle, the liquid trickling down his unshaven chin and splashing onto the ragged black coat, which he had acquired fourth-hand when he arrived; his breeches and puttees were filthy and covered in mud; he wore a black turban on his head and the soles of his boots had come away from the uppers.

After lunch they all slept, fuzzy-headed in the hot afternoon sun. At about five o'clock they roused themselves and Rendel set off with his escort. Moss watched Rendel walking away, a gnarled stick in his hands, his pace measured and the soles of his shoes flapping time with his steps: the sometime correspondent of *The Times* looking for all the world 'like Old Nod the shepherd'.

Leigh Fermor and Moss passed another hour waiting for the mules to come back. The mules arrived at 6.30 that evening and were loaded up, and the small party set off in daylight for Skinias, where they were to spend the next day. When they left, John Stanley was still asleep in the place where he had collapsed at lunchtime. As they passed his inert figure Leigh Fermor commented: 'See what a year in Crete does to one.'

The route to the sheepfold was much easier than it had been the day before. Instead of going up every peak they followed the contour lines. The shepherd showed no surprise when he was introduced to them and Moss thought that the whole area must know of their presence, if not their mission. The old man welcomed them with milk in a communal glass and *mizithra*, a soft unsalted cheese with a pungent aroma and mild flavour, stored in a basket hanging, dripping from the ceiling of his tiny stone hut. After a short rest they moved on. In every village they passed, the dogs sensed their presence and began to bark. Leigh Fermor's solution to the problem was to draw attention to themselves, shouting orders in a loud voice and in German, and singing German military songs including 'Bomber über England', 'Lili Marlene' and the unofficial German national anthem so loved by Hitler, the 'Horst Wessel Lied'. Moss was introduced to one of the Cretan methods of judging distance – how many cigarettes could be smoked before the next rendezvous was reached.

As they got nearer to Skinias the danger of discovery grew. One of the mule handlers warned them that a few months earlier the Germans had set up an ambush on a bridge which they would soon have to cross and that even the track they were on was regularly patrolled. Another of the muleteers went ahead to check that all was clear; the others waited in a ditch until they heard him whistle, the signal that they could go on in safety. They walked along the deserted streets of the village, the noise of their boots echoing off the walls. Ahead, in the moonlight, they saw two uniformed men. Manolis Paterakis recognised them: they were part of the local gendarmerie, the force to which he had belonged before the invasion. He decided to lead the group straight past them, warning, 'Don't say anything, don't catch their eye.' The kidnappers walked on, single file, heads down, faces hidden. The two gendarmes took no notice of them, dragging on their cigarettes and chatting quietly, as though the band of desperadoes did not exist.

At the end of the village they reached the house where they were to have supper before moving on. Their arrival was the cue for another display of Cretan hospitality. The house was owned by a shepherd called Mihalis, who lived there with his elder sister. The party was immediately offered glasses of raki and Mihalis insisted they stay with him until the following night as they had no chance of getting to Kastamonitsa in the remaining hours of darkness. He would not take no for an answer and said he had already made the arrangements.

Then dinner was prepared, a feast in spite of the wartime shortages: mutton, chopped up and cooked in olive oil. Then lentils, also prepared in oil, creamed goat's cheese and hard-boiled eggs, washed down with Cretan red wine. Moss says that ten people sat down to the meal and, 'I was introduced to the Cretan custom of making a toast not only for each round of drinks, but also as often as anyone at the table lifted his glass to his lips. With ten people present our eating was so punctuated by glass-raising that the meal seemed to continue for hours.'

After the meal a stream of visitors visited the house, all wanting to set eyes on the strange men who had arrived from the sea. Soon the small room was filled with smiles and noisy enthusiasm for the resistance team. Two of the callers were the gendarmes they had so recently passed in the square. The officers were greeted like long-lost brothers.

It was nearly dawn when the party ended. The next day they were served a breakfast of eggs, goats' milk, wine and more raki. Moss came to realise that 'wine takes the place of one's morning cup of tea and one often drinks a liberal quantity before brushing one's teeth'. After breakfast more visitors arrived, each one subjected to a charade of mock security with the door half open and whispered passwords. The most important visitor was Kapitan Anastasios Boutzalis. Originally from Anatolia, Boutzalis looked like a kindly Cretan uncle. He sported a thick moustache and was six feet tall with broad shoulders and a comfortable paunch. His gentle aspect concealed a man who was a great patriot to Crete and an enormously useful ally to the British agents on the island. Like Manolis Paterakis, he had distinguished himself in the battle for Crete and then became one of the first resistance fighters in the mountains, taking part in the battle of Viannos. He struck Moss as something of a Falstaff: he used a dagger to eat the mutton; seeing that Billy Moss was looking at him he suddenly spiked a sheep's eyeball and offered the delicacy to him. Moss found he was unable to accept the gift. Boutzalis shrugged and popped the orb into his own mouth. Moss watched him chew in fascination. 'I could see its shape like a skinned golf ball riding in his cheek.'

Another visitor was a young woman carrying a baby who turned out to be Leigh Fermor's god-daughter. She had been christened 'England Rebellion' in a hilltop ceremony some months before. The child's father had been wounded and evacuated to Cairo, the mother was now in hiding with the infant in the mountains. To be a godfather to a Cretan child is an honour and a solemn undertaking; the role is binding and as deep as a blood tie. The responsibilities last until death. Leigh Fermor presented the child with a gold sovereign. Another person at the lunch was an old man who had been ejected by the Germans from his house in Chania and was now taking refuge with his relatives. He was dressed like a priest and looked to be in his mid-seventies. He claimed to have worked in a restaurant in Los Angeles and his conversation was peppered with phrases like 'Hot dog' and 'Goddam son of a bitch'. The two policemen who had seemed so menacing in the moonlight made a return visit. They were eager to help with the next stage of the journey and were full of helpful suggestions.

After so much social activity the small team was grateful when, as darkness fell, they headed off into the rain on the last leg of the trek to Kastamonitsa. A surreal moment came when, ahead of them, they saw what appeared to be fireflies dancing on the mountain slopes; the lights turned out to be the lanterns of villagers foraging for snails, which crawl out from under rocks after rain, and which are fried or roasted with wild rosemary to make a popular Cretan dish, and a necessity in a time when food was being stolen from them by the German army.

Just before dawn on the morning of 7 April, on the brow of the next hill, the tired walkers saw the village of Kastamonitsa. In three nights' tough trekking they had covered little more than sixteen miles. Billy Moss now knew what they were in for and how demanding the mountain country could be. He regretted wearing hobnail-studded boots and wished that he had the rubber, Vibram soles that had been developed by the Italians for mountaineering and adopted by the British commandos.

As they arrived at the Zografakis house, Kimonas decided to split the team up. He sent the guerrillas who had guided the abduction team across the mountains to shelter in a disused building. Leigh Fermor, Moss, Paterakis and Tyrakis were to stay in the main house. The family were not well-to-do but they were prosperous by Cretan mountain standards, living in a two-storey building with a living room, bedroom and kitchen. The family had often sheltered Allied agents, despite the astonishing risks: there was a German garrison and military hospital in the village; and off-duty German soldiers were in the habit of just wandering into islanders' houses demanding food and drink.

By day the brothers and sisters of the house kept lookout, coming in to warn them when soldiers were loitering nearby or even walking towards the front door; the men were told to keep well away from the windows. Nearby was a dried riverbed full of trees, bushes and large rocks which provided a hiding place where the kidnap team could hide if they had enough warning. Zografakis's wife, whose son had been murdered only months before, found the ordeal of concealing the SOE men distressing. Zografakis himself appeared to be unmoved. He was a handsome, silent man, unsmiling but with an honest, open face, white hair and sparkling bright eyes. He moved over the rough terrain with a nimbleness given only to men who have spent their lives farming on mountain slopes.

Later, the women of the family, Kimonas's wife and two daughters, prepared a banquet for the group. Again many toasts were made, including some swearing revenge for the death of Kimonas's son. By the time they were allowed to climb the rickety ladder up to the bedroom, the team were drunk and half asleep. They slipped gratefully into beds that had been prepared with clean sheets, falling immediately into a deep stupor, oblivious to the fleas that crawled all over them. The first phase of the mission was over: they had landed and reached the base that was to be their headquarters while they finalised the details of the kidnapping.

14

First Base

The next day they woke late to find 'pretty plump girls' bringing their lunch and waiting on them hand and foot. As they ate the four men discussed their next move. The plan was to break into the Villa Ariadne, overpower Kreipe's guards and spirit him away. First they needed to make a study of the villa, the guards, the route in and how they were going to escape with their prisoner.

After lunch they dressed and clambered down the wooden ladder to the ground-floor room. Waiting for them was a happy-faced man of about thirty. Unlike the mountain men, he wore a grey pinstriped suit with a button-down shirt and polished black shoes. He had come by bus from Heraklion. This was Micky Akoumianakis, head of counter-intelligence with Force 133 SOE in Heraklion. It was Micky's father, who had worked for the archaeologist Sir Arthur Evans, who had been killed fighting in the battle for Crete. Micky had inherited his father's house, next door to the Villa Ariadne, the perfect place from which to watch General Kreipe's comings and goings. Leigh Fermor asked Micky to take him to the villa, a short bus journey away.

The presence of the military hospital in Kastamonitsa quickly made it too dangerous for the kidnappers to spend much more time in the Zografakis house. Members of the family kept coming in to warn them that Germans were loitering nearby or even walking towards the front door. They decided that when Leigh Fermor and Akoumianakis left to reconnoitre the villa, the rest of the party must move to a new hideout.

That evening they filled in Leigh Fermor's false identity cards, sorted out maps and papers, and ate and drank. Leigh Fermor's cover name was Mihali Phrangiadakis, twenty-seven, a farm worker from the Amari valley. When they finished the four men climbed the stairs to bed, serenaded by drunken German soldiers singing at the other end of the village.

The next day a new recruit arrived: Grigorios Chnarakis, sent for by Leigh Fermor, who knew him to be an expert in guerrilla fighting. Chnarakis had already taken part in several armed raids and knew the terrain well. Before heading off towards the city, Leigh Fermor turned himself into what he termed a 'Heraklion gadabout': a smart suit was found for him and he used a burnt cork to darken his eyebrows and moustache, his face already tanned nut-brown from years under the Mediterranean sun. A cap, pulled hard down, disguised his fair hair. He and Micky left in the late afternoon and walked to the nearby town of Kasteli to catch the bus.

Kasteli was next to an airfield and was full of army and Luftwaffe personnel. The two men clambered aboard the bus; it was nearly empty, with just a few people carrying poultry and vegetables to sell at the market. Micky nodded to the driver, who was a friend and a trusted member of the resistance. He handed over the fare and settled into a seat; Leigh Fermor slumped beside him, and quickly pretended to have fallen asleep, his head lolling forward.

Outside Heraklion the bus was flagged down at a temporary roadblock. A military policeman climbed aboard demanding that everyone produce their papers. The two agents fumbled in their pockets and produced their forged documents. In the half-dark the soldier glanced at Leigh Fermor, looked at his photograph and handed his papers back. The bus was waved through into the noisy city. On arrival the two men got off, and vanished into the crowds of civilians and uniformed soldiers.

Military vehicles thronged the streets, parked in roads still lined by the ruins of buildings destroyed in the fighting nearly

four years earlier. Soldiers manned roadblocks, stopping the locals
to check their papers and to enforce the civilian curfew that started
at seven every night. Others strolled in the evening light, crowd-
ing the pavements, or sat drinking raki and coffee in cafés and
bars. Some of the more impressive buildings had been taken over
by the invaders and turned into offices. Draped down the facades
were enormous, billowing red and white flags emblazoned with
the swastika.

Military policemen with whistles controlled the garrison traffic; unease and tension pervaded the streets. The German soldiers
were aware that the Cretans detested them and were waiting for
the day when they could take revenge on their conquerors. Leigh
Fermor found that there was 'something bracing about these
descents into the lion's den: the swastika flags everywhere, the
German conversation in one's ears and the constant rubbing shoulders with the enemy in the streets. The outside of Gestapo HQ
particularly, which had meant the death of many friends, held a
baleful fascination.'

Back at the Zografakis house, the rest of the group, Moss,
Paterakis, Tyrakis and Chnarakis, started moving the base with all
its equipment higher up the mountains. Kimonas's father offered
to guide them on the first leg of the journey. They waited until
dark, loaded the mules and slipped out through the deserted
streets into the country. In the clear moonlight they followed the
old man up a twisting mountain path out of Kastamonitsa. Once
safely on their way he left them; for a second they watched his
white hair bobbing as he walked back down to the village towards
the military hospital, its lights ablaze. The kidnappers walked for
three hours, climbing higher and higher. The going was slippery
and dangerous; even the three mules carrying the equipment had
trouble. Eventually they were forced to stop and spend the rest of
the night in the bitter cold under an overhanging rock. When the
sun rose the next morning, Moss was amazed to see the mountains
towering all round him. To the east the white slopes of Mount

Ida, and beyond that the White Mountains where legend has it that Icarus once tried to fly. In the far distance they could see smaller peaks and on the horizon 'a tiny cluster of white doll's houses – Heraklion'.

In Heraklion, Micky led Leigh Fermor through the backstreets and narrow alleys that crisscrossed the ruined town, introducing him to an astonishing array of resistance workers – lawyers, dentists, teachers, headmasters, artisans, students, secretaries, wives, even the clergy. These were the people who had monitored Kreipe's movements on his way to his new home. They were the eyes and ears of the network, secretly logging every move the Germans made, filling hundred of sheets of precious paper, some of it scrap, with number plates, unit badges, the ships coming and going in the harbour and the aircraft landing at Heraklion or Maleme; memorising the defences round the harbour and later drawing plans on brown paper showing every change in gun and sentry position, each bit adding another piece to the intelligence jigsaw.

Leigh Fermor was taken into cellars where resistance workers hunched over clandestine radios, listening to the news from the BBC. Items were scribbled down and turned into stories to be printed on secret presses and distributed to the population. Others worked on propaganda leaflets designed to demoralise the German soldiers, reminding them that while they languished in the hot sun of the island, back home their wives and girlfriends were being seduced by strangers.

Leigh Fermor could not resist pushing his luck. On one of his evenings in the city he and Micky attended a party given by General Sergiou, whose daughter, Kyveli, had infiltrated the *Kreiskommandantur*. In the room Leigh Fermor spotted three German NCOs, who he went over to talk to and ended up trying to teach them the 'Pentozali', a vigorous Cretan dance the name of which implies that the dancers will make themselves dizzy five times over: the Pentozali dancers hold each other by the shoulders and improvise acrobatics. The SOE agent and his non-commissioned German dance students lurched drunkenly round the room, the soldiers blissfully unaware that the friendly and dashing Cretan plying them with more and more raki was a twenty-nine-year-old, blond-haired British major who liked to quote chunks of Latin and spoke near-perfect Greek.

Leigh Fermor's bravado nearly backfired when Micky offered round his cigarettes. They were in an English packet and the dance came to an abrupt halt while the Germans asked where they had got them. Thinking on his feet Micky said he had bought them on the black market, which was flooded with stuff left behind by the retreating Allies. The soldiers fell for the story, drank more raki and the dizzying lesson went on.

On 10 April, Leigh Fermor met a young man in a Force 133 safe house in Heraklion. His name was Ilias Athanassakis and he was Micky Akoumianakis's second in command. He was a student and very good at collecting and collating information. A natural undercover agent, he combined daring and prudence with caution, not rushing in if he was uncertain what was going to happen or how he was going to escape. Ilias had a compendious knowledge of the distinguishing marks of the German units in the Heraklion province and a keen instinct for which units had just arrived on the island and where they were going.

The Cretan undercover network discovered that the Germans believed the guerrilla activity in the past two months on the Omalos Plain was proof that a British commando force had arrived on Crete and was hiding in the mountains in the region of Kastamonitsa. German search parties were said to be moving into the area near the Zografakis house. Micky thought that his men at the hideout with Moss were in danger and that they should send a runner to warn them; he did not know that they had already moved to safety higher up the mountains.

Micky and Leigh Fermor's next step was to reconnoitre the Villa Ariadne – a ten-mile bus ride out of Heraklion. From the safety of Micky's house next door to the villa, Leigh Fermor discovered for himself the extent of the security at the general's heavily guarded residence: troops patrolled the perimeter and heavy machine guns watched over weak points in the defences. The building was surrounded by three separate fences of barbed wire, one of which was stretched on to white ceramic insulation fittings, suggesting that it was electrified. Anyone driving to the villa had to go through a guard point, fortified with heavy concrete blocks, and stop at an orange and white steel pole, which was raised once visitors had presented their identification papers and had been given clearance to enter. Getting in and out of the compound was going to be difficult. Getting into the villa itself, finding and overpowering the general and then making a run for it was impossible. They had to find some other way to kidnap him.

The general's military headquarters at Archanes was about three miles south of the villa. Micky's sister, Philia, and Kreipe's driver, Alfred Fenske, whom he had inherited from General Müller, were on relatively good terms. She reported that, for a German soldier, he was a nice man. Fenske had a wife and small son whom he had not seen for over a year. In his wallet he carried pictures of his young family: his son posing in a dressing-up military uniform; his wife sitting with her family at a picnic. Before the war Fenske had unsuccessfully tried to avoid being called up by getting himself arrested and imprisoned for petty crimes. The general's car was the latest Opel Kapitän, with a 2.5-litre, six-cylinder engine, all-steel body, front independent suspension, hydraulic shock absorbers, hot-water heating (with electric blower), and a centrally mounted speedometer. It was comfortable and luxurious. Fenske was proud of the car and spent a lot of time cleaning and polishing its black bodywork and chrome trim to an immaculate deep shine.

Philia used her friendship with Fenske to find out about General Kreipe's routine, which turned out to be very straightforward: she reported that every morning, at the same time, Kreipe was driven to his military HQ at Archanes, and every evening he returned home. On some evenings he stayed later to play bridge with some of his officers and on others, if there was a military exercise on, he worked late.

In April the sun set about 8 o'clock, and Leigh Fermor and Akoumianakis wondered if it was possible to stop the general's car, in the dark, somewhere on his way home. They walked the route to Archanes and discovered a bend in the road which forced traffic to slow down almost to a stop. While they stood in the warm sunshine, wondering whether this was the place to ambush Kreipe, a huge shiny Opel staff car appeared on the road ahead, each wing bearing triangular pennants: the one on the nearside wing striped in black, white and red, like the German flag; the other green with a gold eagle carrying a wreath with a swastika at its centre. The car slowed and, through the open passenger window, they glimpsed General Kreipe himself. The two men stood to the side to let the car pass; as it swept by Leigh Fermor waved. Kreipe turned his broad pale face, surprised perhaps to see two Cretans who seemed to be friendly, and raised his brown leather-gloved hand in salute. Like watching a film in slow motion, Leigh Fermor noticed Kreipe's jutting chin, large nose and his coat fastened with glittering brass buttons. There were decorations sewn onto his chest and an Iron Cross at his throat. The two men's eyes met, then the film speeded up and the car swept on.

That night in Heraklion, Leigh Fermor and Micky thought about the problems: how could they stop the car; how were they to deal with any escort; most of all, in the dark, how would they know they had the right car? Ilias was ordered to watch the general's movements and to make detailed notes about his itinerary.

The next week was the Greek Orthodox Easter. By the Saturday, Ilias confirmed that Kreipe travelled to the villa not once, as Micky's sister thought, but twice a day. He left the Villa Ariadne at 8.30, arriving in Archanes to start work at the dot of nine. At 13:00 hours he returned to his villa for lunch and stayed there, until 16.15 when he returned to his headquarters and worked late into the evening. Philia found out that Kreipe's aide-de-camp had a passion for bridge and often persuaded the general to play a late rubber: after all it passed the time, there weren't many things on the island to entertain the troops, even high ranking ones.

The kidnappers urgently needed a hideout near the ambush spot where they could spend the day before the kidnap. Mickey had a friend, Pavlos Zografistos, who owned a farm about half an hour's walk from the new proposed kidnap point. Without telling him exactly what was going on, Micky asked Pavlos if he was prepared to house a band of guerrillas for a couple of nights. Zografistos was a keen patriot and hated the German invaders; he agreed with pleasure, though he had no idea what this armed and dangerous band was up to.

In the remote cave where the rest of the team were hiding, the time passed slowly. The monotony was broken by the arrival of a runner with a letter from Leigh Fermor updating Moss on progress in Heraklion. After six days the weather changed, and it began to rain, a fine mountain drizzle. While Moss lay reading, smoke from the fire hovering in the low room, a face appeared at the door. It was a shepherd who said that two men had turned up at his hut claiming to be Russian prisoners escaped from a German labour gang at Kasteli airfield. The shepherd was afraid that the men were actually German Secret Police. Moss's mother was Russian and he was fluent, so he and Tyrakis pulled on their coats, grabbed their weapons and went to see what all the fuss was about. When they arrived at the shepherd's hut the so-called Russians had vanished.

Two days later the shepherd reappeared and said that the Russians were waiting in a gulley close by and willing to talk. Moss found them huddling in the drizzle, looking anxious and exhausted. They introduced themselves as Ivan and Vasily and said they had been captured in the Crimea in 1942. At first they were held on the Greek mainland, used as forced labour on roads and construction sites by the Nazis. In the summer of 1943 they were transported to Crete to help build the new runways at Kasteli. Three of them had escaped by crawling under the wire and heading into the mountains. The third man was shot during the break-out. Vasily and Ivan had been on the run for nearly five days.

Both men were starving: rations for the forced labourers were meagre – generally soup and potatoes, which were usually rotten and all but inedible. They were shivering with cold, their clothes were threadbare and their boots had disintegrated, revealing feet that were in a terrible state, blistered and bloody. Moss took them to the shelter of the cave, gave them clothing and fed them like prize bantams; Moss lent one of them his old service dress jackets, making him look like an oddly down-at-heel Guards officer. As they recovered, the men threw themselves into the life of the camp and spent the evenings teaching Moss and the guerrillas haunting folk songs, including many beautiful Ukrainian melodies.

While waiting for the party to come back from Heraklion, Moss began to understand the Cretans better. On the beach he had seen only comic opera clothes worn by piratical villains; he had found Grigorios Chnarakis particularly irritating – he always seemed to do the wrong thing, like blowing his nose into his hand, especially when the wind was in the wrong direction, spitting, trampling on Moss's head when he was asleep. But forced together in the cave, Moss saw through his off-putting habits, and found Chnarakis to be a likeable, humorous and valiant man. Chnarakis was grandfather to six children. He had become a mountain fighter after helping two British airmen who had baled out over the island and landed in his small olive grove. He rescued them by hiding them under a pile of wood and telling the German search party that he had seen some parachutes landing half a mile away. The search party left, Chnarakis stayed with the airmen and that night took them into the mountains, from where they were fed into the escape networks and eventually returned to England. After this escapade he chose to stay and fight with the guerrillas.

Leigh Fermor, Micky and Ilias arrived back from Heraklion just after midday on 19 April, Easter Sunday – a day of great feasting in Greece. In the mountain hideout the war stopped for the day. A sheep was selected, a shepherd drawing his knife across its throat, ending the animal's life in a bleating gurgle. A demijohn of wine was produced and dozens of boiled eggs were offered round, each dyed red with cochineal for Easter. The Cretans crushed the eggs together 'like conkers', shouting 'Christ is risen!' To which the response was, 'He is risen indeed.' The abductors and the Russians joined in the spirit of the Cretan party, singing and dancing. Uneaten eggs were flung into the air and used for target practice. Vasily turned out to be a crack shot: standing, swaying with his glass in one hand, waving his pistol around in the other, and hitting egg after egg, shouting 'Christ is risen', bang 'He is truly risen', bang. He got so drunk that one round thudded into the gravel at Moss's feet. Leigh Fermor coaxed the revolver out of his hand, after which Vasily sank to the ground, pole-axed, and lay comatose in the shade of a beech tree.

The revels went on through the long hot day, though some men dropped out, too drunk to continue. Others lay snoring on the rocks, recovering in the sun so that they could drink and eat more. They sang songs in what Moss thought was 'every language of the world'. By midnight, Moss and Leigh Fermor were alone in the cave drinking the whisky that Moss had brought with him from Cairo. Eventually they too fell into a deep drunken slumber. Outside the last die-hards fired their weapons into the air, not caring whether they attracted the attention of the Germans, the noise of the shots echoing round the mountains. The andartes felt invulnerable, like eagles, perched in the safety of their high mountain fastness.

Easter Monday dawned, the sun shone bright and the hungover
kidnap team reluctantly turned to the business in hand. Everyone
agreed that a direct attack on the Villa Ariadne was impossible
and that only an ambush on the road had any chance of success.
For two days they worked over the same problems: What would
they do if Kreipe's staff car had an escort? How could they recognise the vehicle in the dark? If they pulled the kidnap off how
could they prevent a Nazi backlash against the civilian population? The team did not want to be responsible for reprisal killings
and the destruction of villages. Ilias offered to go back to Heraklion
and spend his mornings and evenings spying on Kreipe's coming
and goings. He promised that in a few days he would be able to
identify the car at night by the sound of its engine, the appearance
of the headlights and its moonlit silhouette. He also promised to
devise a way to give advance notice that the car was on its way, and
soon began experimenting with a battery and wire attached to a
buzzer or light.

Ilias had another worry: the spot chosen for the ambush. The
bend in the road where they planned to stop the car had a restricted
view and any escort or vehicles following would be hidden until it
was too late. Fenske was a good driver, equipped with the latest
model Opel. Ilias did not think the bend was sharp enough to
slow him down. Much better he argued was the junction further
along, where the road joined the Heraklion–Houdetsi road. The
car would have to make a hard left turn, forcing even a good driver
to come almost to a stop. The junction had another advantage: on
the approach there was a line of hillocks with excellent views in
both directions, an ideal place for the lookouts. At the junction
itself, the road was flanked by ditches deep enough for the guerrillas to hide in.

After some argument Leigh Fermor conceded that Ilias was
right: they would jump the general's car at the junction, which
they now called Point A. The plan was taking shape. Next a
runner was sent to contact the 'Falstaffian' Kapitan Anastasios

Boutzalis, asking him to come to the hideout bringing some of his fighters to provide a back-up team to deal with Kreipe's escort or any other troops appearing on the road.

The next problem was how to stop the car. They thought about putting rocks in the road, or overturning a cart. Both methods were cumbersome and dangerous. Anything involving animals, rocks or trees would take time to set up, and the appearance of other cars on the road could lead to a traffic jam. Any sign of trouble and the general's escort would hold him back until the obstacle was cleared. They decided that if Leigh Fermor and Moss were disguised as German military policemen they stood a chance of being able to wave down the car. The two Englishmen had the right complexions and Leigh Fermor could speak German, though his accent and grammar were not perfect. The light-haired Moss could not speak the language but would at least look the part. It was the best they could do. The rest of the team could hide in the ditches on either side of the road, ready to spring out when the car stopped.

The original Villa Ariadne plan had all the attackers disguised as German soldiers, but the uniforms had been left in the plane that returned to Cairo after only dropping Leigh Fermor. The disguises had to be found locally. Micky thought he might be able to track down the right clothes and equipment.

The next day, while the group were munching their lunch of goat's cheese and hard bread, eighteen RAF bombers appeared over the airfield at Kasteli, visible on the flat plain a few miles to the east, and flying in a tight wedge formation. Black bombs tumbled from the fuselages, wobbling down to earth and exploding with dull bangs, sending sound waves which rumbled round the mountain hideout. Vasily and Ivan stood on the rocks waving their arms, shrieking and laughing in Russian. Tyrakis took off his beret and waved it, shouting 'Rooly Britannia'.

The German anti-aircraft guns opened up, puffs of grey smoke blossomed, masking the attackers. The spectators groaned and then cheered when the planes reappeared, unharmed. Their bombs delivered, the planes banked, flying south to the coast and the sea, heading for home and North Africa. Leigh Fermor and Moss clapped as if they were watching a cricket match. Black smoke billowed over Kasteli where German planes and fuel burned in the hot summer air.

By 18 May, the kidnappers were ready, Leigh Fermor announced that the abduction was on for the 24th, when the moon would be new and the night dark. His announcement was greeted with much shaking of hands, back-slapping and laughter; they were accomplices in a great plot of heroic Cretan proportions, bonded by the shared experience of what was to come.

In the late morning of the next day, Kapitan Boutzalis arrived with his fighters; they had set off as soon as the runner arrived and marched through the night. The landscape was filled with a sudden blaze of colour – blue and turquoise shirts, black turbans, silver knives held by purple cummerbunds contrasting with the scrubby green trees and the reddish brown rock. The new arrivals sat talking quietly in the shade of the trees, 'bristling like lobsters' in their criss-crossed bandoliers stiff with pointed brass cartridges. Cigarette smoke drifted through the air and the sunlight glinted dull on their rifle barrels.

To Leigh Fermor and Moss they appeared to be a tough lot; Paterakis and Tyrakis were less impressed, saying they were not as hard as they looked. While some of the men were seasoned mountain fighters, others had scarcely started to shave. They had all joined the resistance out of a deep-rooted sense of patriotism, prepared to defend their country with their lives.

The talk flowed round them like a quiet stream. After a while they began to clean their weapons, enjoying the metallic snap of rifle bolts sliding shut on to breeches shiny with clean oil. Since the German invasion, most of the firearms had been hidden up chimneys or buried in gardens. Moss thought some of them looked as though they dated back to the last Turkish invasion. Two of the guerrillas looked similarly ancient. Boutzalis explained that they had come along for the adventure, not wishing to be left out. Leigh Fermor and Moss wondered whether they were going to be up to the rigours of the coming days. Later, Leigh Fermor encouraged the fighters to change into British battledress tops and berets so they would look more like a coherent unit of fighting soldiers and not like civilian *francs-tireurs*, the punishment for which was execution.

Grigorios Chnarakis provided lunch: potatoes baked in the fire, soft-boiled eggs, fried onions, all mashed together with butter and salt in a large bowl. It was Boutzalis's turn to be taken aside and briefed by Leigh Fermor, who spoke softly to him in Greek. The kapitan unsheathed one of the long knives he carried round his waist and began to clean his nails, looking more than ever to the Englishmen like a bearded pantomime villain. The guerrilla leader learned that his men were to deal with any escort, or other enemy vehicles that suddenly appeared, and keep the enemy at bay while the German general was seized and spirited into the hills. After the kidnap his andartes were to provide guides and lookouts for the first leg of the journey to Anogia, from where they would move to a beach in southern Crete and the rendezvous with the Royal Navy.

When Leigh Fermor finished speaking Boutzalis grinned and gripped Moss around the shoulders, his eyes ablaze, grasping him in a whiskery bear hug and kissing him hard on both cheeks, laughing and chattering incomprehensibly. The briefing over, Moss scrambled into the cave and took a camera from his haversack which he had asked Micky to find for him. He was keeping a written and photographic record of the mission. Had they been captured the pictures and the diary would have incriminated everyone involved. Nevertheless a Leica was found on the black market in Heraklion. This was Moss's reckless, unthinking side: even purchasing these objects was dangerous and could have given

the game away. Back in the bright light he motioned to the guerrillas that he wanted to take their picture. Delighted, the men
clambered to their feet. They posed together in a group on the
rocks, instructing Moss in fast, excited Greek how they wished to
be recorded for posterity, striking serious warlike poses, thrusting
out their chests, holding their chins up like the heroes they were.
After the first few shots one of them grabbed the camera, gave it
to Vasily and then made Moss and Leigh Fermor sit in the middle
of the group: Leigh Fermor resplendent in his battledress blouse
with showy parachute wings above the left pocket; Moss with his
captain's pips on his shoulders and black beret oddly askew.

After the excitement of the photo session everyone packed their
belongings ready for the night march to Knossos and the
Zografistos house. The kidnap team pulled their rucksacks from
the cave that had been their headquarters and home for the last
twelve days. There was little talk and tension filled the air. At
dusk the twenty-five-strong column set off; there was no moon
and it soon became pitch black. The steep shingle screes gave way
beneath their feet, creating small landslides, the men flailed their
arms trying to grab the vegetation to keep upright. The young
found the going hard; the old found it almost impossible.

After an hour they stopped to rest by a stream, splashing the
icy water on to their faces, scooping it into their parched mouths.
Around them the cicadas chirruped and the heavy scent of wild
herbs filled their nostrils. A few minutes later they set off again,
till one of the band, Zahari, stopped, cursing: he had left his
sub-machine gun by the stream. He went back to find it, urged
on by the others swearing at him because they had to wait and
hide until he came back. Four hours later the same thing
happened again, but this time it took Zahari half an hour to
pluck up the courage to confess that he had mislaid his weapon
for the second time. The wait was much longer, the cursing
greater, as precious time and the possibility of moving in the
safety of darkness were lost.

As they marched the landscape changed, the hills became less steep and the going easier. They stopped sliding about on the screes and waded through hundreds of small streams; the song of a nightingale floated across the dark landscape accompanied by the raucous croaking of frogs.

After six hours they marched in an exhausted dream. At each stop their guide promised that the destination was only one more hour away. High in the hills around them were more fighting mountain men, positioned all along the fifteen-mile route, protecting them from the German patrols. The abductors passed unseen, like phantoms, across the landscape.

Progress slowed and Leigh Fermor realised that they were not going to reach Knossos before dawn. Boutzalis reassured him that one of his band had relatives in the nearby village of Kharasso. A man was sent ahead to warn that the abductors were on their way and to organise somewhere for them to hide. After fifteen hours marching they stumbled along the goat track into the village. Two figures appeared out of the gloom: it was the scout who had gone ahead accompanied by his cousin. In a rapid exchange of Greek they explained that the house where they were to hide was too small to accommodate everybody, the group had to split up. Boutzalis and his men were led to another place while Leigh Fermor's kidnap group was taken through the dark hamlet to a building with external stone steps leading to a small loft. Inside they found it was full of sacks of beans, olives and barrels of wine, and flung themselves down and fell asleep on the flea-ridden bedding.

They were woken soon after dawn with an earthenware basin of hot sweet milk, after which they flopped back into sleep. Around the village, the andartes continued to keep watch, guarding the team with the same fierce care that they guarded their sheep. The hot sun rose in the sky, the day passed and the men in the loft received bowls of cheese, hard-boiled eggs and onions. They drank what Moss described as resin-tasting wine from the barrels. Some of the older members of Boutzalis's group had found the night march too hard. Their footwear was useless – often little more than the rubber pads cut from car tyres – hardly enough for walking on the flat, let alone a steep, narrow, slippery mountain goat track. The old ones hugged the younger men, kissing them on the cheeks and wishing them luck with the mission, and then disappeared down the slopes, heading sadly for home and safety.

In the loft the kidnappers passed the day sleeping, chatting smoking, and tending to the bloody sores on their feet. At dusk they gathered their kit together and tramped down the stone stairs, where they found the owner of the house, his family and some of his livestock crammed into the living space. On the table was a feast of boiled snails, mutton, eggs, cheeses, fresh almonds and a variety of boiled grasses. The men ate through the evening, murmuring over and over 'Efkaristo poly' ('Thank you very much') and drinking the health of their hosts. Shortly after ten they set off into another black, moonless night. Boutzalis and his men had now been on the move for three gruelling nights. Moss found the going slightly easier than the night before, not so steep, but still slippery and difficult. In his diary he describes the journey as being like going up and down an ancient, rotten staircase where every other step is broken and every third step missing. His misery was increased by the fact that the old staircase itself was very narrow and the whole operation had to be carried out in the pitch dark.

Two hours before dawn they reached the house of Pavlos Zografistos, the base camp from which they were to carry out the operation. They were now in farming country, over which the Germans could move easily on foot and use their military vehicles. A few miles to the north was the Villa Ariadne and further on, the garrison town of Heraklion, teeming with the enemy; to the south was Archanes, Kreipe's headquarters. The ambush point, Point A, was just over a mile away to the west.

At the house they were met by Pavlos Zografistos himself.

Again the group split into two. Boutzalis, his men, and the Russians were led to an old tumbledown building, about three-quarters of a mile away, at the end of the track. It was an old wine press, where they were to hide until they moved off; the kidnappers were to stay in the Zografistos house itself.

The Zagrofistos house was small, clean and tidy, with no pictures or photographs on the walls. It stood on its own surrounded by olive trees and vines. Zagrofistos's nearest neighbour lived just under a mile away. The house was like the one they had stayed in the night before: two rooms, one above the other. This time it was a wooden ladder that gave access to the storage area upstairs . . . Micky had used his contacts in the Heraklion black market to provide chocolate, tinned butter, Greek coffee and plenty of white wine. The men settled down to wait.

15

The Waiting

In the afternoon Micky and Ilias Athanassakis arrived from Heraklion. They brought more black market food and two German uniforms. A resistance worker in the city, Demetrios Balahoutis, had a brother who owned a tailor's where the Germans got their uniforms mended. The tailor had made up two suits from offcuts and old pieces of uniform lying around his workshop. Micky had also laid his hands on a military police traffic paddle, a circle of tin fastened to a handle, the disc was red on one side and green on the other. The police used it to wave down vehicles.

Under the critical eye of ex-gendarme Manolis Paterakis, Moss and Leigh Fermor tried on the uniforms. The larger of the two jackets had a corporal's stripes on the sleeve: this one went to Leigh Fermor, the taller of the two men. Micky had found some military decorations and two small cloth cap badges. Leigh Fermor's jacket had a small round swastika badge pinned just under the left-hand chest pocket. The crowning touch to their disguise was two leather belts with silvered buckles bearing the words 'Gott Mit Uns' set around an imperial crown. When the staff car was stopped and the two SOE men approached the windows, their buckles would be the most prominent things the driver and the general saw. For good measure the leather scabbards of their lethal British commando daggers were added to the belts, plus holsters for their Colt automatics.

The two men paraded in front of Micky and Manolis. Micky

said that Moss looked like a typical disappointed German of 1944; Moss posed for a photograph and Leigh Fermor said that he looked like an Englishman dressed up as a German propping up the bar at the Berkley. Leigh Fermor was told to shave off his moustache; when he did so Moss found that his companion had a presence that was unnervingly close to the genuine article. They all agreed that, given the cover of night, the uniforms would pass muster, even if the sleeves were a bit short.

They took the uniforms off for Pavlos's sister to sew on extra bits and pieces, including some campaign ribbons. Her work was interrupted by Pavlos storming up the ladder. A group of German soldiers, possibly a patrol, was heading towards the house. They all waited in the small, stuffy upper room to see what the soldiers wanted. Moss, Leigh Fermor and Paterakis sat on their beds, cocked their weapons and waited for developments. Micky and the others sat with them, unarmed.

The soldiers hammered on the door, shouting for it to be opened. This was followed by the creaking of the hinges as Pavlos opened it and asked what the soldiers wanted. Upstairs the abductors kept their eyes and their guns trained on the entrance. Below them an argument took place, steel-shod boots tramped about on the stone floor as if the owners were looking for something. Then the door slammed, the sound of heavy footsteps followed by silence.

Moss peered through the dusty window. He saw four dust-covered German soldiers slouching away, their rifles over their shoulders, their kit hanging heavily from their belts. The men in the room let go their breath, put away their guns and waited for Pavlos to appear and explain that the Germans had come looking for food. He had persuaded them that there was none to be had.

Later that night Leigh Fermor composed a letter to be left in the car, stressing to the German command that the abduction was a purely British initiative. He wrote:

To the German Authorities in Crete

Gentlemen. Your Divisional Commander, General KREIPE, was captured a short time ago by a British raiding force under our command. By the time you read this both he and we will be on our way to Cairo.

We would like to point out most emphatically that this operation has been carried out without the help of the CRETANS or CRETAN PARTISANS, and the only guides used were serving soldiers of his HELLENIC MAJESTY'S FORCES in the Middle East, who came with us.

Your General is an honourable prisoner of war, and will be treated with the consideration owing to his rank.

Any reprisals against the local population will be wholly unwarranted and unjust.

Auf baldiges Wiedersehen! [See you soon!]

PATRICK LEIGH FERMOR

Major

WILLIAM STANLEY MOSS

Captain.

P.S. We are very sorry to have to leave this beautiful car behind.

The two men signed the paper and added the imprints of their signet rings for good measure. Then they folded it and put it carefully in a heavy, important-looking envelope.

While the work was going on in the house, Boutzalis and his men sat doing nothing in the gloom and heat of the disused wine press. After twenty-four hours they were getting restless. At first the kapitan only allowed his men out to answer the demands of nature. Before long he found it impossible to stop them crawling through the tiny passage that led to the tempting, bright, green outside world. He argued to himself that they had lookouts posted and were not likely to be surprised by a German patrol, so he too came out of hiding, followed by all the others.

It is difficult to keep a secret in any rural community, and no more so than on Crete, where even the most deserted, scrubby hillside vineyards have eyes. A rumour began to spread in the village that something odd was happening in Pavlos Zografistos's old wine press.

Later that day Leigh Fermor told Pavlos what the mission was really about. The Cretan was horrified, asking if they had any idea of the reprisals the abduction could cause. He ordered the men to get out, 'Leave my house I don't want people to be killed.' Leigh Fermor tried to persuade him that the letter he had written was going to make it clear that no locals were involved in the kidnap. Zografistos demanded to be allowed to talk to his father in the nearby village of Patsides about the wisdom of collaborating in 'a big job' with such potentially lethal consequences.

Other men arrived to support the abduction team. Nikos Komis from Thrapsano and Mitsos Tzatzas, from Episkopi, two 'silent mountain men' who were to act as guides once the general was a prisoner. Another guide appeared, Yanni Vitoros, a young man who was to lead them from the abandoned car up to the village of Anogia, where they were to rendezvous after the kidnap. Anogia was one of the strongholds of resistance fighters, an almost impregnable and remote village, which the German soldiers hated going near. Another man joined the group, Stratis Saviolakis, a serving policeman from Sfakia, stationed in the Archanes area. The Germans knew and trusted him, which meant he could move about without causing suspicion. He had already reconnoitred the road from Archanes to the Villa Ariadne, pacing the junction and driving by in a car to see how long it would take to drive from Heraklion to the kidnap site. Stratis reported to the team morning and evening, keeping them abreast with events at the garrison in Archanes.

The next day Zografistos returned from the meeting with his father. He had calmed down and said he would do everything he could to support the operation; he later confided to Tyrakis that his father had got angry with him and told him that he 'was not a man' if he did not help with the operation, even if it meant the ruin of the whole Heraklion region and the death of many hostages. Tyrakis wondered who else Pavlos had spoken to.

Ilias Athanassakis was as good as his word. He had kept the general's car under constant observation, night and day, until he could distinguish it from any other vehicle on the road. He knew the sound of the engine, the silhouette of the car and how the headlights looked at night: even though they were covered by slotted blackout cowls, they were still bright. He and Micky Akoumianakis had abandoned the plan to use a warning system of wires and buzzers; they would rely on torches alone. Ilias's plan was to watch Kreipe leave and then jump on his bicycle and pedal to a spot where he could signal by torch to Mitsos, who would relay the signal to the abductors who were in his line of sight. One flash meant the car was on its way and on its own; two flashes meant that it had an escort.

On 24 April, the day earmarked for the operation, Micky brought bad news: Kreipe had gone to his office as normal after lunch, but had returned to the Villa Ariadne before sunset. The team did not know why he had he done this. They wondered whether someone had tipped him off that bandits were in the area. Pavlos thought someone might have noticed the amount of activity near the normally quiet farm, and that perhaps this was the real reason for the visit by the four-man patrol the previous day.

Pavlos Zografistos began to lose his nerve. What would happen, he wondered, if the Germans searched the area? They were capable of throwing a cordon of two or three hundred heavily armed men round a suspicious area and searching it with a fine-toothed comb. The abduction team had grown to twelve men; together with Boutzalis's back-up men they were putting a strain on the villagers' resources. Twenty-four extra mouths could not be fed for long. Pavlos Zografistos told Leigh Fermor that he had to do something to reduce the risks.

In the evening, after the sun had set, the SOE men moved quietly along the goat track, through the olive groves to the wine press for a conference with Boutzalis. The big Cretan leader was devastated when Leigh Fermor told him that he and his men were no longer part of the operation and must go back to their base hideout at once. He was to take the two Russians with him in the hope that they could form the basis of the resistance group of escaped POWs that Moss planned to lead later in the year.

In spite of their kapitan's disappointment, Boutzalis's men themselves did not seem to be too upset at having to go. They filed off into the night, shaking hands and each taking the gold sovereign which Leigh Fermor offered them. The Russians were given a Marlin sub-machine gun each and some ammunition. Then they embraced their English rescuers, and left. They were a real loss, being strong walkers always ready to carry twice as much as anyone else. With Boutzalis gone the team had no armed escort to protect them during the kidnap. Things would get worse later in the operation when they had to lose Micky and Ilias, whose job was to clear up the kidnap area, and then get back to Heraklion, where they could not be spared from counter-intelligence work. Moss and Leigh Fermor considered abandoning the plan.

Micky knew that an old friend of Leigh Fermor's was in the area, Antonis Zoidakis, another policeman, based in the Amari valley. A runner left with a letter begging him to join the group. Zoidakis had been with the resistance ever since fighting in the battle of Crete. In 1943, SOE had arranged for him to go to Egypt to be trained at their irregular warfare school near Haifa. According to Giorgios Tyrakis, Antonis's favourite sport was 'throat slitting'.

Antonis Zoidakis appeared at around two in the morning full of enthusiasm and worried that he might have missed out on the big adventure. Leigh Fermor was delighted to see him and the two men spent the rest of the night reminiscing. He described

Antonis, 'sitting on my bed in his old policeman's jacket, his cheerful face lit by an oil lamp. We talked and smoked until dawn.'

The waiting and the constant threat of German patrols began to wear the group down. 'Spirits were low,' wrote Leigh Fermor, 'anxiety hung in the air. It needed much outward optimism and cheerfulness to keep spirits from flagging. We talked, read out loud and worried.' The man who found the stress most difficult to deal with was the guide Yanni Vitoros, who was becoming physically ill. Pavlos's sister was also breaking down under the strain of hiding guerrilla fighters in her house. In the early morning of 25 April news came in that there was more enemy activity in the area; she could take it no longer and asked them to leave.

On the border of Pavlos's property was a deep dried-up river bed. It had an overhanging rock that formed a sort of cave. The area was surrounded by saplings; not as comfortable as the upstairs room they had just vacated, but much more peaceful. The men spread their blankets and slept. The next day they were brought eggs, cheese and wine and they ate under a warm sun, enjoying the peace and quiet of their new hideout.

At midday Pavlos Zografistos appeared, creeping up the dried river bed, his clothes and boots covered in dust. In his hand he held a letter from the National Organisation of Crete, the EOK, an organisation normally sympathetic to the SOE. The letter warned Leigh Fermor that they knew about the plan and demanded that it be called off because the risk to the local population was too great. If he refused they threatened to expose him to the Germans. A special envoy arrived from the EOK, Dr Lignos, a senior member of the group. He repeated that the proposed operation was madness and must be abandoned because of the harm it would do to Crete, even if it was successful.

The usually resourceful Leigh Fermor was stumped; he had no idea how the plan had become so widely known. Gathering the kidnappers together, he told them that he was calling the whole thing off. He ordered them to pack up and leave the area at once. The men looked at him in grim silence, shifting their weight, the rocks crunching under their feet.

The silence was broken by Paterakis, who had been Leigh Fermor's right-hand man for more than two years. 'Major,' he said, 'we have come here to carry out a mission, and carry it out we must!' One of the others added: 'Dr Lignos is waiting for your answer in Pavlos's house. Do not let him browbeat you, we are not leaving without the general, alive or dead.' The others murmured their agreement. Leigh Fermor threw down his cigarette, trod it into the ground, and said: 'Right we'll talk to him again.'

Before going back to Dr Lignos he wrote a letter to the EOK, which he hoped would confuse them about the timing of the kidnap, making them think that the abduction was not going to happen for at least another twenty-four hours. Then he trudged up the gulley to the house and spoke to the doctor, spinning him the same story. Lignos went away satisfied. Leigh Fermor gambled that they would capture Kreipe that night, before his letter reached Heraklion.

After the departure of the doctor, two figures came crawling up the gorge, Stratis, the policeman and Ilias, both hotfoot from watching the general's movements. He had not left the Villa Ariadne all day. In the last three days his routine had changed dramatically, making it even more likely that the Germans had discovered the plot. The group tensed, expecting to hear the grinding gears of lorries moving along the hill, disgorging soldiers armed with machine guns, grenades and rifles. If they were attacked the small band of kidnappers would not have a chance.

They resolved to do nothing until dark, to stay under cover and not move about. The slightest sign that there were men in hiding in the area might bring the German army down on their heads. Darkness fell, Leigh Fermor drew an outline of the car in the dust, and made the team rehearse the ambush for the hundredth time.

The two torch men stood in for the general and his driver. The group mimed dragging them out of an imaginary vehicle, spraying sub-machine-gun bullets at an imaginary escort, flinging themselves into imaginary ditches. At last they stopped for the night.

Tired and depressed, the two British officers lay on their backs, talking, smoking, staring at the stars and singing softly. It looked as though the whole enterprise might come to nothing. They decided to give the operation another twenty-four hours before abandoning it.

The next day dawned lonely for the kidnap team. Leigh Fermor wrote later: 'Between the acting of a dreadful thing and the first motion, all the interim is like a phantasmal or hideous dream.' No one knew whether there was German activity in the area. No one seemed to know anything for certain; rumours were everywhere, unsettling the small band. To pass the time Leigh Fermor recited snippets of Shakespeare which he had taught himself to say in German.

Around noon it began to rain and Pavlos Zografistos again rushed up the gorge saying they must move at once. Down in the valley they could hear the raised voices of men, women and children, hunting for snails, heading straight towards them. The team scrambled on up the hill, dragging their weapons and equipment. Their next hideout was a damp, chalky cave, its walls running with rainwater, soaking their clothes. They wondered whether General Kreipe had taken a good lunch and was now speeding back to his headquarters in the comfort of his staff car. Leigh Fermor kept spirits up with pep talks in Greek. Manolis Paterakis and Giorgios Tyrakis worried that Pavlos and his sister were losing their nerve. They thought it might be safer if Pavlos joined the kidnappers. The two men agreed that if he was with them he would be a sort of hostage, he would not be tempted to talk to anyone and neither would his sister.

Without warning, Yanni, the guide, began convulsing:

frothing at the mouth, gibbering, moaning. He started to hallu-
cinate, grabbing Moss's foot and banging the toecap with a cigarette tin. Next he tried to fling away his boots, ripping his socks
off and holding them up in front of his eyes, chattering incoher-
ently. Finally he lay on the ground in the pouring rain making
strange clicking noises. The group dragged him into the shelter of
a rock, where he lay, refusing to stand up. They were going to
have to abandon him and leave him lying among the myrtle
bushes with the rain dripping off the end of his nose. Moss hoped
that the snail-hunters would not find him, or, if they did, that he
would be too deranged to tell them anything. Stratis, the policeman, was deputed to take over to guide them to Anogia; he assured
them he knew the route. The rain stopped, the snail hunters'
voices trailed away into the distance.

In the morning Ilias appeared with the news that General
Kreipe had left for his headquarters; he was back in his old routine.
Calm descended on the group, 'as though everything was out of
our hands'. Leigh Fermor and Moss changed into their German
uniforms and sat smoking, tense and silent as they waited for
dusk.

16

The Trap Springs

That evening, in the officers' mess at the German garrison in Archanes, Kreipe's aide-de-camp asked him if he would care to join him in a game of cards. Kreipe accepted the invitation and asked his ADC to telephone the Villa Ariadne to say he would be late: he would dine later, at half past nine rather than eight.

In his hideout above Anogia, Tom Dunbabin was running a fever. His radio was the only link the kidnappers had with GHQ and it was protected by Kapitan Petrakoyiorgi and his andartes. Dunbabin told his radio operator that he was going to retreat to the Amari valley until he recovered and would be out of contact. The operator would have to make sure that any news was sent to Cairo. Access to his radio was vital to the success of the kidnap. Dunbabin did not know that he was in the early stages of malaria.

The sun set and the abductors walked through the darkness towards the ambush area, Point A. There were others out that night, shadows slinking through the dark, poachers and sheep rustlers. Leigh Fermor grunted at them in German, scaring them off. When they reached Point A, the team were surprised at how steeply the road from Archanes dropped to the junction; neither Ilias nor Stratis had warned them of this and the British agents had not spotted it on their first recce. Moss worried that if the chauffeur stopped without using the handbrake, the heavy Opel could roll forward, giving the general a chance to escape; he was also concerned that if they pulled the driver out of the car it might roll down the road and crash into one of the ditches, leaving them

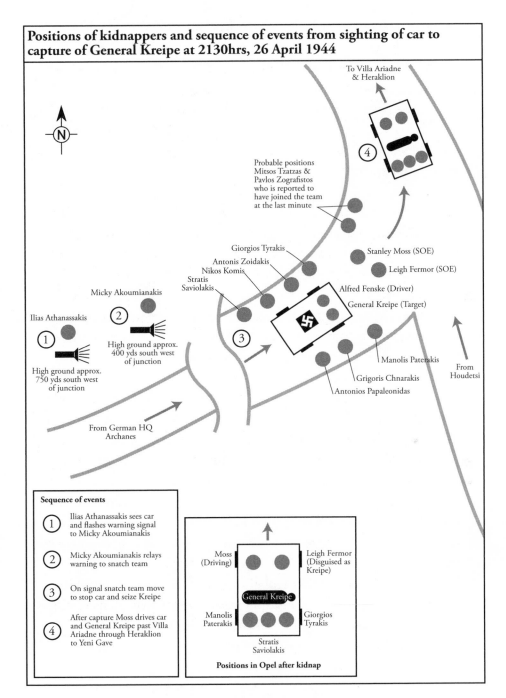

Positions of kidnappers and sequence of events from sighting of car to capture of General Kreipe at 2130hrs, 26 April 1944

To Villa Ariadne & Heraklion

N

④

Probable positions Mitsos Tzatzas & Pavlos Zografistos who is reported to have joined the team at the last minute

Giorgios Tyrakis

Stanley Moss (SOE)

Antonis Zoidakis
Nikos Komis

Leigh Fermor (SOE)

Stratis
Saviolakis

Micky Akoumianakis

Alfred Fenske (Driver)

General Kreipe (Target)

②

Ilias Athanassakis

High ground approx. 400 yds south west of junction

③

Manolis Paterakis

From Houdetsi

①

High ground approx. 750 yds south west of junction

Grigoris Chnarakis

Antonios Papaleonidas

From German HQ Archanes

Sequence of events

① Ilias Athanassakis sees car and flashes warning signal to Micky Akoumianakis

② Micky Akoumianakis relays warning to snatch team

③ On signal snatch team move to stop car and seize Kreipe

④ After capture Moss drives car and General Kreipe past Villa Ariadne through Heraklion to Yeni Gave

Moss (Driving)

Leigh Fermor (Disguised as Kreipe)

General Kreipe

Manolis Paterakis

Giorgios Tyrakis

Stratis Saviolakis

Positions in Opel after kidnap

For a full list of the kidnap team see p. 255.

without a getaway vehicle. There was nothing they could do, it was too late to change the plan.

The team split up and moved into their positions. Micky and Stratis ran towards Archanes, disappearing into the dark, heading for the positions where they could relay Ilias's torch signals to the main group at the junction. Leigh Fermor and Moss took up their positions on the junction itself, Antonios Papaleonidas, Grigorios and Manolis, their guns slung over their shoulders, slid into place beside them; on the other side of the road, the driver's side, Nikos Komis, Antonis Zoidakis and Giorgios scrambled into the ditch. Mitsos Tzatzas ran across the junction towards Heraklion to watch for traffic coming towards Archanes; neither Leigh Fermor nor Moss knew that he had Pavlos Zografistos with him.

Leigh Fermor checked his red torch and Moss balanced the police paddle against the side of the ditch, ready to pick up when the time came to run into position. The noise of feet crunching on stones stopped. For a moment there was silence, then low whistles signalled that everyone was in place.

In Archanes, Ilias leant on his bicycle, hidden in the shadows, staring at the entrance to the German headquarters, waiting for the general's car to appear.

In the ditches, the kidnappers heard the sound of a vehicle travelling fast. A Kübelwagen, the Volkswagen version of a light jeep, bucketed round the bend, the engine revving as the driver changed down, slowing towards the junction. Hidden by scrub, the kidnappers saw that the vehicle had its hood up, making it impossible to see who was in it. The Kübelwagen drove on, silence returned to the junction. Then another Kübelwagen travelling from the opposite direction swung right, heading towards Archanes its headlights sweeping over the bushes hiding the crouching figures.

After a long wait the grinding gears and revs of heavily laden lorries echoed across the rocky landscape, coming from the direction of Archanes. The headlight of a motorcycle combination lit up the road, the vehicle roared round the bend, the driver changed down and braked hard to a halt at the junction; in the sidecar next to him sat a machine-gunner. The two men peered about, the driver glanced back over his shoulder. The gunner traversed his MG34 Spandau across the unseen men in the ditches. The weapon was capable of firing 1,500 rounds a minute, faster than any other machine gun in the world. The powerful BMW engine ticked over while the driver waited, pulled up his goggles, and again squinted back into the darkness. The noise of the heavy engines got louder, two lorries ground into sight, the motorcycle driver slipped his goggles back over his eyes, revved his engine and drove on, the gunner leaning expertly into the bend as they swung left towards the Villa Ariadne.

The lorries lumbered after them, their big black wheels passing close to the kidnappers, spraying them with grit, diesel fumes belching from the exhausts. In the back, troops sat motionless, their steel helmets and shoulders silhouetted against the night sky, unaware that nine pairs of eyes were watching them like foxes. They jiggled and swayed as the vehicles, followed the motorcycle. A lit cigarette end landed in the road in front of Paterakis and rolled into the ditch at his feet, still glowing red. Further up the road Mitsos and Pavlos Zografistos hunched into their ditch as the vehicles rumbled past.

Billy Moss, who had fought with the Coldstream Guards in the desert war, found that the experience reminded him of night patrols near enemy trenches when he could hear careless German soldiers talking or whistling quietly, and even see them lighting their cigarettes, hunched over the flame, trying not to give their position away. He and Leigh Fermor shivered in their German uniforms, which were too thin to protect them from the night wind blowing across the hills. The general was an hour behind schedule.

At 21:15, Heinrich Kreipe was still immersed in the card game. Glancing at his watch he said he was sorry but he must return to his residence where dinner would be waiting. The other players looked disappointed, Kreipe stood, told them to finish the game and follow on in another car with the ADC. The officers clambered to their feet, saluting as Kreipe left the room and headed for the front door where his driver, Alfred Fenske, waited with the car. From his hiding place in the shadows, Ilias heard the starter motor run and the staff car's engine kick into life. The shiny black sedan purred up to the orange and white security barrier. The guards came to attention; a soldier swung open the barrier, holding the counterweight in one hand, and saluted with the other as the second most senior officer on Crete passed by on his way home. Fenske nodded to the guards; they were his friends and he had been chatting with them earlier. Kreipe settled into the leather front passenger seat, talking to Fenske, asking him if he thought his instruction to put a security barrier on the junction between the Archanes and the Houdetsi roads had been followed. If he was going to be kidnapped, he said, that would be where it was going to happen; he admitted to Fenske that he had a strange feeling about it. The car disappeared into the night.

Ilias was certain it was the general: he had seen the number plate which he had memorised days before: WH 563 850. He jumped on his bicycle and pedalled as hard as he could towards his signal point. At the junction Leigh Fermor asked Moss the time: it was 21:30 hours. They wondered whether their quarry was already home, a passenger in one of the Kübelwagens that passed earlier in the evening. Then, from Micky's position on the hillock, came a torch flash: the car was on its way, unescorted.

Leigh Fermor and Moss heaved themselves out of the ditch, grabbing the red torch and the tin traffic signal, and sprinted to the centre of the road, brushing grit and leaves from the fronts of their uniforms. Each had a cocked Colt automatic pistol tucked into the back of the 'Gott Mit Uns' leather belts. Moss had a ten-inch steel cosh hidden up his sleeve, the bulbous metal end wrapped in plaited leather, its strap twisted round his wrist.

In the distance they heard the noise of a car changing down. The two men tensed, stood bolt upright and tried to look as official and military as possible. Ahead lights lit up the bend; they hoped that the signalling system had worked and that they were not about to confront a German convoy.

A car swept round the corner and the other kidnappers got ready to spring. Ilias was right: in spite of the slitted blackout cowls the headlamps were dazzlingly bright. Leigh Fermor and Moss screwed up their eyes against the glare. Moss held up the tin sign, red side towards the car; Leigh Fermor flashed the red torch and held up his hand, shouting '*Halt!*', his voice almost drowned out by the sound of the engine.

In the car, Kreipe was pleased to see his orders about the security barrier had been obeyed. Fenske slowed down, the synchromesh gearbox revving hard as it braked the vehicle. Fenske applied the footbrake and the Opel Kapitän purred to a halt. He pulled on the handbrake and, just as he had been trained, left the engine idling so that he could drive his way out of trouble if anything unexpected happened. Through the windscreen General Kreipe saw the two policemen walking towards him, one on each side of the car, moving past the stiff metal pennants out of the glare of the lights. Fenske did not recognise them. Kreipe got ready to congratulate the men on their efficiency. The driver and passenger windows wound down to reveal the general in a peaked cap, red and gold trim on his uniform collar. Fenske was bare-headed. The two SOE men drew level with the windows, blocking the view of the other kidnappers. Leigh Fermor pulled the automatic from behind his back; Billy Moss let the tapered leather grip of the heavy 'life preserver' slide into the palm of his hand.

Kreipe glanced up and began to smile, Leigh Fermor saluted and leant down, looking across the general at Fenske, asking: '*Ist dies das Generals Wagen?*'

'*Ja, Ja,*' replied Fenske.

Behind the driver's head Leigh Fermor could see Moss's belt buckle glinting.

'*Papieren bitte,*' said Leigh Fermor, holding out his hand in a respectful manner. The general nodded and reached into his coat pocket for his identity card.

Instantly, Leigh Fermor and Moss tore open the car doors. The interior light snapped on flooding the driver and his passenger in dazzling white. The andartes leapt out of the ditches and dashed forward. Leigh Fermor grabbed Kreipe by the lapels, knocking off the general's gold-braided hat. He jammed his automatic into the German's chest shouting '*Hände hoch!*' The driver twisted towards Moss, fumbling to drag his Luger from its holster. Moss grabbed the man's collar and hit him as hard as he could across the temple with the cosh. Fenske sighed and slumped sideways, as if he had been hit with a hammer, blood streaming into his eyes from the gash on his head. Moss dragged him out of the car and Tyrakis ran up, hitting Fenske another hard blow to his head. Together they pulled the man's body onto the ground, twisting his arms behind his back and snapping handcuffs onto his wrists. Fenske lay in the road, a moaning gurgle coming from his throat. Antonis Zoidakis knelt down and pulled the driver's Luger from its holster.

On the other side of the car Kreipe bellowed in rage, trying to break free, cursing and lashing out with his fists and feet, hitting Leigh Fermor violently on the cheek. The Cretans fell on him, shouting and screaming, forcing him to the ground with their weight. Mitsos and Zografistos ran up just in time to join the fight. They too leapt on the general. As Kreipe lay pinned to the ground, Chnarakis handcuffed him and the others tied his legs with rope. The rear doors were wrenched open and they bundled him, head first, struggling and writhing, into the back of the car, forcing him to lie lengthways on the floor. Zografistos saw something glinting on the road, it was the general's Iron Cross and he scooped it up, unnoticed in the confusion. Giorgios barged past him and leapt into the back, his feet trampling the general, Stratis and Manolis followed, their feet stamping on Kreipe's chest and shins. They slammed the doors and wound down the windows, their Marlin sub-machine guns poking through ready to spray fire. Chnarakis and Zoidakis dragged the driver to the side of the road, out of the way of the car. Zografistos tried to help them. Fenske's feet scraped along the ground, his head lolled forward, blood ran down his neck.

Moss leapt into the driver's seat, checking that the handbrake was on and that the fuel gauge read full. Leigh Fermor thumped into the passenger seat, pulling Kreipe's peaked cap onto his head. The general began to struggle again, heaving around; Tyrakis drew his long, sharp, silver-bladed knife and held the point against the officer's throat, muttering threateningly in Greek. Kreipe stopped resisting.

By the ditch Zoidakis and Chnarakis tried to get the driver to stand up. At each attempt his knees buckled. Moss depressed the clutch, pushed the car into gear and got ready to take off the handbrake. Leigh Fermor gave his last instructions to the others. They were to go, at once, with Fenske, to meet up with Dunbabin at his wireless base. Micky pushed everyone aside, his face grotesque through the car window, screaming hysterically in a voice full of venom: 'Long live freedom. Down with Germany!' Leigh Fermor pushed him back, shouting at him in Greek to shut up. At the same time he smashed the interior light bulb with his Colt, shards of glass and plastic sprayed the front of the car, then darkness and dead calm descended. Moss released the handbrake, slowly let in the clutch and felt the powerful engine take the weight of the vehicle. Then he revved hard, the rear wheels skidded and they sped off, heading for Heraklion and its 15,000-strong German garrison. In the mirror he could see some of the others dragging Fenske off the road and into the darkness. The ambush had taken less than ninety seconds.

Inside the Opel, the kidnappers erupted into excited, relieved gabbling, punctuated by the moans of the general, muffled by Giorgios's hand clamped over his mouth. Ahead of them were headlights, lorries driving towards Archanes. The three guerrillas in the back of the Opel ducked down, the lorries roared past, the soldiers in the trucks sitting bolt upright like toys, rifles between their knees.

Through the Checkpoints

Kreipe began to shout above the noise, repeating over and over in German: 'Where's my hat, where's my hat?' From his position on the floor, trampled under the feet of the three kidnappers, he could not see that it was on Leigh Fermor's head.

After a few minutes they were flagged down by soldiers manning a checkpoint with no barrier. Paterakis, Stratis and Tyrakis crouched low. Giorgios once more clamped his hard mountain farmer's hand, rough as sandpaper, over the general's soft mouth, crushing his face between his fingers. Moss slowed down, giving the soldiers a chance to see the pennants on the wings of the car. Then, when they were within yards of the soldiers, he accelerated, passing the checkpoint, tensing in expectation of a rifle bullet blasting through the rear windscreen. The car cruised into a bend and the roadblock vanished behind them. The kidnappers knew that if the guards suspected anything they would telephone ahead to have the vehicle stopped.

From the floor of the Opel, Kreipe asked how long he was going to be forced to remain in his undignified position. Leigh Fermor lit a cigarette and spoke in German. He told the general that if he was prepared to give his word that he would not shout or do anything to attract attention, then he would be treated as a comrade in arms, not a prisoner. Leigh Fermor found it difficult to make out the general's muffled reply, but assumed that he had agreed.

Another security point loomed up. The splendour of the staff car and the sight of the pennants worked the same magic; the kidnap vehicle was waved through, the guards snapping to attention and saluting. Seconds later they were speeding uphill. Ahead of them on the left lay the Villa Ariadne, where Kreipe's staff were waiting to welcome him home and the kitchen was standing by, ready to serve dinner. The soldiers on the gate heard the car approaching and got ready to raise the barrier; one of them ran towards the house to be there to open the car door and usher the general up the steps. The car drew level with the orange and white security bar, Moss put his hand on the horn and drove past. To the delight of the kidnappers the guards saluted, ramrod straight, staring ahead. Leigh Fermor asked the general if he spoke any English.

'*Nein*,' he replied.

Moss asked if he spoke Russian.

'*Nein.*'

'Greek?'

'*Nein.*'

'*Parlez-vous français?*'

'*Un petit peu . . .*'

The two Englishmen could not resist 'the Cowardesque reply': 'I never think that is quite enough.'

After this interchange they talked to Kreipe in stumbling French which Leigh Fermor translated into Greek for the benefit of the others.

Moss drove fast through the deserted flax fields towards Heraklion. Houses began to appear along the sides of the road. On their right they passed a large, lavish building which had been requisitioned as a garrison post office. A few hundred yards further on was the officers' club; outside were chairs and tables where members sat in the warm evening air being served by white-coated mess stewards moving about taking orders and delivering trays of drinks. Military traffic into the town was building up, forcing Moss to slow down. From somewhere on the terrace outside the club a voice shouted: *'Der Generals Wagen'*; officers and men on the crowded terrace rose to attention, saluting, barging into the waiters and sending trays of drinks flying. The Opel rolled on past Heraklion cemetery along King Giorgios II Street, towards another checkpoint and the centre of the city. The pennants saw them through, the barrier swung obligingly into the air. The silence of the fields gave way to the hustle and bustle of the garrison town.

Ahead Moss could see lights around the gardens of Liberty Square and throngs of soldiers milling in front of the huts which were the *Soldatenheim*, the Wehrmacht's equivalent of the Naafi. Through the huts a swastika billowed from the pillars of the Kreiskommandantur, where Moss would have to turn right into King Giorgios I Street. This was the riskiest part of the journey: the road was very narrow and full of German vehicles and soldiers, illuminated by pools of light spilling from cafes and bars. The car slowed outside the Kommandantur and the soldiers on guard saluted. Moss swung on to the main road through the town and headed towards the crowds coming out of the civilian cinema. Soldiers poured from the building, blocking the road. More flags bearing white-circled, black swastikas flapped in the evening breeze. Drunken German soldiers sang songs and walked with their arms round each other's shoulders, shouting greetings and elbowing aside any local unfortunate enough to get in their way. Moss blasted the horn, sending uniformed men scurrying out of the path, saluting and stumbling as they as they cleared a way for the general's sedan. The car was waived through checkpoint after checkpoint, Leigh Fermor muttering directions from the passenger seat.

They drove on towards Lion Square. During the day the area was usually full and bustling with people bartering whatever they could lay their hands on. The white marble bowls and lions of the fountain were permanently covered in dust; the water that fed it had been cut off soon after the invasion. Ahead the road turned slightly to the left: this was where three years earlier Colonel Tzoulakis had lost his life firing at the first paratroopers to enter the town.

The kidnappers were on the last leg of the journey through the town. From the back of the car the general's muffled voice burst out: 'This is marvellous; where are you taking me?'

'To Cairo,' replied Leigh Fermor.

'No. But now?'

'We are in Heraklion.'

Kreipe was flabbergasted. *'Heraklion?'*

'You must understand that we want to keep you out of sight,' said Leigh Fermor. 'We will make you as comfortable as we can later on.'

Leaving the centre behind they headed towards the biggest challenge of all, the heavily guarded West Gate, leading them out of the city and onto the road to Anogia. If things went wrong it was here that they planned to abandon the car and the prisoner. If forced to run they were going to blindfold Kreipe and leave him tied up in the car, using the vehicle to block the road. All around there were hundreds of narrow alleyways, flat roofs, cellars, culverts, skylights and the ruins of bombed buildings into which they could disappear. The band had hand grenades, automatic weapons, ammunition and rations enough to last until they could be smuggled out of the city. In their pockets they carried suicide pills.

Traffic approaching the gate had to turn left and was then funnelled between large concrete blocks, painted with broad black and white stripes. The Opel joined the short queue of military vehicles and drove slowly up to the massive stone arch, weaving between the anti-tank blocks. Now it was Stratis who clamped his hand round the general's mouth, pressing his dagger against Kreipe's throat.

Manolis and Giorgios slid back the bolts on their Marlin guns, holding them low and ready to fire through the thin steel of the car doors. Leigh Fermor and Moss cocked their pistols; Leigh Fermor held his ready to fire; Moss's lay on his lap.

There were more soldiers than usual on guard at the gate, milling about on either side of the arch. A military policeman, holding a red torch, stood stock still in the middle of the road, silhouetted by bright arc lights. Leigh Fermor wound down his window and shouted out: '*Generals Wagen*,' ordering the soldiers to kill the lights. Through the windscreen Moss could see the men passing the word back, '*Generals Wagen*' and stiffening to attention. The military policeman hesitated, then stood aside and saluted, the barrier rose into the air, and the car swept through. Leigh Fermor shouted '*Gute Nacht!*' and they were out of the city where there was one final checkpoint, and then they were heading west along a road that ran through moonlit fields.

Back at the kidnap junction, Micky and Ilias finished clearing away the evidence of the kidnap and then set off on foot for Heraklion, where they were planning to start a propaganda campaign against the general.

In the hills, Fenske the driver, had come round and was walking unsteadily under the guard of Nikos, Antonis, Chnarakis, Pavlos Zografistos and Antonios. They were making good progress and were two or three miles from the kidnap scene. Even so, Antonis decided that they could never make it: soon the Germans were going to send search parties and the driver would be a guarantee of their capture. They stopped for a rest; Antonis walked behind the German, taking out his knife and nodding to the others. He held Fenske's hair, yanked his head back and slit his throat as if he were slaughtering a lamb. The man's body jerked and arched in spasm, his feet drumming on the ground until after a minute they became still. Antonis ran his hands over Fenske's tunic and removed his wallet, his paybook and his driving licence; finally he decapitated him, wiping the knife clean on the leg of his breeches. Together, the kidnappers threw the corpse into a deep hole and hid the head, leaving it to be collected later as a macabre souvenir. The abduction had claimed its first victim.

In the Opel everyone was cheering, singing, shouting and lighting cigarettes. For the first time since his capture, the general was allowed to sit up and made as comfortable as possible. Leigh Fermor turned and knelt on his seat, leaning down towards Kreipe, saying in German, '*Herr General*, I am a British major and beside me is a British captain. The other men in this car are Greek patriots; they are good men. I am in command of this unit and you are an honourable prisoner of war. We are taking you away from Crete to Egypt. I am sorry we had to be so rough. Do everything I say and all will be well.' Then he returned the general's hat.

'*Ja, Danke Herr Major*,' said Kreipe. '*Sagen Sie einmal Herr Major, was für ein zweck hat dieser Husarestück?*' ('Tell me Herr Major what is the point of this Hussar stunt?')

Leigh Fermor said all would be clear in the morning and then joined in the singing.

From the back of the car Moss was handed a cigarette made from fiery peasant-grown tobacco rolled on rough paper. He drew the smoke into his lungs and thought that he had never known better. The group gabbled on about what sort of celebration they would have when they got to Cairo. Moss put his foot hard down on the throttle; the car sped on towards the mountains, filled with smoke and singing men. Far to the north lay the makeshift grave of John Pendlebury and overhead a new moon bathed the landscape in pale light.

An hour or so later, they came to the track near Yeni Gave, where Moss and the others would have to get out and make their way on foot to Anogia, while Leigh Fermor took the vehicle the last mile and a half to abandon it just above a cove which had been used for submarine landings. They hoped that the position of the car, plus a broadcast from the BBC telling the world that General

Kreipe was already off the island and on his way to Cairo, would fool the Germans into giving up their search for him.

Ahead of them a familiar figure stepped into the road, illuminated by the headlights, waving his arms, indicating that they should stop; it was Nikos Stavrakakis from Anogia, a member of the resistance. Moss brought the car to a halt, and the general was hauled out, his handcuffs unlocked and the rope round his legs untied. Kreipe looked frightened. Leigh Fermor gave the general a formal salute and once more told him that he was a British prisoner of war. Then Moss saluted, as did the Cretans. Kreipe looked relieved at this show of respect towards his rank. With a final reassurance to the general that he would not be harmed, Leigh Fermor, who had not driven for over five years, got in the car with Tyrakis and set off. The car shuddered forward in kangaroo hops then stalled. The gears crunched and for an instant it rolled backwards. Leigh Fermor struggled with the big heavy vehicle until, at last, the engine revving hard, the clutch slipping and the car in low gear, he zigzagged up the road. The others watched the tail lights vanish from sight. Then they set off up the steep hill to Anogia.

A few miles later, Leigh Fermor reached the track leading down to the submarine cove and stopped. He and Tyrakis threw cigarette ends onto the floor of the car and left an overcoat and a torn copy of an Agatha Christie paperback on the rear seat. A Cadbury's milk chocolate wrapper added to the sense that British commandos had hijacked the vehicle. Finally they pinned the letter of explanation to the front passenger seat and left the staff car with one of its doors open. Before abandoning it they ripped off the pennants that had helped them pass through the checkpoints; Tyrakis danced about waving them in the air shouting 'Captured standards! Captured standards!' A hundred yards down the track they left a green commando beret and an empty tin of Player's cigarettes. Then they headed for Anogia, guided by the white peak of Mount Ida towering in the distance.

Moss's party made slow progress into the mountains: Kreipe

had hurt his leg when they dragged him out of the car and he was limping badly. Stratis walked in front, followed by the general and then Moss, holding his revolver pointing at Kreipe's back. Manolis brought up the rear. Scrambling up steep, crumbling rocks, then down into small streams and heavy undergrowth was hard for the prisoner. Moss decided that having his gun in his hand was pointless. He searched the general for any concealed weapons and, finding none, put his automatic away, freeing his arms to help the older and much less fit man across the many streams that crossed their path. Stratis, the policeman, who had earlier assured them that he knew the route, kept getting lost.

The party became very thirsty and regretted not drinking the water they had so carefully helped the general to cross. The ice-cold, crystal-clear water courses had given way to trickles in deep ravines that were impossible to reach. In desperation they used an emergency ration tin as a scoop, lowering it down on a string, a laborious process which produced about a quarter of an inch of water each time. Kreipe complained that he was hungry and had not eaten since lunch. Moss gave him a few raisins which he had in his pocket. They drank the muddy water from the tins and trudged on towards Anogia. Kreipe asked his captors if they were regular soldiers and kept wanting to know what they hoped to achieve by the 'Hussar stunt'. He warned Moss that it was unlikely they could get him off the island, that his men were going to rescue him.

On the final stretch of the trek Kreipe became more and more morose. He told Moss that he had fourteen brothers and sisters and that he was the thirteenth child. His father was a pastor with no money and as his own pay as a major general was very good he had become the one that the family looked to as the breadwinner. He was soon to be promoted lieutenant general and had already put on the badges of his new rank. Outside the village they reached a dried river bed, where they had been told to hide until dawn. Stratis noticed that the general was shivering with the cold, and gave him his police overcoat. Kreipe talked about his premonition that something bad was going to happen on his road home. He thought the T-junction was a dangerous place, where he could be assassinated; the possibility of kidnap had not occurred to him.

Tyrakis and Leigh Fermor, still in his German police disguise, made their way in the dim light over the hills to the rendezvous point. They did not have far to go, five or six miles, but the lack of light, and the rough going, clambering up the steep mountain-side cut about with rocky precipitous gorges, ravines and streams, made the distance feel much longer. They lost their way and came across two boys, hunting for eels with flaming torches made of pine. The boys gave them directions, obviously frightened and wondering what a German corporal and a Cretan shepherd were doing on a lonely hillside in the middle of the night. The two men walked on, the silence of the night broken by the tinkling of goat bells, the soft croak of frogs and the song of the nightingales. They felt low, overcome by tiredness and feelings of anticlimax. At last the village loomed ahead of them, white houses spreading like a fortress on a tail of rock, a natural gateway to the snow-capped peak of Mount Ida, glittering far above them in the moon-light, silent and brooding.

With the dawn Moss saw that Kreipe had what he thought of as 'typical Teutonic looks', a fixed bullish expression, thin lips, short-cropped hair, shaved and greying at the temples, and pale blue eyes. Moss estimated him to be anything from forty-five to fifty-five. Kreipe sat silent and quiet, a melancholy look on his face.

Moss scribbled two urgent signals, one to Tom Dunbabin, higher up in the mountains, asking him to radio Cairo telling them that Kreipe was a prisoner and requesting that the BBC World Service broadcast news of the general's capture. The BBC should make it clear that Kreipe was already off the island and en route to Egypt. Finally he asked for leaflets to be dropped on Crete telling the islanders the same thing. The second letter was to Sandy Rendel, telling him about the kidnap. Moss gave the two messages to Stratis who folded them into tiny squares and hid them in his turban before setting off for Anogia to find two runners. He promised to bring food and wine back to the group, who had not eaten for nearly twenty-four hours.

Suddenly Kreipe began to fuss, shouting and scrabbling at his tunic, then searching in the folds of his coat, which he had taken off to sleep under. He was upset because his Knight's Cross, which he wore on a ribbon around his neck, had disappeared. Moss told him that it must have come off in the struggle round the car and that there was no possibility of going back to look for it. Eventually, tiredness overcame the general and he lay down to sleep, his fitful snores drifting across the floor of the gulley.

In the early morning Leigh Fermor and Tyrakis reached Anogia. Smoke from wood fires floated between the buildings, backlit by the low sun, throwing beams of light and shade across the narrow streets. The villagers setting off for work treated the two men with contempt. They turned their backs, fell silent and spat on the ground, slamming their doors shut as the two men passed. Leigh Fermor knew these people well and was used to being welcomed and treated like one of their own. He heard a woman wailing 'The black cattle have strayed into the sheep.' Then more mysteriously, 'Our in-laws have come.' At last the penny dropped: he was still in disguise and looked like a German soldier.

He approached a woman he knew, the wife of the priest, who he was sure would recognise him: 'It's me Pappadia, Mihali.' Mihali was the name that the Cretans had given him. The woman would not look at him, keeping her gaze on the ground. The priest, Papa Yanni Skoulas, appeared accompanied by Leigh Fermor's godbrother Giorgios Dramoudanis. The priest, a brave man and an early member of the resistance, assured the villagers that all was well and that the strange German was indeed Mihali.

Stratis arrived and found two runners to take the messages to Dunbabin and Rendel. He confirmed that Moss and the others, plus General Kreipe, were safe in a gulley about two miles away and that it would be better to wait until night before joining them.

Baskets of food and wine reached the hungry kidnappers in the afternoon. As they ate Kreipe explained that he had commanded troops in the Khuban in Russia, where the fighting had been very heavy and drawn out; with sadness in his voice he told Moss that his main diet in those days had been caviar. As he spoke, Kreipe 'tucked into the meal like a schoolboy'. The lost medal was still on his mind.

While the general moaned about his loss, the others enjoyed themselves eating and drinking in the hot sunshine. Then they fell asleep, guarded by armed guerrillas, the first of many who would risk their lives guarding the crew on its passage to the south coast and safety.

18

Radio Silence

Tom Dunbabin lay low at Fourfouras, still ill. He only had a few men with him, one of whom was Giorgios Frangoulitakis, whose Cretan nickname was 'Skoutello' (a type of bowl). Unsurprisingly, SOE called him Scuttlegeorge. Dunbabin had left his radio set back at the hideout of Kapitan Mihali Xylouris near Anogia. As it got lighter Dunbabin told Skoutello to go to Anogia and make contact with Xylouris: 'Take this note. Go to the Mytheria area where the wireless transmitter is and you'll find Captain *Livermore* there, perhaps he'll want you to help him – he'll tell you all about it. Nothing else.' Dunbabin looked worried and depressed. Skoutello asked him if he was ill; Dunbabin claimed to be fine. The Cretan set off at once.

In Heraklion lorries full of troops lumbered through the West Gate, heading for the mountains, taking the same route as the kidnappers in the Opel, the soldiers scanning the roadsides for signs of an ambush. At the heavily guarded docks down by the port, a lorry protected by military outriders swept along the quays heading for the German-controlled press which was churning out leaflets threatening harsh reprisals for the kidnap.

At dawn the soldiers who had been on duty in the night, including the men on guard at the Villa Ariadne, were arrested and asked why they had let a car full of guerrillas drive straight past them. Among those in the cells was the general's bridge-playing ADC, under suspicion of collaborating with the andartes. All over the island the occupying forces were on edge, unnerved that a senior officer, their second in command, had been abducted from outside his heavily guarded home.

In the afternoon the first German patrol drove into Anogia: three lorries bounced to a halt and disgorged nearly fifty nervous men, carrying rifles, sub-machine guns and heavy weapons. Some formed up in the square while others fanned out to cordon off the village. The people waited. Nothing happened. A runner slipped into the fields, crouching low, running to alert the men in the gulley. Leigh Fermor and Tyrakis were still in the village, trapped in the priest's house.

The lorry with the leaflets drove across Heraklion airfield towards a Fieseler-Storch spotter plane, engine running, red dust billowing everywhere. The Cretans had nicknamed the plane 'The Cockroach' or 'the Germans' only daughter', because it was the only Fieseler-Storch on the island and had been scrounged from another part of Europe. The parcels were loaded and the small insect-like aircraft took off, climbing slowly into the sky; in the back of the plane sat an observer with a powerful set of field glasses. The Storch banked west, towards Anogia, where the search parties were loitering in the square, or sitting about in cafés making no effort to search the village. Heavy machine-gun fire and explosions could be heard in the distance.

At the gulley the runner arrived with the news that a large number of soldiers were in the area. Paterakis shook the sleeping Moss by the shoulder, shouting: 'Germans coming. Plenty of Germans in village.' They all scrambled to their feet and stuffed their kit into rucksacks. Even the general lost no time, lacing up his boots. A guide led them along the bank of the stream to a more remote hiding place. Kreipe was limping, complaining about the pain in his leg, which he said had got worse. The guide led them across a stream and up a near-vertical bank which the general found impossible to tackle on his own. The group hauled him up, struggling from foothold to foothold, to the mouth of a very small cave, scarcely large enough to hold more than two men. Kreipe, followed by Paterakis, Moss and Stratis, squeezed in, then the abductors covered the entrance with bracken. Through the fronds they watched for the approach of patrols. The general sat with his knees pulled as close in to his body as his stomach would allow, and fell asleep, his snores filling the cave.

At just after five in the afternoon the Fieseler-Storch arrived. Through the bracken Billy Moss could see the plane circling slowly, scarcely a hundred feet above him, the observer clearly visible. Then the plane flew over the village itself, releasing hundreds of leaflets that rained down like confetti. The black print read:

TO ALL CRETANS

Last night General Kreipe was abducted by bandits. He is now being concealed in the Cretan mountains, and his whereabouts cannot be unknown to the populace. If the general is not returned within three days all rebel villages in the HERAKLION DISTRICT will be razed to the ground and the severest measures of reprisal will be brought to bear on the civilian population.

The frightened villagers retreated to their homes. The soldiers peered over their gunsights at empty streets. Overhead the spotter plane flew up and down for three hours, searching for the kidnapped leader. Eventually it headed back to Heraklion; the soldiers clambered into their lorries and drove off. It was six o'clock in the evening; the sun was sinking towards the west.

The drone of the spotter plane died away, the light faded and the men in the cave decided it was safe to leave their cramped quarters. They heaved the general down the steep slope to the bank of the stream. Paterakis recalled the time when he had been caught by a reprisal squad in his family village of Koustogerako, south-west of Chania. German soldiers had arrived, cordoned off the area and rounded everyone up, men, women, boys and girls. They were led to the church and lined up against a wall. Paterakis remembered the fear, the children crying, the anxious muttering of the adults, the soldiers shouting in German and the noise of the machine gun as they set it up in the back of a lorry: the clinking of the long chain of brass rounds being taken from the ammunition box and fed into the firing mechanism; the click as the rounds were locked into place; the final sawing clunk of the weapon being cocked and the silence that followed.

The children stopped sobbing, staring at the soldier behind the gun, who squinted back through his sights, waiting for the order to fire. Paterakis held his breath, wondering whether his death would be quick and easy or slow and painful. He braced himself for the impact of the bullets and closed his eyes. A shot cracked through the afternoon air. The lieutenant in charge tumbled backwards, hitting the ground. Another shot and the soldier behind the machine gun slumped forward, a hole drilled between his eyes.

Pandemonium broke out, the villagers fled from the square, running crouched to dodge the bullets. The soldiers panicked, dragging the body of the officer onto the machine-gun truck which sped off in clouds of dust, the soldiers firing wild, unaimed rounds at the hillside.

Unhurt and amazed, Paterakis opened his eyes to see his brothers and cousins running down the hill towards the village, waving their rifles over their heads. These men were lethal marksmen, as good as any military-trained sniper, with a lifetime's experience of shooting wild goats at long distance on the hills. The Paterakis brothers embraced, weeping with joy, while the villagers clapped their saviours on the back, laughing and shouting. Within the hour the people collected whatever they could carry and fled to the safety of the mountains.

In Anogia the villagers came out of their houses, peering around, picking up the leaflets and reading them, wondering who had organised the kidnap and how such an audacious plan had been pulled off. Someone shouted: 'The horn wearers, they came for wool, we'll send them back shorn.' An old man said: 'Mark my words, they will burn down our houses for this, but then so what? My house has already been burnt down four times by the Turks, the Germans can burn it down a fifth. They have already killed scores of my family and my child, yet here I am. We are at war and war is terrible, but you can't have a wedding feast without killing the sheep for the meat.'

In Heraklion, Micky Akoumianakis rallied his men. Graffiti appeared on walls declaring *'Kreipe befiehl wir folgen'* a parody of the Nazi phrase, *'Führer befiehl wir folgen'* ('Führer lead we will follow'). It implied that Kreipe, like General Carta, had allowed himself to be captured so that he could escape to Cairo and get out of the war, which he knew Hitler was losing. The graffiti were written in heavy gothic script as though painted by German soldiers wanting to desert and follow their general. The Cretans did not know that this black script was banned in Germany, having been condemned as Jewish.

In the mountains, Paterakis went into Anogia to find Tyrakis and Leigh Fermor and lead them to the gulley. At the rendezvous Kreipe asked about his driver. Leigh Fermor told him the driver was fine and would join them in a few days.

They ate a meal of boiled eggs, cheese and bread. Kreipe was given the codename Theophilos, so that he would not know when they were talking about him, and loaded on to a mule, which had been hired in the village. Then they set off, heading for the lair of the Kapitan Mihali Xylouris where they hoped to find Dunbabin and the radio with which they were going to contact SOE Cairo and organise the Royal Navy motor launch to pick them up. The journey would take all night and was made slower because the heavily laden mule had to be led along meandering goat tracks.

By two in the morning, a long way short of their destination, they blundered into a sheepfold where the owner, an old shepherd, invited them to rest in his hut, a primitive conical, stone structure. Crawling through the tiny entrance they entered a small smoky room hung with cobwebs and bags of dripping whey; round the walls were wooden shelves on which lay cheeses, and beneath the shelves were stone seats. A bracken fire burnt in the middle. The shepherd offered them cheese and rock-hard bread, which they soaked in rough wine. Kreipe fell asleep, overcome by the heat of the fire and the food and drink. The others asked the shepherd to wake them in two hours, then they too fell into an exhausted slumber. The rest of the route would take them over the Ida Mountain, a 'forbidden zone'. It was a place where many shepherds preferred to live, risking death by putting their knowledge of the caves, tracks and hiding places at the disposal of the guerrillas. After the short rest they pushed on.

By dawn they could see the Lasithi mountains, the general on his mule silhouetted against them. Kreipe jolting along surrounded by the rag-tag andartes reminded Moss of the Emperor Napoleon leading the remains of the Grand Army back to France across the freezing wastes of the Russian steppe. The group's progress was monitored and guarded by guerrillas hidden in the hills; they could be heard whistling to each other, signalling the band's progress as they approached Kapitan Xylouris's hideout. A lookout bounded down the hill, a beautiful young man with wild green eyes, who embraced them all, smiling and laughing and chattering in excitement. He was soon joined by others, more embraces, kisses and laughter. Kreipe was astonished at the affection the Cretans showed to the British officers – something he and his men had never experienced.

They were led along a gulley to a cave concealed halfway up a rock face. In the entrance stood Kapitan Xylouris himself, a striking white-haired man with sparkling eyes and a lavish moustache. He was famed for his bravery and courage, and Leigh Fermor regarded him as 'one of the best and most reliable leaders in Crete'. The kapitan embraced the two British agents and solemnly saluted Kreipe, who returned the salute with military dignity, trying not to look nervous, surrounded as he was by armed men dedicated to the overthrow of the Nazi regime. The hideout was crowded with many representatives of Anogian families; they had all come to see the prisoner.

More English agents appeared from the darkness of the cave, including John Houseman, a former cavalry officer turned SOE man, who looked every inch the long-haired Cretan peasant; next to him stood a handsome man with a thick beard, long black boots, a dagger in his belt, which held up a pair of filthy breeches. His name was John Lewis, a British Army corporal under the command of Dunbabin. A third Englishman appeared, a wireless operator who had also been working with Dunbabin. The kidnappers were told about Dunbabin's illness and that he had temporarily gone into hiding, though no one quite knew where he was.

Then the situation got worse. The runner that Moss had sent off with the signal for Dunbabin appeared with the news that he had not got through: the British authorities had no idea that Kreipe had been captured and the BBC had not been instructed to broadcast that the general was off the island and on his way to Cairo. Moss became more and more angry that the RAF had failed to drop any pamphlets about the capture. He was baffled and confused by Tom Dunbabin's disappearance and unexplained silence.

Dunbabin's wireless, which was at the cave, was faulty. Leigh Fermor scribbled a new signal to be sent at once. The operator set to work but the radio started cutting out, then stopped working altogether. Unscrewing the cover plates to reveal the guts, they found that one of the valves was broken. The nearest replacement was in Cairo. The SOE had only two other transmitters on the island: Sandy Rendel's and a set operated by another agent, Dick Barnes. Two more runners were immediately sent off with messages for Barnes and Rendel. The return trip to either radio would take nearly four days, and that made no allowance for the time Cairo took to reply. The man heading for Rendel would have to scale two mountain peaks.

The runners vanished into the hills and a little while later the party who had been escorting the driver, Fenske, appeared: Nikos Komis, Chnarakis, Antonis Zoidakis and Antonios Papaleonidas. They had narrowly escaped capture and been delayed by German search parties, which were becoming more and more frequent. It was the machine guns of these patrols that Moss's group had heard firing earlier in the day; the soldiers had fired at random into wooded areas. When he was asked what had happened to Fenske, Antonis Zoidakis became sheepish, unable to look anyone in the eye. He explained that the driver was too badly injured to make the journey and that he had been disposed of: he mimed whipping out his knife, slashing at a man's throat and wiping his knife quickly on his trousers; he shrugged and asked what else could they do? He did not mention the head. Leigh Fermor told Kreipe that the driver was unharmed but, for his own safety, had been left in the hands of some guerrilla fighters in the hills, where he would stay until he had recovered from his injuries. Kreipe seemed satisfied.

Later that afternoon, 29 April, the reconnaissance aircraft crept across the sky, dropping leaflets with another message from General Bruno Bräuer:

NOTIFICATION

Paid bandits under British leadership abducted a senior German officer on the night of 26th to 27th April. Without the support of a section of the urban population, which, as I have observed for some time, collaborates with the bandits and the traitors to the people, his abduction would never have been possible.

For the past weeks the bandits have been brutally murdering, on the orders of their British and communist paymasters,

Greek patriots who, for the good of the Cretan people and peace, security and future of Crete were working for greater Greece.

I will from now on, with the utmost severity and the intervention of German arms, ruthlessly strike the guilty parties and exterminate them.

This decision in no way alters the fact that I will also further attempt, in the spirit of the political pacification, peace and security of the population I have announced, to achieve a friendly co-existence of the Armed German forces and Cretans.

The Commander of Fortress Crete

General BRÄUER.

That afternoon more lorries sped through the West Gate of Heraklion, heading into the White Mountains where the kidnappers were hiding. The spotter plane was now a permanent feature in the sky. The abductors waited, desperate for news of what was happening and what beach they were to head for.

John Houseman spent some time trying to persuade Kreipe to allow himself to be photographed. Eventually he agreed, but said that Houseman must promise that the pictures would not be used by the press. The SOE man snapped away while the general set his jaw in grim defiance, adopting the pose of a conquered hero. Later they watched the guerrillas playing a game called 'buzz buzz', in which participants repeatedly slapped each other on the face; the point of the game was to see who could take the hardest knocks.

As darkness fell, Kreipe, Leigh Fermor and Moss talked quietly, drawing on cigarettes. The cold was intense but they could not light a fire in case it drew German patrols. From the mouth of the cave they could see the snow on the peak of Mount Ida. Kreipe stared at it for some time and then began to recite quietly to himself an ode by Horace, beginning: 'Vides ut alta stet nive candidum Soracte . . . (Lo Mount Soracte glitters deep in snow . . .).' Leigh Fermor, who knew the ode by heart, joined in and completed the next five stanzas. He remembered that: the 'general's blue eyes swivelled away from the mountain-top and when I'd finished, after a long silence he said "*Ach so Herr Major*" it was very strange. "*Ja Herr General*". As though for a moment the war had ceased to exist. We had both drunk at the same fountains long before; and things were different between us for the rest of our time together.'

Eventually they tried to rest, Kreipe, Leigh Fermor and Moss huddled together under the only blanket they had, with ticks, fleas and vermin as companions. General Kreipe could not settle. Lewis gave him his own bedding and plied him with shots of raki; in the end the general nodded off, snoring heavily and still thrashing about. Two hours later Kreipe woke up and complained bitterly that the kidnappers had interrupted his sleep by kicking him.

All the while Manolis Paterakis and Giorgios Tyrakis guarded the cave, sitting quietly, their automatic weapons at the ready in their laps.

19

Situation Ugly

The next afternoon the runner reached Sandy Rendel. Leigh Fermor's message was sent at once to SOE Cairo, from where it was relayed to London, arriving on 30 April at 21.55. It read:

General Heinrich Kreipe. RPT. KREIPE. kidnapped night 26 April by Major Leigh Fermor and Capt Moss. Now held in mountains. Hope evacuate party on three or four May. Germans dropped leaflets stating KREIPE RPT KREIPE captured by Greek bandits and threatening direst reprisals against villages and population if not surrendered within three days. ESSENTIAL RPT ESSENTIAL fullest possible broadcast made by all stations be made by midday tomorrow FIRST RPT FIRST May to effect that KREIPE RPT KREIPE captured by BRITISH RPT BRITISH party and ALREADY RPT ALREADY arrived in CAIRO RPT CAIRO. Most urgent as Cretan party report situation UGLY RPT UGLY.

The request went from SOE Baker Street to the home of the BBC Overseas Service at Bush House in London's Aldwych. It was from here that the BBC transmitted to the conquered peoples of Europe, and had become a beacon of truth and honesty, as well as a useful weapon in the endless war of deception being waged against the Axis powers.

SOE emphasised the urgency of the request, asking for a broadcast to be made not later than noon the next day, Monday

1 May. The night duty officer realised that the request was urgent and serious but did not have the power to authorise the transmission. He rang the BBC Balkans Section for clarification and was told not to worry, 'there was no point in trying to do anything during the night'. The message, which was headed 'Most Urgent', was placed in a tray to be worked through the next day.

At 8.30 the next morning, Miss Barker, a BBC employee, set off from her digs in the World's End, Chelsea, to walk to work at Bush House. Her route took her along the Embankment north of the Thames and past evidence of the battering London had taken over the last few years from bombing and incendiary attacks: the ruins of Chelsea Old Church, next to it Jacob Epstein's studio, now just a huge hole in the ground; Bush House itself bore the shrapnel scars of the two 800-pound bombs that had exploded nearby.

Miss Barker was on the committee that liaised with SOE about special broadcasts. She reached her office at nine and began to sift through the signals that had come in during the night. Leigh Fermor's urgent signal now read:

Festungskommmandant Generaloberst Heinrich Kreipe kidnapped night 26th April . . . now held in mountains. Hope evacuate party on 3rd or 4th May. [The Germans] are threatening direst reprisals against villages and population if not surrendered within three days. Essential fullest possible broadcast that Kreipe captured by British party and already arrived in Cairo. Matter most urgent as Cretan party report situation ugly. Endeavouring arrange from here to drop leaflets this sense.

At the same time, Lieutenant Colonel David Talbot Rice, Head of SOE's Balkans desk and on the same committee as Miss Barker, read Leigh Fermor's signal. He had been waiting anxiously all week for news that his agents were safe and that the kidnap mission had been successful. He was alarmed by the words 'situation ugly' and telephoned the senior officer on the liaison committee, and the man in charge of the Political Intelligence Department (the cover name for the Political Warfare Executive, which had offices at Bush House).

By 10.30 that morning, Talbot Rice had failed to make contact with any person in authority. He decided to break protocol and contact the BBC direct, ringing his opposite number at the corporation and asking him to prepare a broadcast along the lines requested by Leigh Fermor. A transmission was scheduled for noon that day. Talbot Rice emphasised that the matter was of the greatest urgency but was forced to point out that nothing could be broadcast without authority from the Political Warfare Executive. In the meantime Miss Barker found her copy of the signal from Crete and immediately took it to the PWE offices; the officer there said he could not approve the transmission, but was willing for it to be referred to the Foreign Office, who could, if it chose, overrule him. Eventually an amended version of the broadcast was authorised and transmitted. It said that General Kreipe was being taken off the island; it did not say that he had already left and was in Cairo.

At just after midday, Talbot Rice telephoned Miss Barker direct to ask her what was going on. She gave him the bad news about the amendment. Later that day Talbot Rice was reprimanded for breaking protocol. By now a frustrated and angry Talbot Rice explained his motives and sent a memorandum arguing that, in future, events like those of the last twenty-four hours should be handled at a higher level by people who had the authority to act without referring their decisions for approval.

On Crete, Sandy Rendel sat in his hideout waiting to hear what arrangements were being made to pick up the kidnappers and their prisoner. While he waited he scribbled a note to Leigh Fermor:

> Dearest Paddy, the word congratulations seems pallid to what I feel inclined to say on reading your triumphant note – it's almost the best true story I've yet heard. Bless you! And all the best of luck of course for the rest of the trip.
>
> We got your message off [...] today and are waiting for an answer now [...] when I will send Drake [codename for a runner] by one route which he knows and the elder of my other Manolis by another to confirm. I hope boat is on way. The messages may both get to you on time but possibly not I fear. As you know Huns are very thick on the ground. In any case the message has got there and I assume you act if it had. I hope you fixed signals beforehand. I sent an additional wire as follows.

> IF NOT. RPT. NOT FIXED WITH PADDY ALREADY SEND SIGS AND TIMINGS FOR HIS BOAT ALL STATIONS. RUNNER HERE MAY NOT. RPT NOT REACH PADDY BEFORE BOAT DUE. PLEASE CONFIRM BOAT WILL COME FOR FOLLOWING NIGHT AS WELL.

> The above is probably superfluous but in case you don't get the message by the night and don't go to the spot the boat comes that night, it still gives everyone a good chance I hope. My second messenger will go to Vasso first and try to find Tom's haunts there and hence you – but I doubt if they can make it. Drake has good chance though everyone as you know is being stopped a good deal on the roads etc. Though tomorrow it may have all blown over.

Just after midnight Cairo transmitted the time and place of rendezvous, enabling Rendel to finish his letter to Leigh Fermor:

Later . . . we have only just got the answer [...]. They are sending a boat to Cape Melissa B605111. The message in so far as it concerns you reads:

BOAT CAPE MELISSA B605111 RPT 605111 THIRD FOURTH RPT THIRD FOURTH STOP CONTACT PADDY URGENTLY STOP EXCELLENT WORK STOP ALL SEND CONGRATULATIONS. YOUR NUMBER ONE SEVEN

'Your number one seven' was the second part of a message you asked me to send and was about leaflets broadcasts etc.

In haste again – our very merriest and most complete congratulations from self, Giorgios and all you know here, love Sandy.

Cape Melissa, the rendezvous beach, was just below the village of Agios Pavlos and was one of many beaches stretching along the south coast of the island. If it was cut off, or the arrangements changed, they might be able to find another, further west.

Rendel wrote the message out twice and handed a copy to each of his two runners, who tucked the folded fragile tissue-like sheets into tight squares and tucked them into their turbans. Assuming there were no hitches and the runners were not captured or shot, it would take at least twenty-four hours to deliver the messages. The abductors would then have less than four days to cross some of the toughest terrain on the island, travelling through occupied territory, at night and leading by mule a lame, middle-aged German general who had no interest in getting to the rendezvous point on time.

Leigh Fermor, in the knowledge that there were patrols every-where and that they must keep moving up and over Mount Ida or be captured, decided to keep going towards Agios Pavlos and hoped that if things changed the runners could catch up with them.

During the morning Skoutello arrived. Leigh Fermor ordered him to go at once to the hideout of Kapitan Petrakoyiorgi, who Pendlebury had codenamed 'Selfridge', and ask him to bring reinforcements. Selfridge's hideout was four hours away, further up the mountain. When Selfridge received Leigh Fermor's request he set off at once, taking with him five units of men. Confusingly each group was led by men with the same name: 'Yiorgi'. Selfridge's men would act as guards to the kidnappers as they moved across Mount Ida. Skoutello described how 'the men turned into swallows, they seized their guns and were like ibexes leaping over the rocks and took up positions all along the hills of the watershed.' These were tough mountain fighters – shepherds who knew every stone, slope, path, ravine and peak of the route.

Leigh Fermor sent Antonis Zoidakis ahead with orders to check that the way was free of Germans and to light fires showing the kidnappers the safe route over the crest of the mountain and down its southern slopes Two runners accompanying him were to keep contact with the main party, who had until dawn to reach the next rendezvous, a village called Nithavri, the highest habitation on Mount Ida's southern slopes. Skoutello asked Selfridge to try to persuade Leigh Fermor to change his route and go through the village of Vorizia instead, which the Germans had already destroyed. The kapitan shook his head saying, 'You don't know the British. Once they have made their minds up they won't change them.'

The group set off in daylight. They moved in single file, cheered on their way by the guerrillas and the British agents. The general travelled in state, astride his mule; as they left, Corporal Lewis whistled in accompaniment the Al Jolson song 'Going to Heaven on a Mule'. The route to Nithavri took them straight over the summit of Mount Ida. On the way, a branch whipped back and hit Kreipe in the arm making him swear loudly; some of the Cretans thought he was exaggerating to cause a fuss and slow down progress. The general's state of mind was not helped by the behaviour of one of the guerrillas, Manolis Tsikritsis, a small, wizened man wearing a sort of red fez like a deacon's cap; Tsikritsis spent a lot of time staring fiercely at Kreipe. On the day of his capture Kreipe had left his home, dressed for work in his office followed by a game of bridge with his staff officers. Six days later, in the same clothes, he was over 7,000 feet above sea level, toiling up one of the most difficult climbs in the Mediterranean, surrounded by people who hated him.

The climb to the summit of Mount Ida took them along paths covered in slippery loose scree that proved too much for the mule carrying Kreipe. The creature kept sliding and falling; the general had to dismount and it was led off. On the way the party found an old leaflet that had been dropped the year before by the British. It ridiculed 'the Hun' with a picture of German soldiers begging for food from two village housewives. Tsikritsis showed the leaflet to Kreipe and grinned at him. The general turned to Leigh Fermor and said in German: 'Don't leave me with these people, they frighten me.'

Progress slowed to a snail's pace. Even the fittest men found the climb exhausting. Kreipe stopped every ten minutes or so to catch his breath, or smoke a cigarette. Tempers frayed and the Cretans muttered that the general was malingering; they nagged the British officers to make the prisoner go faster, making sinister throat-cutting motions with their hands. As they climbed the general noticed Selfridge's men watching over them from the heights and asked how many there were. Skoutello said he did not know the exact numbers but there were a lot.

The party crossed the snow line, leaving the last of the ilexes and cedars below them. The temperature dropped, it began to drizzle and a freezing wind blew the sleet into their faces, scouring their cheeks like sandpaper. The world turned into an icy white hell where every footstep might lead to a bone-shattering fall on to the rocks or a lethal plunge into a deep gorge. One of the Yiorgis went in front, followed by the general, a forage cap on his head and wearing Stratis's gendarme jacket against the bitter temperatures. Leigh Fermor brought up the rear, carrying a curved-topped mountain walking stick. From time to time Paterakis and Tyrakis stood to one side watching progress, their Marlin sub-machine guns slung casually over their shoulders. The sun sank in the west and Bill Moss took a photograph of the group as they ploughed on into the failing light.

The mist cut visibility at the summit down to less than a few hundred yards. Paterakis worried that German patrols, some of whom were trained mountain troops, might have already climbed the south face and be waiting to ambush them. The group came to a ruined shepherd's hut, roofless with only two walls left standing. They huddled in its shelter, not daring to go on until they got word from Antonis's runners or could see the signal fires. The mood darkened. Even Tyrakis and Paterakis became antagonistic towards Kreipe, who could not fail to understand the murderous tone of their grumbling.

Thousands of feet below, at the foot of the mountain, where the sun was setting on a balmy evening, lorries full of German soldiers crawled across the landscape heading for the villages. Frightened men, women and children peered from their homes wondering what hell the invading soldiers were about to unleash. The lorries arrived and the villagers heard the crashing of tailboards followed by the sound of hundreds of steel-shod feet kicking up clouds of dust. NCOs shouted commands at nervous soldiers, bullying them into formation before marching them off, weapons clinking, up the mountain.

Above the snow line the abduction team shivered in the hut.

They had not eaten for twelve hours. Leigh Fermor and Moss foraged in the mist for the bitter, edible, mountain dandelions which everyone wolfed down, even though they had nothing with which to wash down the grey leaves.

They had been on the run for six days. Twice in the last twenty-four hours the BBC had broadcast the item stating that the general was being 'taken off the island'. The leaflets that Leigh Fermor had asked to be dropped over the island's main cities never materialised: flying conditions had made any such expedition too difficult.

Night fell. Selfridge's guides peered into the darkness, straining for Antonis Zoidakis's fires. Enemy patrols moved slowly up towards them. Nearly two thousand men had been trucked into the area with orders to throw a cordon round the south-west side of the mountain. The soldiers did not like leaving the safety of the tracks and the protection of each other, fearing that ambush and death lay waiting for them in the craggy, frightening corners of the steep landscape. To keep up their morale they fired flares into the air and their weapons into the undergrowth.

At last the mist cleared and a fire was spotted on a distant ridge; the time had come to move on. For the first two hours the descent was very steep, and the snow-covered ground treacherous. Once back below the snow line barren rock gave way to vegetation and cedars so exposed to the prevailing winds that they grew as streaks of wood almost parallel to the rocks. They made their way down slowly, not helped by whipping branches slapping them in the face, thorns ripping at their clothes and slashing into the skin on their hands. The andartes grew more and more hostile to the General, muttering threats of violence and death in a way that only a Cretan knows how. Leigh Fermor and Moss began to worry that they would lose control and be unable to guarantee Kreipe's safety.

They went down hand over hand, trying to support Kreipe's weight as they slithered and slipped down the steep ilex- and thorn-tangled rock faces. Before long they lost sight of the signal fire. They realised they were not going to reach Nithavri before daylight. The guides knew that somewhere nearby lived a shepherd, a trusted man, well known to the guerrilla band. They could hear the jangling of sheep bells and sometimes came across the animals themselves huddling in groups. Then at last they found the shepherd who greeted them like old friends. The peasant chatted away in Greek, telling them that it would be an honour to have them all in his hut, his only refuge and shelter in the long days tending the sheep on the hills.

It was three o'clock in the morning when the exhausted band reached the sheepfold. The shepherd ushered the freezing men into his hut and soon they sat around the fire trying to dry their clothes, their eyes running from the smoke. He offered them all he had: water, stale bread and hard cheese. At dawn, after a few hours' sleep, the men filed out of the hut like zombies and followed the shepherd to their hiding place for the next day: a cave, the mouth of which was tiny and hidden by ilex trees. They fell to their knees and crawled through the branches to find themselves in a huge cavern. The shepherd told them that it had been used as a hideout in the war against the Turks and it had enough room to hide hundreds of men. The walls dripped with water. They dragged in logs and lit a fire which filled the air with more smoke than heat. Then they covered the entrance with branches and bracken and tried to sleep, one of the Yiorgis always awake, his gun ready in case the snoring Kreipe tried to escape.

Outside, a mountain storm raged. The thunder echoed inside the cave as though they had stirred the anger of the mountain gods. Paterakis, Tyrakis, Kreipe and the two British officers huddled together and slept as best they could while far below the general's men prowled the foothills, moving inexorably towards the hideout.

The next day they gathered more wood and lit a second fire. Leigh Fermor and Billy Moss scrambled through an opening 'no bigger than a coal hole' and discovered a tunnel that led to a huge cathedral-like chamber dropping away from them for storey after storey. The bottom was strewn with rushes and animals' skulls. This led to an even bigger chamber 'thickly speared with stalactites and stalagmites [we] had the impression of standing at the end of some vast and colonnaded hall'. Moss wondered if this was the mythical cave where the Goddess Rhea hid her newborn son Zeus from the fury of his father Cronus.

They crawled back through the tunnels to find Kreipe shivering in the cold, despite wearing Stratis's gendarme jacket and, now, Leigh Fermor's coat. The English major joked to Kreipe that if they were captured they would both be shot for impersonating the enemy.

Inside the cave they could just hear the noise of the spotter plane droning overhead and the occasional sound of soldiers shouting to each other as they combed the mountainside. The abductors had no choice but to wait. They had been cut off from the outside world for a week. No message had reached them and they had no idea if GHQ Cairo even knew that they were holding the general prisoner. They ate their last ration of bread and cheese — they had run out of water. Leigh Fermor found the day very stressful, one of the worst he had experienced. Kreipe sat silent and depressed, lost in his own thoughts.

In the afternoon, a runner arrived with a message from Antonis Zoidakis. Paterakis unfolded the damp, thin paper and read out the barely legible Greek. Zoidakis reported that more and more lorries were pouring into the villages round the foothills, bringing reinforcements. The Germans were preparing to sweep the slopes en masse and would start a major search the following morning. They should leave the cave at once and head for the south. Paterakis read out the important words: 'For God's sake come tonight, a mule waits for you.'

Moss asked the general what he thought about another night march. Kreipe shrugged and said that physically he would be alright, but mentally he was feeling very down. Moss wrote in his diary that the general 'smiled as he spoke – a hopeless sort of smile – in a way that made one feel a kind of sympathy for the mental anguish from which he was so obviously suffering'. The guerrillas were very worried about leaving the safety of the hide-out; they were surrounded and knew that the soldiers in the cordon must hold all the key points on the descent. It would, they argued, be safer to wait for two or three days. In the end they bowed to Leigh Fermor's insistence that they must get the general off the island as soon as possible. The Cretans worried that if they refused to go on, Leigh Fermor would think they were cowards.

They slipped out of the cave just before sunset and moved down the mountain, freezing rain water from the cedar trees dripping on them, soaking their heads and shoulders. They found Antonis Zoidakis waiting with a mule and a guide, another mountain man called Panagos. The animal had a comfortable padded saddle and coloured blankets and had been borrowed from Antonis's mother. Round its neck it wore a string of blue beads from which was slung a bell that the guides muffled with cloth. Like most of the other mules used by the andartes, the mule's vocal cords had been cut to stop it braying and giving away their position.

They planned to head down the south side of Mount Ida in the direction of Nithavri. Zoidakis would again go ahead to reconnoitre the route. On the way they came to a crossroads where the roads from four villages joined. The place was danger-ous and Germans could be seen moving about the tents they had pitched in the area. The guide Panagos suddenly disappeared and the group became anxious. Leigh Fermor held a quick conference. He suggested they head for the village of Agia Paraskevi: 'there's a deep stream there covered with myrtles, we've hidden there before'. Skoutello was impressed by the Englishman's firm leadership.

Agia Paraskevi was Zoidakis's home village in the Amari valley. For centuries the valley had been a sanctuary from the armies that had invaded Crete. It was twenty miles long, with olive groves, vineyards and shady ravines lined with walnuts and figs. Drifts of poppies streaked the green patches of young wheat. Its gushing springs were studded with derelict mills, Turkish bridges and white-walled villages where the guerrillas came to hide from the enemy.

As they moved through the darkness they could see the glow of searchlights around the hugely expanded airfield at Timbaki. The lights were aimed out to sea and were working in conjunction with coastal probing batteries, placed to fire on any British ship that might try and approach the beaches at Agia Galini or Sahtouria. Every now and then the sky above them was lit by flares fired by the searching soldiers, and echoing German voices shouted, 'Kreipe, Kreipe, speak up, don't be afraid!'

Soon the ladder-sided steepness of the mountain gave way to the gentler slopes of the Amari valley and paths free from the treacherous scree. Progress was much faster than it had been the previous night; they marched for the first three hours non-stop, sloping past the high fastness of Nithavri and on towards Agia Paraskevi. At midnight, they reached the rendezvous, a tree, hollowed out for animals to drink from. There was no sign of Zoidakis. Leigh Fermor thought they must have mistaken the route or come to the wrong place. Paterakis and Tyrakis went to scour the area for other groves. For half an hour they searched, whistling and making owl hooting noises, but returned empty-handed. The team wondered if Zoidakis had been captured and had been forced to reveal where they were; perhaps the Germans were all around, waiting to pounce on them as soon as the sun rose. They decided to press on. It began to drizzle, a cold penetrating rain, which quickly turned into a downpour soaking through their already wet clothes. Paterakis muttered that the weather was good for the olives if not for the kidnappers. Eventually, somewhere near the village, they flopped down into a ditch, inches deep in water, sodden and forlorn.

Leigh Fermor had another look at the letter, holding it under his coat to hide the light of his torch. To his horror he realised that what the letter said was the reverse of what Paterakis had read out in the cave. Antonis had written: 'For God's sake DON'T come tonight.' The letter had been heavily folded and was wet, the 'DON'T' had been obscured in one of the folds.

At dawn Tyrakis set off for the village in the hoping that he could track down Antonis. The others could do nothing but wait in the cover of the ditch as it slowly filled up with water. They felt abandoned. Kreipe was the most dejected of all, sitting with a blanket over his head, water running down his face.

The sun rose and at mid-morning Tyrakis arrived with Antonis Zoidakis carrying baskets of food. When he saw the bedraggled abductors Antonis exclaimed: 'What are you doing boys, you ought to be dead! How did you get through? There are hundreds of Germans crawling all over the mountains, especially where you came down.' He made the sign of the cross and said: 'God exists and you ought all to build churches, – No! cathedrals! You are lucky to be here my children.'

In the dark, they had somehow slipped through the cordon. They were shaken by the narrow escape and the near-fatal blunder. German search parties were now high above them and the voices of the soldiers calling '*Kreipe, Kreipe, Generaloberst Kreipe!*' still echoed round the mountains, bouncing from peak to peak.

Antonis distributed the food, and served Kreipe first with exaggerated deference. Then he passed the food round to the others, handing round the cheese fritters and announcing: 'White flannel vests all round.' After which he pulled a gallon jar of dark mulberry raki from the basket, saying: 'Next, red overcoats for all!' Even Kreipe was amused by Zoidakis's antics, although as he ate he muttered in German: 'I wish I had never come to this accursed land, it was supposed to be a nice change from the Russian Front.'

20

Marooned

The following day more lorries rumbled down the primitive dusty roads that followed the broad sweep of the beaches below Sahtouria, dropping over two hundred soldiers along the route. The infantry set up defensive positions with mortars and heavy machine guns, while engineers ran out miles of telephone cable linking the positions, cutting off the approaches to the beaches from both the land and the sea, including the one that Cairo had designated for the rendezvous, Cape Melissa.

At the same time Ilias Athanassakis and Micky Akoumianakis clambered aboard an ancient bus in Heraklion, and travelled south to try and track down the abductors. They had much to report, especially the fact that so far there had been no reprisals. After nearly three hours bouncing south they left the bus and began to walk, heading for where they thought the abduction party would be. They were both wearing very light shoes, suitable for the city but not for the rough hill areas where they were headed. It was another hour before they arrived, with torn shoes and blistered feet, to be reunited with the kidnappers.

They found Kreipe sunk in a dazed torpor, seemingly oblivious to his surroundings. When they told him that his ADC and the guards at the villa had been arrested by the Gestapo he perked up for a second and shrugged, saying that his ADC was a complete dunce whom he had been about to replace. He added that he felt sorry for the guards because it was not their fault. Then he shook his head and slumped back into silence.

Micky and Ilias reported to Moss and Leigh Fermor that the Germans were worried the kidnap might trigger an uprising on the island. Bräuer had strengthened the guard round his head-quarters and would not move from it without an escort. Worse, there was a German detachment in the village of Krya Vryssi, which was only three miles away. There was a possibility that the garrisons at Rethymnon and Mesara would be mobilised to close the whole of the Amari valley, trapping them. The kidnappers still did not know whether their signals had got through to Cairo, and had no idea of the time or place of the rendezvous.

At times German troops passed very close to the hideout, some-times no further than a few hundred metres. When one patrol came especially close, stretching the nerves of the kidnappers, Kreipe said to Leigh Fermor: 'Perhaps you and your company will soon be my prisoners.' The Englishman snapped back, 'Don't dream of shouting for you can never escape these men. I warn you, they will despatch you on the spot.'

Leigh Fermor had to find a radio set. He was fairly certain that Dick Barnes was only a day's walk away. If he could find him his problems would be over. He decided to set off in search at dusk, taking Giorgios Tyrakis with him.

The same day, 3 May, Dick Barnes, who had no idea what was happening along the coast, picked up a message confirming that a launch would be off Cape Melissa in the evening and, if the party failed to make the rendezvous, would return for a second try the following night. Giorgios Psychoundakis was with Barnes and offered to take the message to Leigh Fermor. He had to leave immediately to have any chance of getting the message through in time and he did not know precisely where the kidnap party had got to. He set off for Yerakari, in the Amari valley, where he hoped to find someone who could help.

While Leigh Fermor was trying to track down a radio, the Germans set up a field headquarters in the schoolhouse at

Apodoulou, close to the main hideout, cordoning off the village and not allowing anyone in or out. The villagers were very frightened; they knew that there was a stack of arms in the roof of the schoolhouse and thought it was only a matter of time before it was discovered.

In the late afternoon, Leigh Fermor and Giorgios, disguised as peasants, set off, heading north towards the last known position of Barnes and his radio set. Soon afterwards it began to rain. Billy Moss and the general settled down for the night under the same blanket. Before he slept Kreipe drank an enormous slug of raki, pulled most of the covers over himself and fell into a deep sleep. Moss could not sleep: he lay under part of the sodden blanket, huge drops of water hitting him in the face, kept awake by the deep droning snores of his prisoner. Around him the guerrillas, equally cold and miserable, took it in turn to keep guard.

On the south coast, off the beach at Cape Melissa, a motor launch skippered by Commander Francis Pool, hove to in the darkness. On the bridge, Pool, a lookout and a radio operator, scanned the shoreline with their field glasses, looking for the blinking of a signal torch. Armed men stood by on the deck, ready to launch a rubber dinghy and paddle for the shore. The motor launch waited for a long time in the darkness, wallowing in the slight swell. After several hours Pool decided he had pushed his luck far enough. He ordered the coxswain to start the engines. An electric motor hauled the anchor back on board, its chain clattering against the metal of the hull. The coxswain reversed from the beach then went full ahead, swinging the bow in a wide curve heading for Egypt, its wake boiling behind in a huge white ribbon.

Leigh Fermor and Giorgios made good progress in their night march along the Amari valley, and broke their journey at Fourfouras, where Giorgios's family lived. On the next day, 4 May, they decided to risk moving in daylight across the foothills of Mount Kedros. The walk was idyllic, and the spring weather fine. They crossed woods and streams and marched through fields of poppies, anemones and asphodels. Birdsong accompanied them and to the east Mount Ida loomed above them. On the Mesara Plain, several miles to the south-east of the kidnappers, German engineers arrived in the villages of Lochria, Kamares and Magarikari and started unloading boxes of high explosives. Infantrymen rounded up the villagers and marched them into the fields. The engineers began to pack charges in the foundations of the houses.

During that day messengers at last arrived at Moss's hideout. One was from Dick Barnes with the news that a motor launch had appeared the night before, had seen no signals from the beach and had left without sending a landing party. He told them the boat would return every night for the next four nights. Moss knew that with hundreds of troops now guarding the beach there was no possibility of making contact with the launch. In his diary he fumed: 'How infuriating it is to know that all this is happening at a beach that is no more than a few hours walk from here and we can do absolutely nothing about it.' Moss decided it would be safer to leave the area and head further west.

On 5 May, Tyrakis and Leigh Fermor walked through a cypress grove into the village of Pantanasa, looking for Dick Barnes. Neither man had visited the village before. They had a contact, the Hieronymakis family, but had never met them and there was no one in the village to vouch that they were genuinely part of the resistance movement. The villagers had to know who they were dealing with and asked: 'You say you are Mihali, Mihali who? And who are Siphis and Pavlos [Stockbridge and Barnes's codenames].'

In the end, and after two hours of haggling, Tyrakis's uncle Stavropol appeared and vouched for the two men. Runners were sent off to Barnes and Stockbridge asking them to come to the village with their radio sets. Leigh Fermor and Giorgios then set off for the village of Yenni, heading for Pantanasa. At Yenni they found out that things had got worse. Both Barnes and Stockbridge had been forced to move their sets and they were each about fifteen miles further away, across difficult Cretan terrain. The chess pieces in Leigh Fermor's game were moving and he was playing blindfolded. He no longer knew where the radios were, he did not know that troops were in the Amari valley and that Moss was about to move camp. Three sets of messengers had been sent to Dick Barnes but none of them had got through. To add to the confusion Giorgios Psychoundakis still had no idea where Leigh Fermor was. Communications had become a nightmare.

Eventually Psychoundakis tracked Leigh Fermor down at Yenni, at the western end of the Amari valley, with news of the motor launch that had been waiting for them the night before. The Englishman was phlegmatic: 'Never mind, we couldn't have gone there because the Germans moved in there yesterday morning.' He wanted Psychoundakis to go back to Dick Barnes and get him to bring his wireless set.

Psychoundakis did not think that such a plan was possible. Moving a wireless station was a difficult task. The heavy charging engine and batteries and all the other paraphernalia required at least six men carrying the gear on their backs, and would have to be moved at night, in pitch black, avoiding the tracks and navigating the steep slopes.

Then they talked about which beaches might still be open for a rendezvous. Leigh Fermor wondered whether the beach at Preveli was a possibility; it was the place from which hundreds of Allied stragglers had been rescued; or maybe the beach at Keramia?

'Not at Preveli,' Psychoundakis replied. 'There is a permanent German guard post there. I don't know the Keramia beach, but we've got a man from that district. He'll tell us all we want to know. He's in Rethymnon. But I'll go and get him without losing a minute. But I think, Mr Michali [another nickname for Leigh Fermor], that the only place you'll be able to leave is from our beach at Rodakino. That's where it will be in the end.'

With alarming speed the beaches were being sealed off. Soon, it seemed, there would be no beaches available at all. Leigh Fermor told Psychoundakis to return to Dick Barnes as fast as possible. Another runner was sent to retrieve some Cretan clothes Leigh Fermor had left in the village of Agyroupolis, and which he said he needed, and a third runner went to Rethymnon to find the expert on the beaches.

Leigh Fermor spent the next three nights marooned in Yenni, 'smoking and staring at the moon'. During the day he sat in the warm sun listening to the sound of the nearby waterfall, trying to work out how he was to lead his band off the island. For once the sky was empty of spotter planes and the landscape silent. The enormous pressure that he was under began to tell. He was exhausted and in a constant state of stress; his left arm had become stiff and difficult to move. The situation was changing hourly; escape options were closing one after the other and no one knew what to do.

Psychoundakis returned the next day, accompanied by Dick Barnes, resplendent in black jackboots, a shaggy, stinking, goat-skin cape and a handkerchief round his neck. With them was Kapitan Yannis Katsias, loping along like a fearsome wolf, 'heavily armed, carrying his rifle at the point of balance, looking like a twig in his massive hands. Katsias was a man you wanted as a friend not a foe.' Katsias was a tough, free-booting giant of a man with great good looks. There was no better person to lead them along the old rustling tracks, hidden and safe.

Barnes told Leigh Fermor that it was impossible for him to bring his set any closer and that it would be best to carry on using the runners. He agreed with Psychoundakis that the beaches below Rodakino would be the best place to organise a rendezvous, although several days earlier there had been trouble there: a

German patrol had marched into the village and started to burn it down; the locals had ambushed the soldiers, opening fire and killing some of them, and two Germans had been taken prisoner. Nevertheless they decided to keep moving west towards the village.

That evening, 5 May, Leigh Fermor, Psychoundakis, Barnes and Yannis sat round a fire drinking wine and eating an enormous hare cooked by Yannis in oil and onions. They sang mountain songs to the tune of the Pentozali dance. Leigh Fermor made up his own verse:

> *Ah, God-brother, the night was dark for the lamb and goat and dam*
> *   sir*
> *But when we saw the branding mark, we only stole the ram sir.*

This was a comic improvisation on a song about a sheep rustler who, realising that he is about to steal his god-brother's flock, has a fit of conscience and only steals thirty instead of the whole flock; in Leigh Fermor's rendition he only steals the ram, the head of the flock: a reference to the general.

The next morning, Lefteris Papayannakis, the reconnaissance man from Rethymnon, hid in the rocks above the beach at Keramia. German boats were beaching from the sea, landing more troops, while from inland he could see dust clouds thrown up by lorries full of troops arriving at the garrison already guarding the beach at Preveli. Keramia too was a non-starter.

At Cairo the SOE Crete desk was becoming increasingly worried about the situation. The motor launch sent to wait off the beach at Cape Melissa had seen nothing but the odd meaningless flash of a signalling torch, and the first time the crew had tried to make contact they had been fired on and forced to make for the safety of the open sea. A message was sent from GHQ to London:

5 ATTEMPTS HAVE BEEN MADE. NONE SUCCESSFUL. SIGNAL BEING MADE SHORTLY. OP REGARDED AS OF FIRST IMPORTANCE. DIFFICULTIES CONSIDERABLE. PARTY IS ON RUN AND COMMUNICATION INTERMITTENT.

To confuse things further the powers at GHQ decided to take matters into their own hands. Without the benefit of up-to-date intelligence on German positions, they ordered a Special Boat Service raiding party to land below Rodakino, somewhere near Sahtouria beach, make contact with the kidnap group and help them fight their way off the island. The raid was planned for the night of 9/10 May.

21

Hide and Seek

Antonis Zoidakis reached Moss with the information that more soldiers had been deployed to reinforce the cordon to the south-west of the mountain, cutting them off from the beaches there; the Germans were organising another sweep of the hillside and the beach at Keramia was closed off. Moss ordered Zoidakis to go back and get an exact idea of how many Germans were in the area and whether it was possible to find a track leading through the cordon. With no path to follow it was too dangerous to leave the hideout. Moss postponed his plan, hoping to set off the next night, knowing that the longer they remained where they were, the more likely they were to be discovered.

Next, one of Sandy Rendel's runners arrived with a copy of Rendel's first and now hopelessly out-of-date message about the rendezvous. With it was a personal letter from Rendel to Moss.

Dear Billy,
All my rosiest and sincerest compliments and congratulations on presenting everyone with quite the best war story yet . . . I shall look forward immensely, needless to say, to hear the full details later. I am glad the old man is a charmer – so much nicer than if he was grumpy. Bless you – and once more I raise an aged battered, almost historic but very respectful hat and all the best for the rest of the journey.
SANDY

Moss spent a tense day, unable to move, with nothing to do and forced to listen to the complaints of the general, who claimed that he could not sleep at night (though he slept whenever he could during the day) and that he had stomach ache as well as severe pains in his leg. After a great deal of trouble Moss had got hold of a copy of *1001 Nacht* (*The Arabian Nights*), a book which the German said he wanted to read, and which Moss now presented to him. He took it from his captor's hands, looked at it and handed it back, saying it was too old-fashioned for him. Moss wrote in his diary: 'I could have killed him.'

At midday the distant boom of detonating explosives echoed from the hills. The engineers had done their work: the villages of Lochria, Kamares and Margarikari, complete with furniture, cooking utensils, clothes, children's toys, farm tools, and all the other objects of simple country life, were reduced to piles of flaming rubble. Some of the villagers were caught in the cordon and arrested, others who had tried to escape were murdered. A messenger arrived at Moss's hideout with news of the destruction. When Kreipe heard this he began to laugh, gloating that it was a simple thing for his men to exact retribution for anything that the British did or incited the guerrillas to do. 'If Bräuer continues the cordon and the search like this,' he said, repeating his taunt, 'soon I won't be your captive but you will be mine.' This was the last straw for Moss; he rounded on the general and warned him that if he did not shut up he would start treating him as a prisoner of war rather than as a sort of distinguished guest.

After this outburst Moss and Kreipe sat side by side, sulking in silence, each unable to get out of the presence of the other. Tension built in the hideout. Moss wrote in his diary: 'All Germans are the same young and old. I take an oath now that if I can humanly accomplish it I shall kill or have killed a thousand Germans before I leave the island.'

Manolis Paterakis began to nag Moss, muttering that he

thought the general was going to try and escape or give the game away by shouting to attract the search parties. The team watched him all the time, cocked weapons in their hands, and followed him everywhere, especially on his frequent excursions to urinate in the thickets.

The sun grew hotter, the rustling impatience of the cicadas filled the air and birds sang in counterpoint to the drone of the spotter plane which had reappeared overhead. The kidnappers could hear the grinding gears of lorries toiling along the few suitable roads and the occasional crump of a hand grenade or the chatter of a heavy machine gun, fired by nervous soldiers at the phantoms they imagined were waiting to ambush them.

In the destroyed villages, the engineers poured fuel on the ruins. Choking black smoke swirled everywhere, towering for hundreds of feet in the air and drifting for miles, cloaking the countryside with the acrid, sickly sweet smell of burning rubble and kerosene. The homeless villagers tried to escape to the safety of the mountains, caught in the misery of life on the run. The German propaganda newspaper *Paratiritis* ran a story about the destruction of the villages:

> The brazen and criminal deeds of the outdoor bandits who abducted and spirited away General Kreipe brought about the inevitable measures against the elements: elements guilty of illegal activity against the security of the occupying forces and the general peace of the area . . . the villages of Lochria, Kamares and Margarikari were surrounded by German troops on 3 May 1944 and emptied in the course of a large-scale operation waged against the bandits of Mount Ida. After the evacuation of the villagers the villages themselves were razed to the ground.

Another, even more ominous leaflet which was distributed, read:

Cretans beware the edge of the German sword
will strike down everyone of the guilty men
and all the henchmen and all the hirelings of the English.

In the evening Antonis Zoidakis returned. There were now enemy troops swarming into the south-east end of the Amari valley, heading for where they were hiding; there were now troops at both ends of the valley and soon they would be surrounded. The good news was that he thought he had discovered a track which would lead them through the cordon of patrols.

The destination, which they needed to reach that evening, was the village of Yerakari, in peacetime famous for its cherries, but since the beginning of the war a hub for guerrilla activity. They moved off as soon as it was dusk, guided up the flanks of Mount Kedros by Antonis and a local schoolmaster. The failing light cloaked the move and prevented General Kreipe from seeing how close his men were to finding him.

The mule that carried Kreipe was small and weak, and the journey took them all night. On the way, they were met by Ilias Athanassakis, leading a goat and carrying brushwood so as to look like a farmer. In one village they saw the light of an oil lamp and Chnarakis went ahead to investigate. It was the local raki factory. Moss peered through the windows and saw men toasting each other in the drink, throwing it down in one gulp between shouts of 'Eviva!' A cigarette-tin full of the potent liquor was brought outside to Moss and the others, who found the taste 'warm and deceptively mellow'.

The rest of the journey passed without incident. Scouts moved ahead checking the villages ahead for German patrols. Moss found that, apart from the barking of dogs, everything had an eerie stillness. Just before dawn they reached Yerakari, and they were guided to the hut where they were to stay. They lit a fire and waited.

*

Leigh Fermor, Tyrakis and Psychoundakis arrived at the village of
Patsos, an hour or so from Yerakari, and met up with another
patriot, Giorgios Harokopos, whose family had helped British
soldiers to escape after the battle for Crete. The Germans had
raided the Harokopos house several times, imprisoning two of his
uncles, torturing his younger brother, and declaring the family
'Not law-abiding', after which they burnt the house down.
Harokopos was now asked go to Yerakari on 7 May and lead the
abduction team to a new, safer hideout where they could all reunite
somewhere near Patsos. Leigh Fermor reminded the young resistance fighter of the seriousness of the task he was about to under-
take. In return the British officer offered to give him safe passage
on the motor launch to Cairo.

That evening, the ISLD officer Ralph Stockbridge received
Leigh Fermor's message requesting his wireless set, and wrote a
long reply:

From Ralph Stockbridge 6.5.44.

Dear Paddy,

Have already sent you two urgent messages with answers to
your previous letter with news and instructions. Neither
presumably reached you they were sent to the address you gave
me. The burning of Sachtomic [the village of Sahtouria] cancels
their news. Whether the news of this reached Cairo in time to
stop them sending boat there last night 5/6 I very much doubt
also. Cairo say they broadcast capture of General and that he
had reached Cairo on 30th and 1st and news also published in
press. Leaflets printed at once, but not dropped because of bad
flying weather. Presumably dropped by now.

I regret I cannot come to meet you. Apart from the fact your
messenger did not get here till midnight nearly, I am, as you
know, my own operator, reluctant to leave the set particularly
at the moment.

Stockbridge knew that there was another SOE agent on the island, Major Dennis Ciclitira.

What I suggest is this. Sachtomic and Rodakino are blown – Dick [Barnes] led a party there 8 days ago and his signals were answered by MG fire from the sea. Since when lots of Huns have snooped around there. But at ASI GONIA RPT ASI GONIA is Dennis and Dennis has a set and an operator with him and nothing to do, he is due to leave by the next boat which is due, I think in about a week's time from the Preveli area. I suggest you send a runner along to Dennis saying you are coming to join him and in fact go over there and keep in touch with Cairo about boats. I will let Dick know also. This is better than runners chasing about all over the place with out-of-date news. I have told Cairo your situation – as far as half way through message about burning Sachtomic when all my batt[eries]s went flat suddenly . . . Will get this off have been up charging all night and will also send second telegraph saying you are out of Amari area and striking west. I will tell them to keep Dennis and Dick fully informed of both possibilities and to do their damnedest to get something in next week, even a destroyer if necessary.

Signals use MK every 20 minutes from 21:00 GMT onwards.

That at the moment is all I can tell you. Obviously you must have a set with you more or less to arrange about boat and Dennis is the obvious man. I personally am moving HQ tomorrow evening because these bloody people are scared stiff and kicking me out . . . If you prefer to stay where you are in any case contact Dennis. If anything urgent comes over my set for you I will send it to Dennis unless by tomorrow midday you let me know – you are staying where you are + Dick is to come and meet you at some given place at some given time. Though again there will be the communications difficulty + I consider preferable you join up with Dennis + I will let Dick know what you say. As I say if you want him with you send messenger (reliable please) tomorrow.

Have already sent you two lots of cigarettes. Here are some more and compo. Sorry about all this business.

Love from us all,

Ralph

MK – 'Monkey King' – was the recognition code to be flashed in Morse by torch from the beach of the rendezvous point to the rescue ship. If the captain of the pick-up vessel did not receive the signal, or if the signal was incorrect, he would cancel the rendezvous and head back across the sea to Egypt.

The huge and deadly game of hide and seek went on: the German searches forced everybody to keep moving from hideout to hideout with no quick way of contacting each other. As Stockbridge's tight-lipped and disapproving message pointed out, even when a runner did get through, the news he carried was usually out of date.

Billy Moss and General Kreipe were still not speaking to each other. Moss had run out of things to read and passed the time delousing himself, sitting on a rock in the sun, stark naked, searched the seams of his clothes for parasites – much to the embarrassment of the guerrillas who found nudity shocking. Kreipe did the same thing though without completely disrobing. The hours passed slowly. An old man and his grandson appeared from the village with a scant meal of a few dried cherries and sour milk. Later the old man came back with a bottle of wine and spent the rest of the day staring at the group in total silence.

With little to eat and nothing to do, the general relented and broke his silence towards Moss. He apologised, explaining that his poor knowledge of French had made his words seem harsher than he meant. The two men passed the rest of the day discussing the course of the war. Kreipe argued that the Allies would never be able to land in northern Europe and that the only way the war would end was with a negotiated settlement. Moss was surprised at how little the high-ranking officer seemed to know. Kreipe admitted that terrible things had gone on in the Ukraine. He thought that the Romanians were the best allies the Fatherland had, followed by the Italians, who he thought were 'very good indeed'.

In the afternoon, the young Giorgios Harokopos arrived, eager and ready to lead the abduction team and their prisoner on their journey to the next hideout at Harakas about a mile beyond the village of Patsos where, although they did not know it, Leigh Fermor was hiding. Harokopos was excited at the prospect of seeing the now legendary kidnap team and their captive general, but found the kidnappers looking tired and worried, their faces etched with the strain and uncertainty of the last two weeks. He shook hands with each of them and congratulated them on their brilliant achievement, hoping in his heart that he would not let down such a magnificent group of men. Then he said a polite 'Good evening' to General Kreipe and helped him mount the mule on which he was to travel.

The route to Patsos took them past the village of Spili, where a German battalion was garrisoned. Paterakis and Harokopos scouted about a quarter of a mile ahead of the main party, checking for ambushes. If they fell into a trap the others would have a chance to get away and hide in places that had already been identified for use in an emergency. The weight of the burly Kreipe became too much for the mule and the general was forced to go on foot; the journey, which should have been completed in three hours, took nearly six.

A string of messengers arrived for Leigh Fermor, all with bad news: the Germans were closing off beach after beach; hundreds of Cretans now knew the kidnappers were hiding in the area and, although most of them were determined to help the team, it was only a matter of time before a collaborator revealed where Kreipe was being kept, or one of the guerrillas was captured and broken under torture.

Most alarming of all was news that Cairo was mounting a rescue attempt led by the commander of the Special Boat Squadron (SBS), twenty-six-year-old Lieutenant Colonel George (the Earl) Jellicoe, who was a maverick. In 1942 he led the commando raid on Heraklion airfield in which twenty enemy aircraft had been destroyed and for which he won the DSO, complemented the following year by the award of an MC for actions on Rhodes. Neither Jellicoe nor Cairo knew that the chosen landing beach at Sahtouria was guarded by nearly two hundred German soldiers. It was clear that Jellicoe's party was on a suicide mission and likely to be massacred. Leigh Fermor sent a runner back to Dick Barnes with a signal asking Cairo to cancel the operation. It was 7 May; Jellicoe was due to land on the 9th. Leigh Fermor hoped his signal would get through in time.

Next he sent a runner with a message to Moss telling him about the raid. From the scribbled address Moss realised Leigh Fermor was very close by. He sent a reply asking his superior to rendez-vous with him as soon as possible. Leigh Fermor and his group broke camp and set off to rejoin the others.

On the way he and Tyrakis discussed what they would do if the raiding party appeared. Leigh Fermor thought they should send Kreipe to the village of Rodakino under an escort of guerrillas. Leaving the rest of the kidnappers to create a diversion, after which they could 'hare over the mountain'. Tyrakis said that no one wanted to stay with the general and suggested they put Kreipe in a cave and roll a huge boulder over the mouth to imprison him. In the last resort they would have to kill him and fling his body into a deep hole where he would never be found, just as they had done with his driver.

In the middle of the night of 9/10 May, Leigh Fermor and Tyrakis rejoined the others at Patsos. In the three days they had been away they had walked more than sixty miles. They arrived to find everyone asleep.

Leigh Fermor shook Moss awake, shining his torch in the young man's face and then into his own. They were delighted and relieved to see each other. The next two hours were spent drinking raki and smoking, going over and over the problem of Jellicoe's raid. Leigh Fermor now wanted to take a 'gang of twenty-five local thugs' down to the beach at Sahtouria to cause havoc behind the German lines as they came under fire from Jellicoe and his commandos. Under cover of the fight, Moss and the others would have to break out to the west with the general. Finally, tipsy and exhausted, they all fell asleep.

In the morning General Kreipe was surprised to see Leigh Fermor, and greeted him, saying, 'Good Morning Major, we've missed you.'

22

Men of Darkness

Later in the morning Dick Barnes's messenger, Kostas Koutelidakis, arrived to tell them that the Jellicoe raid had been postponed until the night of the 11/12th. Koutelidakis confirmed that the beach at Keramia was guarded by German patrols. There was nothing to do but go further west, which meant looping north-west towards the village of Fotinou, after which they had to face a stiff climb over another mountain before once more dropping down south to the coast.

The Germans were hard on their heels: the group learned that they were raiding Yerakari, where the kidnappers had hidden only the day before. Other villages in the valley had also been raided. It was even more dangerous to move about in daylight. Yet again they were forced to wait until dark. Members of Giorgios Harokopos's family arrived with food, including a lamb which they roasted on a spit. One was Giorgios's uncle Eleftherios, a retired soldier and a member of the armed National Organisation of Crete, the EOK. Eleftherios had persuaded a friend in the village to lend the group a mule, one of the strongest around and capable of taking the general's weight.

At midday a wonderful lunch was laid out for the kidnappers. Kreipe was once more amazed at the generosity which the Cretans showed towards the British. A few days before he had seen an example of how thoroughly the occupying forces had been subverted: a member of the resistance had needed some false papers to travel to Heraklion; to the general's amazement, not one, but three sets were immediately produced for him, all bearing the distinctive thin red line across the top. Kreipe requested Leigh Fermor to ask Harokopos's sister why they were treating the British with such kindness and affection. 'It is because the British are fighting for our freedom,' she replied, 'while you Germans have deprived us of it in a barbarous way.' The SOE officers told Giorgios Harokopos's father that they were planning to take his son to Cairo. In compensation for the loss of the boy the British offered the old man some of the gold pieces. With great dignity he refused to take anything even though he was very poor.

Darkness fell, they heaved the general onto the mule and set off, leaving the nearby village of Patsos and the Harokopos family behind. By the end of that night's march they needed to reach the village of Fotinou. They walked towards the rising moon, now bright and more than half full. In their propaganda the Germans called the resistance fighters 'Men of Darkness'; young Giorgios pointed at the moon and said 'Our sun is rising!' They passed a spring whose freezing water was supposed to give the gift of immortality. They all drank, including the general, who asked for a second cup.

The jolly mood brought on by the prospect of eternal life was soon spoiled. The caravan passed a village recently burned to the ground by the Germans. The ruins of the buildings stood like skeletons in the dark; dead animals and pet dogs scattered in the main street. At the next village, Karines, they were met by 'Uncle' Stavros Zourbakis, his wife Kiria Eleni and their daughter Popi. Kiria Eleni was a formidable woman and a crack shot with a rifle. She greeted them with a welcoming tray of raki, wine and dishes of peeled walnuts.

They pushed on down a steep valley, the mule slipping and sliding; Kreipe swaying 'like a bride' on the animal's back, and four guerrillas walking alongside to stop him falling. At the bottom of the valley ran the main north–south road, which connected the two enemy garrisons at Spili and Armeni. Even at night military traffic on the road was heavy, made worse by the troops searching for the kidnappers. Taking no chances, the party hid on the east side of the road checking that the coast was clear. Then they crossed two at a time, running crouched, covered by the guns of the others. Kreipe dismounted to be escorted over the obstacle. The mule followed, a guerrilla thrashing its hindquarters.

On the approach to Fotinou, guerrilla fighters appeared at regular intervals. They could be heard whistling signals to each other, shepherding the caravan on its way. These men were under the command of an eighty-year-old, whose fighters were his sixteen sons and twenty-eight grandsons. The noise of the whistling changed, and became more urgent. A guerrilla scrambled down to the party, a German patrol was heading straight for them.

The group fanned out behind a ridge, vanishing into the darkness, weapons cocked, ready for a fight. Kreipe was dragged off the mule and flung into the heather. Other men headed for higher ground, spreading out in an ambush. Everyone peered into the darkness, gently easing off their safety catches, trying to spot the bobbing steel helmets of the Wehrmacht soldiers.

They heard the crunch of boots on the gritty track. A guerrilla clamped his hand over Kreipe's mouth to stop him shouting. The noise of the boots got louder. Then a shrill whistle echoed round the moonlit hills, followed by another, then another, and finally a voice shouting in Greek followed by laughter. The German patrol was a party of guerrillas who had come to escort the group into the village. They were now under the guardianship of Kapitans Andreas and Sifis Perros, both members of the Tzsangarakis family.

At last the tired band walked into Fotinou, where the villagers could not take their eyes of the high-ranking prisoner. Leigh Fermor thought it was as though the Sheriff of Nottingham was being led bound into Robin Hood's lair in Sherwood Forest.

They spent the next day in an olive grove, an idyllic but not very hidden setting, which they were assured was safe. Guerrillas flitted, shadow-like, between the trees, constantly vigilant. The quiet of the morning was broken by gunfire coming from the nearly village of Armeni, where there was a German fuel dump. Flares wobbled into the air, burning bright against the blue sky and trailing orange-grey smoke; nobody knew the reason for the commotion. Lunch was brought to them by a little man who was a shepherd. He and his wife had been forced to marry to resolve a long-standing feud that had its roots nearly a century in the past; Billy Moss renamed them Mr Montague and Mrs Capulet.

In the afternoon, the group was joined by four Russian POWs. They were engineers who had broken out from a cage at Rethymnon barracks. They were in bad shape, starving, with ragged clothing and worn-out boots. One of them, Peotr, was very ill with a stomach complaint. It was decided that Chnarakis would take most of them to Kastamonitsa, where they could join another small band of escaped Russians who Moss hoped would form a fighting force for future escapades. The Russians were given money, food and weapons and sent off with a distraught Chnarakis, who did not want to leave the main party and who had to be persuaded that his was a job of great importance. As they left the Russians raised the two fingered 'V' for victory sign. Peotr was left behind with the kidnappers. Too ill to walk, he lay on the ground writhing, groaning and retching. Now a second mule was found to carry him.

The route then took them to a tiny remote village, Alones, where Kapitan Yannis Katsias waited to rejoin them. With him were wild young fighters, mountain men, who shared Katsias's familiarity with every twist and turn of the tortured terrain. One of them was the son of the village priest, Father John, a brave supporter of the andartes and whose other son had been executed by the Germans. They were to guide the kidnappers to the village of Vilandredo. Yannis himself went ahead to warn of the group's progress. The escort that had led them so safely from Fotinou shook hands and said their farewells; the work done, they returned to their villages.

The mule clambered and lurched from perch to perch, jolting and jerking the German general. Suddenly the leather girth snapped and the saddle slid down the animal's flanks, sending Kreipe tumbling into a ravine. A rock caught his arm, wrenching it back, making him scream in agony. He landed on his shoulder, bellowing in pain, and lay clutching his arm, crying out that he was dying. After a while he began to thrash about like a baby, rolling from his back onto his stomach and shouting blasphemies at his captors. Then he began to whimper: 'I've had enough, why don't you shoot me and get it done with.' Eventually he stopped and allowed the guerrillas to help him to his feet. They pulled the heavy man back onto the path and improvised a sling for him, bodging a repair to the girth strap.

Kreipe could now only hold on with one hand and needed someone constantly by his side to stop him tumbling off again. He winced every time the mule stumbled or heaved itself onto another ledge. The groaning and retching figure of Peotr, on another mule, was becoming an unpopular liability. Moss took a deep dislike to him, and later wrote scathingly in his diary that Peotr was a typical prejudiced product of the Russian proletariat. He resented the Russian's tiresome claims that life under the Soviets was a form of paradise compared to what he imagined life in England to be like. Paterakis nicknamed the Russian 'Pendamorphi' ('the five times lovely one' – a princess in a Greek fairy tale). His personal habits, though probably caused by stomach illness, were considered so repulsive that at one point the guerrillas suggested leaving him behind or pushing him into a gorge.

Very behind schedule, they reached Vilandredo, where they were greeted by Leigh Fermor's godbrothers Stathis and Stavros Loukakis, carrying their baby sister, Anglia, another of Leigh Fermor's goddaughters. The group was led to the base of a cliff face, halfway up which was their next hideout, impossible to reach from below. They were forced to climb above it and then lower themselves down, using branches and roots as handholds, man-handling Kreipe as they went.

After an hour of scrabbling they reached a tiny ledge at the mouth of a cramped cave. From the dark silence came the sound of deep snoring. In the cave's gloom they made out the outline of a man sleeping against one wall. He slowly woke and disentangled himself from the stinking goatskin cloak that was his blanket. The man was heavily built, with swarthy dark features, black eyes and a huge black beard which he began to stroke, staring at his new-found companions. Then he said, in perfect English, 'I wondered when you two schoolboys were going to appear.' This was Major Dennis Ciclitira, the man Ralph Stockbridge had recommended Leigh Fermor link up with. Ciclitira had heard of their predicament from Stockbridge and had come to find them.

Ciclitira was a businessman of Greek origin, brought up in Westcliff-on-Sea in Essex, and had connections in the olive oil trade on Crete. After serving with the South Staffordshire Regiment at the start of the war, and on SOE's Crete desk in Cairo, Ciclitira had spent the last five months on the island. During this time two of his men, sergeant majors, one a New Zealander and the other from the Coldstream Guards, had been captured and killed by the Germans.

The group breakfasted on searingly strong cheese and sour milk, talking about how they were going to get General Kreipe off the island. Ciclitira, who was himself due to leave in a week, said he would go back to his wireless station and ask GHQ if his pick-up launch could come earlier and take them all off, although exactly where the rendezvous would be was still not known. He then left for the two-hour walk back to his radio base at Asi Gonia, where he was scheduled to make a transmission to Cairo that afternoon. The kidnap group felt relief, delighted that they might soon be back in communication with Cairo.

At noon Leigh Fermor's godbrother Stathis reappeared and insisted they move thirty fleet further up the cliff face to a better spot. Kreipe did not want to move: he complained that he was very happy in the cave and that his shoulder was shattered and causing him great pain. It took six men half an hour to haul the general to the new hideout. When they arrived they found that the area had been prepared for a feast. Cushions and coloured blankets had been spread on the ground; a suckling pig was slowly roasting on a glowing red fire and the aroma of cooking meat filled the air.

The men examined the general's shoulder. It was badly bruised, but not in nearly such a bad condition as he claimed. They bathed it and wrapped it in a sling made from handkerchiefs, mollycoddling their prisoner, telling him how brave he had been and congratulating him on his uncomplaining stoicism. The general, looking a bit shame-faced, apologised for his behaviour, excusing himself by saying that he thought his shoulder blade was broken and had been in such great pain that he had no idea what he was doing. After eating, most of the men dozed. Some stayed on guard, scanning the hills for German patrols and watching over Kreipe snoring in the afternoon sun.

The tensions of the last ten days eased. The coast was only a few hours' walk away and they could relax until they heard from Ciclitira that he had received confirmation of the arrival of a boat at the rendezvous beach. For two days they waited in the sunshine, guarded by Katsias and his men. For the first time in weeks they felt safe, soothed by the sound of crystal-clear water rushing down the mountain, sleeping on comfortable cushions, their heads pillowed by Malotira plants, the soft springy source of Cretan mountain tea, their noses filled with the scent of wild oregano which the ancient healer Hippocrates regarded as a valuable medicine. As darkness fell they sang songs in harmony, including 'Good Night Ladies', which they repeated over and over again. When their voices failed and sleep overtook them, nightingales began to sing, while the Milky Way twinkled in the deep blue sky above their heads.

*

On 13 May the quiet was shattered by the shouts of Kapitan Katsias's men. Lorries full of German soldiers were arriving in the vicinity. More trucks were heading for Vilandredo. The cushions and blankets were cleared and wine poured on the fire, which went out in a billow of steam. Then the kidnappers made the laborious descent down the cliff face to the safety of the first cave.

While the scrambled to hide, Katsias moved his men to the cliff opposite the cave, where they could cover the entrance and drive off any German patrols. Then they waited for the onslaught, screwing up their eyes against the sun, peering into the hills. During the afternoon they heard automatic gunfire, the crump of grenades and saw more flares rising into the sky. The commotion came from the west, where Katsias had sent men to shoot up German trucks and create a diversion to draw the enemy away from the hideout.

At dusk a runner arrived. The patrols were moving north, heading for Asi Gonia, where Dennis Ciclitira was hiding and trying to transmit to Cairo. More soldiers were in Vilandredo, kicking in doors, terrorising the inhabitants and searching every house, trapping Stathis and his brother Stavros.

In Asi Gonia, Ciclitera struggled to take down a Morse signal from SOE Middle East. He could hear lorries revving, soldiers shouting and the spotter plane droning overhead. He turned off his set: it was too dangerous to go on transmitting.

At the cave, Katsias decided to move them further up the mountain. Kreipe declared that he was cold and would walk, but only in order to warm himself up. The move took about an hour, after which they waited for Stathis and Stavros. Several hours passed by and they did not appear. Night fell and Katsias told them they must move again, even higher up the mountain. The route was difficult. Trees cut out the moonlight, and the path was lined with bushes that hid a steep drop to a dried-up, rocky river-bed. They trekked slowly and in single file, each man straining to keep his eyes on the person in front, panting hard as they struggled with the climb. An hysterical, feminine cry broke the silence, then the noise of breaking branches and a heavy object sliding down the crumbling rock, followed by a sickening thump and the deep groans of a man in pain. Kreipe had stumbled, staggered against the bushes lining the path and fallen through, tumbling nearly twenty feet to the ravine below.

A torch flashed to reveal the German officer groaning, spread-eagled in a deep pile of dead leaves. Some of the men slid down the hill, gripping on to the vegetation growing out of the rocks. Kreipe hauled himself onto his hands and knees, his groans turning to a series of bad-tempered insults as he cursed his captors. He was scratched, bruised and shaken, but otherwise, not hurt; nothing was twisted or broken. After a short rest the group moved on, keeping close watch on the prisoner to prevent him stumbling again in the darkness. Kreipe stopped swearing and relapsed into a silence broken only by the occasional whimper.

It took until three in the morning to reach the new hideout. There they wrapped the general in all the blankets they could muster and he fell into a asleep. Leigh Fermor and Moss thought that the two falls, the strain of capture and the seventeen-day mule ride and route march under guard had shattered Kreipe's nerves. They worried that he was not in a fit state to finish the journey. There was still no sign of Stathis and the promised provisions.

Without blankets the two agents found it impossible to sleep. The misty air was damp, the rock walls ran with slime, and the cold cut right through their battledress tops. Leigh Fermor talked obsessively about their comrades back at Tara who he compared to beasts gorging themselves on drink, the pleasures of the house and life in the nightclubs of Cairo. As the edge of the sky began to lighten they heard boots crashing on the rocks below. Everyone sprang into action, cocking their pistols, chambering rounds into the rifles and machine guns, then crouching in the undergrowth, waiting for the appearance of the dreaded field-grey uniforms. Stathis's voice rang out, and he burst among them with his brother Stavros, carrying two bottles of raki and a basket with bread and cheese. The brothers explained that they had been trapped and that finding nothing in the village, the soldiers had headed south, circling round towards the beaches. Another unit of around a hundred Germans were looking for their missing general in and around Rodakino, about twenty miles to the south and overlooking the possible rendezvous spots.

In an attempt to warm themselves up, Leigh Fermor and Moss drank the raki very quickly and soon became 'pretty tight'. The day passed with no message from Dennis Ciclitira. They decided to send a messenger to him, but the boy they chose refused to budge, saying that it was too dangerous and that the Germans would capture and torture him. A runner arrived with news from Ciclitira: he was safe, still in hiding, but for the moment unable to receive or transmit. The Germans had come very close but had not discovered him. Before the raid he had picked up a message from Cairo that a motor launch was scheduled to pick them up the following night, the time and place of disembarkation still to be confirmed. If he could get back on air and receive the coordinates and timings for the rendezvous he would try and make his way through the German lines to meet them in time to join them on the launch to Egypt.

The group could only guess at the possible beaches, which were all several miles due south across the mountains. They had to wait for the cover of darkness before moving, but until they knew where they were going they could not move at all. Once more they were marooned.

Leigh Fermor's arm was getting worse and he was in a great deal of pain. The general sat in a depressed lump, complaining about his shoulder and leg but otherwise not talking, almost unaware of his surroundings. The Russian Peotr was managing to swallow liquids, though his sneering manner, his temper and his personal habits had not improved. The day dragged. The sun and the temperature rose while the kidnappers waited for news. In Cairo, the wireless communications room had been trying, with no luck, to raise Ciclitira and send him the rendezvous information. Jack Smith-Hughes, the head of section, suggested they try Dick Barnes.

The sun set, the temperature dropped and still no word came to the kidnap group. They resigned themselves to another night in the damp and the cold. Stathis and Stavros agreed to go and fetch more food.

The men returned after dark. Somehow they had found warm clothing, blankets, food and wine, all of which was received with gratitude by the fugitives, especially the general. With still no news from Ciclitira, there was nothing to do but eat, sleep, and wait.

Their slumbers were interrupted an hour later by a man softly ordering them to wake up. It was Dick Barnes: 'A boat is coming to pick you up from a beach near Rodakino at 22:00 hours tomorrow night, 14/15 May. Here's the map reference. You'd better get a move on if you want to get there in time.'

Leigh Fermor woke Kreipe: '*Wunderbar, Herr General.* We're leaving!'

On the map it looked as though the beach was a full day's trek away. Once more Leigh Fermor decided to split the group. He proposed to take Kreipe the long way round, through the Kryoneritis mountains, a bleak, empty area ringed by craters with deep crevices, no paths and no flat areas. Without a mule the general would have to walk, guided by Yannis Katsias and his men. Billy Moss and the others were to make a dash for it through much easier terrain, but more dangerous straight into the 'forbidden zone' and the German patrols that ringed the coastal beaches.

It was a bright clear night, and the moon nearly full. Yannis Katsias left at once, heading for Rodakino, to warn the guerrilla bands that the kidnap party was making its final approach. Moss and his group left soon after him. Finally Leigh Fermor, the general, Paterakis and Yannis's guides headed for the mountains and some of the steepest and worst going on the island; but at least, once the sun rose, they could keep moving in broad daylight, safe from German eyes.

23

Home Run

As they moved across the mountains, Leigh Fermor's group was joined by more than twenty new andartes, all under the command of Kapitan Andreas Kotsifis. Most of the men had fair hair with black eyebrows, 'like pen strokes with their light blue eyes, blazing out from beneath'. Their homes at Rodakino and Kali Sykia had been destroyed by the Germans, dynamited and dive-bombed. They had nothing to lose and everything to fight for, optimistic, reckless spirits moving round the forbidden zone with impunity, defying the invaders to come into the mountains and take them on.

Billy Moss made fast progress over the easier, though still vertiginous, route, running up and down the steep slopes like 'a madman's switchback'. They had no water with them, although Tyrakis had a bottle full of raki at which they all sipped when they stopped to get their breath back. They arrived at the rendezvous point above the beach just before dawn.

Five hours later the guerrillas led Kreipe and his captors to the same spot. The general's epic journey had taken thirteen hours. Leigh Fermor was in a bad way. He was finding it hard to move, had terrible cramps, was walking stiffly, and complained that he did not know what was wrong with him.

The party sat overlooking the wide beaches stretching below them to the east and west. On the nearest was a German garrison. Through field glasses they could see soldiers bivouacking inside a barbed-wire enclosure, protected by heavy automatic weapons and mortars mounted, behind sandbags and piled high with boxes of ammunition. Kreipe asked if he could have a look. He peered through the binoculars at the men who, only a few weeks ago, had been part of his command. He watched them hanging out their washing, sunbathing, preparing the midday meal, even playing leapfrog. The garrison was oblivious to the presence of the kidnappers, their captured leader and a band which had grown to more than a hundred guerrillas. Kreipe handed back the field glasses, sighed and said: 'You must be pleased. I sometimes wonder who is in charge of this island, us or you British.'

Less than a mile to the west there was another garrison with about forty more Germans and more guard posts at intervals all along the beaches, linked by telephone and all heavily armed. The party had no choice but to sit hidden in the heather above the cliffs and wait until it was time to get on to the pick-up point. From time to time they heard guerrillas in the hills blazing away with their Tommy guns in a defiant challenge to the oppressors. The group hoped that if they were spotted they would be mistaken for the same homeless, wild men and that the Germans would be too nervous to take them on.

At four in the afternoon they began to move surreptitiously along the cliffs, travelling in groups of two or three, the rocks concealing them from the soldiers on the beach. The journey took less time than they had anticipated and because it was still light they stopped about a quarter of a mile from the rendezvous spot to wait. They were in a tiny vegetable garden created by a shepherd, and which even had a fountain. Towards the end of the day the shepherd himself arrived to tend the plot. Unaware that a few yards from him sat the fugitive general, he offered the kidnappers onions and lettuces and water from the fountain. They sat eating what they hoped would be their last meal on the island while, to the west, the sun set, turning the glittering Libyan Sea a deep midnight blue.

At eight o'clock it was time to move down to the beach, ready to meet the motor launch. More andartes arrived to see them off. The beach was set in a cove sheltered by steep rocks and it began to turn into what Leigh Fermor described as a 'sort of drawing room': men smoked cigarettes, lounged and talked. Kreipe sat by himself on a rock at the water's edge, his arm in a sling and the sea lapping softly at his boots, ruined by the rigours of the last nineteen days, their once-gleaming surface scraped bare.

At 21:30 hours Leigh Fermor and Billy Moss decided it was time to start signalling. They climbed on to a rock and fished out a torch from Moss's haversack. The codewords had been changed from Monkey King to Sugar Baker, 'SB'; they realised that neither of them knew what that was in Morse code, and stared at each other in dazed silence. Then Leigh Fermor said that he knew how to do S.O.S. If they flashed two Ss, they would be fifty per cent correct and the commander of the motor launch, knowing they were not signallers, might make allowances for them. There was a clear problem with this plan: if the skipper thought it was Germans playing a trick, and trying to lure him on to the beach, he might just sail away.

They decided to risk it and flashed two lots of three dots, '. . .' (S S), over and over.

The temperature dropped; a sea mist crept over the water and visibility fell to a few hundred yards. The two agents thought they could hear the deep throbbing of the motor launch's powerful 650 bhp petrol engines. The noise got louder and they peered into the fog, hoping to hear the muffled clatter of the anchor chain or the paddle of oars in a rubber dinghy. The guerrillas too stared out to sea, straining to glimpse the vessel's silhouette or hear the throb of its engines. Someone said: 'She's going away.' The sound of the engines faded, the ocean lapped gently against the shore and the three men stood in the silence, defeated.

At that moment the huge figure of Dennis Ciclitira appeared, scrambling down towards the water line. With him were two captured German soldiers and a Gestapo agent who had given

himself up. The prisoners were bundled out of sight: no one
wanted them to catch a glimpse of the general. Ciclitira strode on
to the beach calling out: 'Paddy? Billy? What are you up to?'

Leigh Fermor and Moss, with one voice, shouted, 'Do you know
Morse?'

'Bloody fools,' replied Ciclitira. He grabbed the torch and
began flashing 'SB, SB' – 'Sugar Baker, Sugar Baker', while berat-
ing them with the fact that had the boat been the enemy's it might
have opened fire.

Ciclitira kept flashing the correct signal but no vessel
appeared. The mist cleared a little and the moon showed them
a sea empty to the horizon, then it billowed in again and visibility dropped to nothing. The group waited, desperate for the
sound of engines. Half an hour later they heard a deep rumble,
bouncing across the water from the west. Once more Ciclitira
began to flash. Through the gloom appeared the familiar outline
of a Fairmile B motor launch, a three-pounder Hotchkiss
outlined in black.

The launch dropped anchor fifty yards from the shore. Two
dinghies full of heavily armed men splashed into the water and
began to paddle towards the beach. Moss shouted 'George!',
assuming it was George Jellicoe and his SBS raiding party.

'He can't make it, you'll have to make do with me, Bob Bury,'
came the reply. This was Lieutenant Robert Bury, the officer
commanding an SBS covering force Cairo had sent along to help
out.

The bow of the rubber craft slid crunching on to the beach and
a sailor leapt out with a mooring line, while men with camo-
painted faces and automatic weapons splashed into the sea, storming on to the beach and demanding to know where the enemy
was. To their deep disappointment they were told that the only
available Germans were the prisoners. For a moment Lieutenant
Bury considered pretending that he had not made contact so that
he could move inland 'searching' for the general's party and engage

the Germans at the same time. He was persuaded that this was not a sensible course of action.

The men heading for Egypt took off their boots, leaving them for those who were staying behind. Then they stripped off their weapons and ammunition and handed those over too. Bury gave up the rations he and his men had brought. Ciclitira handed over his revolver and compass. Leigh Fermor gave Antonis Zoidakis the remaining gold coins from his money belt.

The men hugged and kissed each other, saying goodbye to comrades they might never see again. The hubbub was interrupted by the sailor holding the landing lines: 'Excuse me sir, I think we ought to get a move on.'

The young Giorgios Harokopos had a sudden change of heart and thought he should stay on the island. He turned to wade back on to the sand. Leigh Fermor caught him by the shoulder and said quietly, 'Your turn Giorgios, get in the boat.'

Surprisingly many of the andartes shook General Kreipe's hand or saluted him before he was helped into one of the dinghies, still wearing his boots. The vessel pushed off, heading away from the beach towards the motor launch where Captain Brian Coleman was waiting to greet his German guest. Royal Navy ratings helped Kreipe on to a rope ladder leading up on to the deck, murmuring confidently: 'That's it sir, easy does it, last couple of rungs, there you go sir, welcome aboard.'

Kreipe climbed on to the deck and stood for a moment, the last chance of rescue gone. Then Bob Bury's disappointed raiders heaved themselves up the ladder. Ciclitira and Leigh Fermor were the last to board. The engines rumbled into life and the motor launch went astern drawing back from the beach. The kidnappers leant on the handrails watching the men on the beach dwindle into tiny waving figures before disappearing into the darkness. The prow of the vessel swung south, its engines opened up as it sped towards Egypt and the port at Mersah Matruh.

High on the rocks surrounding the cove the guerrillas watched the motor launch surging away, shouldered their weapons, lit cigarettes and headed back into the mountains to continue the fight for the liberation of their home, and to wait for whatever reprisals might be visited upon them. They knew they had done well. They had worked day and night to make sure the kidnappers and their prisoner got off the island. They had risked their lives, handing the party on like a baton, hovering like eagles above them, ready to die to ensure the operation was a success. In the end more than 400 men had been in on the plot and many more knew the story. Not one of them had betrayed the secret. In the mountains and on the boat thrashing towards Egypt there was sadness that the Hussar stunt was over.

Crete dwindled into a tiny speck and vanished into the night, Leigh Fermor and Billy Moss were shown to the wardroom, where they were plied with cigarettes, rum and best of all, lobster sandwiches, a speciality of Coleman's command. They had come up with the idea for an audacious mission and seemed to have got away with it. They knew their exploits had caused the death of Kreipe's driver, but apart from that, they hoped that the kidnap had not provoked the anger of the German authorities. They believed that the destruction of villages as they spirited the general to the coast was not connected to the kidnap or the beginning of mass reprisals. As the night wore on they smoked and ate and drank, toasting each other and talking until dawn. The general did not take part in the celebrations.

24

Returning Heroes

The boat made its way through the night with the SOE officers in a state of such high excitement that sleep was impossible. The weary Cretans, sad and uncertain at leaving their homes, were more subdued and went below.

In the morning people wandered about the deck free from the tensions of the last few weeks. Kreipe sat by himself, his arm in a new sling made from torn sheets, his mood even more distant and withdrawn. Around mid-morning a klaxon sounded; Coleman bellowed from the bridge, ordering all non-sailors to take cover below. The Hotchkiss and the twin Bren-gun crews slid into place, the operators twirling the elevation handles, scanning the sky for sight of the intruder. An airplane appeared high overhead, a tiny speck among the blue; Coleman and the rating on watch peered through their powerful Barr & Stroud naval field glasses. 'It's one of ours sir.'

The aircraft was a Lysander, a light reconnaissance plane sent out to check up on the progress of the launch. The anti-aircraft crews stood down and the andartes came back on deck, peering at the horizon for the first sight of land.

Night fell and they slid into the blacked-out harbour at Mersah Matruh. Waiting on the quay were a collection of officers, other ranks, military policemen, staff cars and lorries, lit by an arc light. They all looked immaculate: the officers with sparkling Sam Browne belts across their shoulders and shiny shoes, the military police in gleaming white gaiters and peaked caps; other

ranks beautifully turned out in neatly pressed battledress, their
toe caps bulled like mirrors. The most senior officer present was
Brigadier Barker-Benfield, the man who had sanctioned the
kidnap. Ratings made fast the mooring lines and a gangplank
was lowered. Coleman left the bridge to say goodbye to his
guests. He shook hands with Leigh Fermor and Moss and saluted
Kreipe.

The reception party watched in amazement as the rag-tag
brigade, many barefoot, jacketless, dirty, stinking, most looking
like music-hall pirates, made their way on to dry land. When
Kreipe stepped onto the quay, Barker-Benfield snapped to attention and gave him a parade-ground salute, as though he were a
visiting, high-ranking Allied officer, welcoming him to Egypt in
fluent German. Kreipe, Leigh Fermor and Billy Moss were escorted
to staff cars. The general received more salutes, which he returned,
pleased, if not surprised, at the courtesy.

The cars roared off, heading for Harbour Station mess, where
they were to spend the night before flying to Cairo and GHQ. The
Cretans, and the stragglers, were taken by lorry to accomodation
provided by Bob Bury, issued with slippers and allowed to clean
up a bit before sitting down to a lavish feast, including soft white
bread and butter, the like of which they had not tasted since the
start of the occupation. Even Peotr the Russian seemed pleased,
crossing himself and saying *Kristos Voskris, pedia* – 'Christ is risen,
boys!' That evening General Kreipe dined with Barker-Benfield,
Leigh Fermor and Billy Moss. Before they sat down Barker-
Benfield sent for a doctor, a Jewish man called Mendlesson, who
took the general into another room and examined him. Mendlesson
said that there was no cause for concern: the general had not
broken anything, but had some bad bruising. Kreipe grinned, no
worse for his encounter with a doctor whose race he had been
taught to loathe. Mendlesson bound Kreipe's arm in a new, pure
white sling. Later, eating a dinner of pilchards and prunes, they
discussed both world wars. Kreipe praised the way he had been

treated by his captors, saying they had shown 'chivalry and courtesy'. He continued to express his regret at losing his Knight's Cross. The gentlemanly Barker-Benfield said he would offer a £5 reward for its return. Before going to bed the two SOE agents gave Kreipe some Greek biscuits, known as *paximathi*, and a water bottle full of raki. Barker-Benfield and Kreipe, men of similar age, shared a room: they could be heard chatting away in German until the early hours of the morning.

The next day Leigh Fermor took the brigadier to meet the rest of the kidnap team. They found the Cretans waiting to be picked up in a lorry by Dennis Ciclitira. The group were still shoeless and unshaven, their baggy and torn clothes stank. Peotr the Russian stood apart, his fly undone and his arms hanging in front of him, a sneer on his face. Ciclitira arrived wearing his best Cretan mountain farmer's clothes and sporting his massive black beard – unrecognisable as a British officer.

Barker-Benfield shook every man's hand and then gave a rousing oration in English, with Leigh Fermor interpreting, praising the Cretans for what they had done and the great help they had given to the Allied cause. When the brigadier finished, the youngest of the guerrillas, Giorgios Harokopos, whose father had refused to take the gold pieces, stepped forward. He made a short speech: 'We thank you British General, for the titanic struggle you are waging for our freedom and the freedom of the whole world.'

The andartes then clambered aboard the lorry and were driven to Cairo, crossing the old battlefields and passing evidence of the 'titanic struggle' – mile after mile of military debris, burned-out tanks, lorries and guns, the destruction from the battles against Rommel and the Afrika Korps. At the Citadella, a Force 133 building in Heliopolis, the Cretans were interrogated for eight days. The British were not always tactful. When the guerillas were about to be issued with identity papers, they were shocked to be told by one brash lieutenant: 'You will be settled temporarily until we see what is to be done with you. We may send you to a refugee camp.' The Cretans were moved to a conventional barracks where several of them, including Giorgios Harokopos, enlisted in the Greek Army, joining the *Hieros Lochos*, 'The Sacred Squadron'.

General Kreipe was driven to an airfield to board an Anson waiting to take him to Cairo. As they flew over the battlefields of North Africa, Kreipe showed great interest, asking who had held which sector. He knew many of the German commanders personally. In Cairo, Kreipe stepped on to the runway to be met by more British officers and by press photographers. His image would soon appear in newspapers in Britain, the United States and throughout the British Empire. Then the general climbed into a staff car and was driven off into captivity.

In Cairo the newspapers trumpeted the kidnapping with banner headlines: 'Amazing Abduction of German General from Outside his Headquarters: Abducted General Arrives by Air'. These headlines were an embarrassment to the Third Reich, and to General Bräuer on Crete. German counter-intelligence put out the rumour that had been started by Micky Akoumianakis that Kreipe had not been kidnapped at all but had deserted, having been in touch with British intelligence for some time. The morale of the German army in Crete, on the wane throughout 1944, fell even further. Many members of the security battalions, Cretans who had enlisted in the Wehrmacht, deserted and fled to the mountains to join the andartes.

GHQ found itself in a small quandary about how it should treat its new prize. On 19 May a signal was sent from London saying that it was assumed General Kreipe 'will be brought to this country for internment and he feels that as a tribute to SOE's efforts in capturing him they ought to be allowed to provide escort'.

In the end Kreipe was taken to England without an SOE escort. He was interrogated on 23 and 24 May 1944 in London.

The general's debriefing provides an insight into the state of the

Nazi leadership and its priorities at this time. Kreipe revealed that his new command on Crete, the 22nd *Luftlande* Division, had been ordered to consider itself cut off and that in the event of an emergency, an Allied landing or a local uprising, it must fight as best it could, unsupported. Kreipe explained to the interrogating officer that Germany no longer had the resources to evacuate troops and that resupply was limited to the occasional meagre 200-ton vessel. He added that replacing the highly trained men of this division with inferior troops who could be sacrificed was not possible. The German army was living 'hand-to-mouth' and could not afford to have two divisions of men out of action for the two months that a changeover would take. At one point he blurted out that Crete would be defended to 'the last cartridge', but would not be drawn on what this really meant.

Kreipe described General Bruno Bräuer as a 'blockhead' for underestimating the scale and danger of the Cretan resistance. Kreipe had now seen the guerrillas at first hand and knew how determined and organised they were. He said that Bräuer shared the general view of the resistance as little more than a few disorganised gangs of sheep thieves. He also provided evidence of disarray among senior officers on the Eastern front. He confirmed that one officer, General Walter von Seydlitz-Kurzbach, had surrendered to the communists and had become a collaborator, forming the anti-Nazi 'League of German Officers'. Seydlitz-Kurzbach's actions had shaken many senior men fighting on the Russian front. He confirmed the rumour that the Luftwaffe's chief of the German general staff, Generaloberst Hans Jeschonneck, had been forced to commit suicide by his old enemy Hermann Göring, for failing to supply the beleaguered troops at Stalingrad.

Kreipe revealed little more, other than a useful piece of gossip: Hitler's future brother-in-law, Waffen-SS General Hermann Fegelein, was now one of the most hated men in the Führer's entourage. Kreipe's interrogator was disappointed when the prisoner claimed to know next to nothing about the so-called 'secret weapon' that Hitler had mentioned in speeches. He thought that whatever it was, it was very accurate and being developed in Peenemünde. The interrogating officer summed up his report:

> My general impression of Kreipe is that he is rather unimport-
> ant and unimaginative. Anti-Nazi, possibly because events are
> trending that way. Might drift into the Thoma group if Thoma
> took any interest in him, which is perhaps doubtful.

(Von Thoma was Rommel's second in command, an anti-Nazi who had been captured towards the end of the Battle of Alamein.)

For Kreipe, SOE's 'Hussar stunt' wrecked what remained of his military career and left him humiliated, a figure of fun, something from which he would never properly recover.

A long time after the war a member of Kreipe's staff in Crete confided to former SOE agent Bickham Sweet-Escott that when the officers in the mess at Ano Archanes heard that their general had been captured, there was at first a shocked silence, broken by an officer saying, 'Well gentlemen, I think this calls for cham-pagne all round.'

After his interrogation Kreipe was flown to Calgary in Canada, where he joined other high-ranking Nazi generals. He was released in 1947 and died aged eighty-one in Lower Saxony. The kidnap may have saved Heinrich Kreipe's life. On 20 May 1947, the anniversary of Operation *Merkur*, General Friedrich-Wilhelm Müller, the island's most violent and vicious commander, together with the notorious Bräuer, were tried for war crimes on Crete. They were found guilty and executed by firing squad. Kreipe might easily have died with them.

Before his execution in Athens, Bräuer was debriefed by a member of the Swedish Red Cross; the German general summed up the consequences of Kreipe's kidnapping for the Wehrmacht by saying: 'Oh we've got boxes of generals in Germany: it's when you lose your master baker you start worrying.' During his imprisonment in Athens, General Müller, SOE's original target, met Patrick Leigh Fermor; when he was told this was the Englishman behind the kidnap of Heinrich Kreipe, the German officer laughed and said: '*Ach Herr Major. Mich hätten Sie nicht so leicht geschnappt.*' (My dear major, you would not have taken me so easily.)

25

Moss and the Battle of Damastas Bridge

In Cairo, Leigh Fermor's physical condition deteriorated: the stiffness in his arm spread to his legs and joints and became so serious that he could not cut up his own food. He said that he was 'as stiff as a board'. He was admitted to hospital suffering from a high temperature, and swollen joints, and was given a provisional diagnosis of polio, later changed to polyarthritis. (A modern doctor might have diagnosed him as having a severe post-infection arthritis, sometimes known as 'reactive arthritis'.) Leigh Fermor took three months to recover his strength. He was visited by the Commander-in-Chief, Middle East, General Sir Bernard Paget, who gave him the DSO for the kidnap operation. He received the medal in his pyjamas, still lying in bed, his battledress top round his shoulders, on to which Paget pinned the medal. Billy Moss received the Military Cross.

For six weeks Moss kicked his heels in Cairo, visiting Leigh Fermor in hospital, smoking with him, drinking champagne and trying to come up with a new adventure. Leigh Fermor's limbs grew thin while his joints became more swollen and red. Moss met comrades who had been badly wounded and heard the sad news of dead friends. He swapped his peasant costume for evening clothes, drinking and flirting with Sophie. In the end even the delights of the undergraduate hooliganism at Tara began to pall.

Moss put an idea to Brigadier Barker-Benfield: he wanted to return to Crete to organise the band of escaped Russian POWs into a guerrilla force. The fact that Moss spoke perfect Russian made the plan plausible. What Moss really wanted to do was either repeat the kidnap operation and abduct Kreipe's newly installed successor, General Helmut Friebe, or lead a raid on the German headquarters at Archanes and kill as many officers and men as he could. Moss shared these thoughts only with Leigh Fermor.

Moss set off for Crete on 6 July in a motor launch, accompanied by Giorgios Tyrakis. On the island several members of the old team agreed to join him, including Antonis Zoidakis and Ilias Athanassakis. Ilias agreed to recce the Ano Archanes German military headquarters, and draw a map showing where the soldiers worked, ate and slept. Moss heard from Micky Akoumianakis, the head of intelligence in Heraklion, that he did not want to be part of another kidnap operation.

From the start Ilias Athanassakis thought that the new kidnap plan was 'utter madness', but kept his thoughts to himself. Instead, he went about his task slowly, telling Moss that, for security reasons, the Germans were changing the structure of their headquarters. In this way he hoped that the plans would be dropped. In the end Moss received a letter purporting to be from the communists threatening to betray him if he went ahead with the kidnapping. The reality was that the letter came from local nationalists and was written by Ilias himself, who feared he might be held personally responsible for the reprisals and deaths that the plan would cause.

Undaunted, Moss dropped the idea and left the Anogia area and moved his headquarters to Embriski to the east of Crete, where he planned to muster his band of former Russian POWs. There a message arrived from Sandy Rendel telling him that the escaped prisoners had all been evacuated on the orders of GHQ Cairo. Rather than cut his losses and ask to be sent back to Cairo, this high-spirited, twenty-three-year-old Coldstream Guards officer and freelance adventurer set off on another escapade. He returned to his 'mountain lair' on Mount Ida above Anogia, the headquarters of the white-haired Kapitan Mihali Xylouris, where he was joined by six freshly escaped Russian POWs. They were all young men and claimed the Germans had told them that whatever happened, no Russian would leave the island alive.

On 7 August 1944, a German NCO, Feldwebel Josef Olenhauer, entered the village of Anogia with an eight-man patrol. Olenhauer was a strange man who could be at once very strict and very lenient. He was not unpopular everywhere, and yet the inhabitants of some villages found him tyrannical and overbearing, an impression heightened by the fact that he was often accompanied by his Alsatian dog and carried a whip. Olenhauer had links with German counter-intelligence; other people thought that he also had links with SOE. A boy who regularly took food and supplies to Ralph Stockbridge thought that Olenhauer knew what Stockbridge was up to and turned a blind eye to his activities.

On that hot August morning, Olenhauer and his men were in Anogia looking for Cretans to press into forced labour. He stood in the village square waving a whip, his dog straining at its leash, Olenhauer demanding that volunteers step forward. There were none. The soldiers began to round up any men, women and children they could find. On the outskirts some of the villagers slipped into the safety of the fields. Others hid in the darkness of their houses, hoping to escape. Olenhauer marched fifty hostages off on the long road leading to Rethymnon. On the way they were ambushed by local armed men who fired their weapons in the air, warning the hostages to lie on the ground; then they opened fire on the soldiers, many of whom fell dead on to the ground. Olenhauer and the remainder of his patron were captured and, after a brief trial, shot, as was the dog.

When news of the executions reached the headquarters of *Festung Kreta* in Chania, reprisals were inevitable. The remaining inhabitants of Anogia fled into the safety of the mountains, carrying what possessions they could on their backs, or piled onto mules and driving their sheep and goats ahead of them. The first refugees to reach the safety of Mihali Xylouris's headquarters told the kapitan what had happened.

At the same time, under the cover of darkness, Billy Moss led a party of fifteen men, a mixture of Cretan andartes and Russians, down the mountain, through the deserted village of Anogia, heading for the Heraklion–Rethymnon road to set an ambush.

At three in the morning they reached Damastas, marked by a bridge at a bend on the main road. The group carried Hawkins anti-tank grenades, small square objects which held a pound of TNT and a chemical igniter. When a vehicle passed over the mine, the box containing the igniter cracked and acid poured onto the explosives, detonating it. Moss planned to mine the bridge with the grenades, which could be easily hidden in the worn, split, tarmac. By five in the morning everything was in place, with the guerrillas crouching in the ditches that lined the road.

Moss could not resist indulging his passion for photography. He carried a camera which he thought could be set to take pictures automatically. He balanced it on a rock, assuming it would snap away on its own. It did not survive.

A whistle warned Moss's gang of approaching vehicles; the men shouldered their weapons, waiting for the fight. Round the bend came not lorries full of men but two boys and a flock of sheep, enough weight to detonate the mines. The guerrillas rushed forward and hustled the lads into a small valley a few hundred yards away. The boys were on their way to a market, others were following them and for the next two hours, unwary market-goers, plus their sheep, goats, and mules carrying produce, were waylaid and taken away to the safety of the same valley.

Silence descended, and the ambushers waited for another whistle. It came just after seven in the morning. The ambush party heard the low rumble of a vehicle. Into view came a three-ton truck: two Germans sat in the front, and a mixed group of

Cretan and Italian labourers in the back. Moss's group opened fire, and the truck blew apart on the hidden mines. Bits of twisted metal rained down, clanging against the road and rocks. The truck was reduced to a buckled, smoking wreck, trapping the bodies of the dead labourers. The driver lay crumpled and dead behind the wheel; his companion lay in the road, his skull smashed. The surviving labourers were taken prisoner. Another truck appeared and was destroyed, then a Jeep-like Kübelwagen drove into the trap, where it too was turned into scrap, and its occupants killed. The wreckage blocked the road, the Kübelwagen burning in a position where it could be seen by oncoming vehicles. The ambushers moved on to a fresh, less well-protected section of the road.

It was now 8.30 a.m. The morning was still and clear, the noise of cicadas mingled with the tinkle of the goat bells. Another whistle pierced the air, followed by the noise of a troop carrier, its thirty-five occupants sitting stiff and upright in the back; sunlight glinting from their helmets. Fifteen guerrilla Sten and Marlin guns opened up: within seconds, 400 rounds of 9mm ammunition had lashed the bodies of the soldiers in the vehicles. Most of them died where they sat, a few managed to jump on to the road or scrabble for the cover of a low stone wall.

Silence returned, punctuated by the hiss of steam escaping from the broken radiator. Blood seeped through the floorboards of the vehicle, mingling with the black oil that leaked from the ruined engine. The smell of petrol and burned rubber drifted through the air. Suddenly a shell landed in the middle of the guerrillas, exploding with colossal force; shockwaves blasting across the scrub. An armoured car appeared, weighing nearly four tons and carrying a 20-millimetre cannon firing high explosive shells. In the turret stood the commander, muttering directions to the driver, ignoring the rounds ricocheting off his vehicle. Grenades exploded against the armour plating, showering rock and hot metal, throwing up clouds of dust which hid the vehicle. The armoured car rumbled on. One guerrilla, Manolis Spithoukis, who stood directly in its path, firing from an ancient, single-shot rifle, was hit in the chest and severely wounded. The Germans behind the wall opened up and some of the guerrillas began to withdraw.

The armoured car was nearly on top of them. Moss tried to get behind it, rushing across ten yards of open ground then flinging himself behind the safety of some rocks; with him was Vanya, one of the Russians. Unflustered, the vehicle commander drew his pistol and fired aimed shots, hitting Vanya in the head and sending him sprawling dead to the ground. The guerrillas tried to give covering fire but were running out of ammunition.

Moss remained behind the rocks, waiting for the vehicle to draw level with him. When the commander bobbed down to reload his Luger, Moss threw a grenade into the turret. The armoured car blew apart. The agonised screams of the men inside died down, the blast turned the vehicle into a blazing mess. The surviving Germans fled under the cover of the thick black smoke drifting everywhere, leaving behind equipment and ammunition which was quickly scavenged by the guerrillas before they made their way back to the hideout. The battle of Damastas Bridge was over.

That night Moss and Tyrakis discussed the casualties. They reckoned that one of the Russians, Vanya, had been killed. The Germans had lost forty or fifty men killed and a few taken prisoner; several labourers had also been killed. When Moss asked Tyrakis what had happened to the prisoners he replied that they had already been taken care of, making a slash with his hand across his throat.

It was well known throughout Crete, and in all the Nazi-occupied territories of the Mediterranean, that the Germans demanded the lives of ten civilians for every one of their soldiers killed in 'unlawful combat'. The guerrillas faced the possibility of around 500 Cretan deaths. Clutching at straws, Moss reasoned that as the dead Russian was wearing British clothing and carrying no identity tags, the Germans might think that the raid had been carried out by a British commando party.

Nothing daunted Moss, who was still keen for action and began to embellish his plans to work with the Russian prisoners of war, more of whom were arriving at the hideout. He sent a wireless signal to Barker-Benfield at GHQ Cairo, outlining his scheme to use the Russian POWs. The plan was approved, but he was ordered to first return to Cairo, on a boat which was scheduled to arrive in three days' time.

In Anogia, once called 'Camelot' by the SOE, a proclamation went up. It was signed by Friedrich-Wilhelm Müller, who had been sent back to the island after Kreipe's abduction:

Order of the German Commander of the Garrison of Crete

Since the town of Anogia is a centre of the English espionage in Crete, since the Anogians carried out the murder of the sergeant of the Yeni-Gavé garrison and the garrison itself, since the Anogians carried out the sabotage at Damastas, since the andartes of various resistance bands find asylum and protection in Anogia, and since the abductors of General Kreipe passed through Anogia, using Anogia as a stopping place when transporting him, we order its RAZING to the ground and the execution of every male Anogian who is found within the village and within an area of one kilometre round it.

Chania 13-8-44

The Commander of the Garrison of Crete

F-W. Müller

On 12 August word reached the village that lorries carrying hundreds of soldiers were leaving Heraklion, heading west. The men of the village fled, heading for the mountains. At dawn on the 13th, the lorries arrived; troops leapt out and quickly

surrounded the village. Machine guns were set up in the main
street and the soldiers rounded up the remaining inhabitants,
about 1,500 people, mainly women and children. They were to
leave the village within the hour. The people did as they were
told, trooping past soldiers who were already looting their houses,
plundering personal belongings, food and livestock.

Sweating soldiers unloaded hundreds of cans of petrol, which
they carried through the village streets, kicking down doors and
emptying them into the houses. Then they threw in stick grenades
turning Anogia into a blazing inferno. Not all the buildings were
empty. In one were two cousins who could not walk; in another a
man who was too mentally ill to understand what was going on;
and in another, widowed sisters who refused to leave each other or
their home. An old man was dragged out of hiding and shot, the
soldiers left two dead piglets in his arms as a joke. When the fires
died down, dynamite was set in the ruins and detonated.

It took from 13 August until 5 September to destroy the entire
village. The work was hard and slow; each evening the exhausted
soldiers withdrew to the village of Sisarha to recuperate. In
twenty-four days, Müller's forces killed 117 people, destroyed
940 houses, and burnt many small vineyards, cheese mills, wine
presses and olive groves. Not a house was left standing; any livestock that could not be taken away in trucks lay dead in the ruins.

Finally the lorries bounced down the hill, heading back to the
garrison at Heraklion, leaving desolation where once 4,000 people
had lived and thrived. The troops covered their faces to protect
them from the stench of rotting carcasses and the grime blowing
across the rubble. The fires burned for days, sending black smoke
towering into the sky, a warning to Cretans for miles around.
Anogia was not the only village to be pulverised. Damastas, where
Moss had ambushed the armoured car, received the same treatment. Dense smoke coiled over the remains of nine villages in the
Amari valley, including Yerakari, where 164 more Cretans were
killed. Some villages were destroyed on a whim: others emerged

unscathed: Asi Gonia, said to be protected by Saint Giorgios, miraculously avoided the kerosene and dynamite.

When Moss got to Cairo, he found that Barker-Benfield had left for the newly liberated Greece. A fortnight later the brigadier returned and told the young captain that the plans had changed: he was to forget Crete and go instead to Macedonia. Moss never returned to the island.

26

Aftermath

As the war drew to a close, North Africa and Crete became military backwaters. German forces in Europe were caught between the Red Army advances in the east and the Allied army in the west. The German high command on Crete lost confidence. On 11 October 1944, after uneasy negotiations, and with German artillery standing by to shell the city, Heraklion was liberated. Kapitan Petrakoyiorgi, codenamed 'Selfridge', sat on a horse watching the Germans retreat through the arch of the West Gate, under which Kreipe had also been driven on the night of his capture.

The retreat was accompanied by triumph, tragedy and farce. Women who had collaborated were paraded and had their heads shaved; in the court of Heraklion traitors from the village of Sarcho were stabbed to death and thrown from a first-floor window. Kapitan Boutzalis shot a rival through the arm for being rude to his daughter. A captured German agent pleaded to be allowed to commit suicide. He was taken to the edge of a cliff where his arms and legs were broken with boulders, before he was allowed to crawl to the edge and fall to his death.

For the next few months the Germans remained inside Chania, their last stronghold. Communists argued with Nationalists about who should govern the island. Civil war broke out in mainland Greece and for a while it looked as though it would spread to Crete.

On 30 April 1945, Hitler took his own life at his *Führerbunker* and the following week Germany surrendered. On 8 May, VE

Day, the new commander of Fortress Crete, General Benthack, who had only been in office since the previous January, contacted the British and capitulated. Major Dennis Ciclitira appeared at Benthack's headquarters in Chania to take his surrender, but the general insisted that he be dealt with by a man of similar rank. When Ciclitira offered to radio to British HQ in Heraklion, Benthack asked him how he proposed to do so. Ciclitira replied that his secret radio set was concealed in the building next door to the German headquarters. It had been there for weeks, its radio signals hidden by the amount of radio traffic coming from headquarters. Benthack was taken to Heraklion, and, in a cobbled-together ceremony at the Villa Ariadne, he surrendered to Major General Colin Callander, commanding officer of the British Army's 4th Division in Greece, who had been flown in especially to take charge of the proceedings. Benthack's men were permitted to keep their weapons until British troops arrived to guard them.

In a surreal moment, undercover SOE agents entered Chania and invited German officers to a party in a nightclub. As a German band played jazz, the British officers revealed who they were and what they had been doing, declaring to the astonished enemy their real names and their codenames.

On 23 May 1945, the German troops were at last disarmed and sent home, but, to the disgust of the Cretans, taking an enormous amount of booty with them: 'They left like tourists, carrying their suitcases.' British soldiers of the Royal Hampshire Regiment were detailed to protect the German soldiers; their regimental history notes: 'The Cretans strongly resented the restraint of the British troops towards their hated and conquered foes.'

Several questions dogged the legacy of the Kreipe kidnap operation after the war, the most important of which were: had it been worth it, and did it lead to any reprisals? These are themes which recur in Leigh Fermor's post-war correspondence with Cretans, fellow SOE operatives and even a German officer who had been a member of Kreipe's staff in Crete.

The abduction of the Divisional Commander from virtually outside his own home stirred the hornet's nest of German fury. Müller's leaflet of 13 August 1944, distributed to the islanders by air, ordered the destruction of Anogia giving the reasons as: the murder of a German NCO; Moss's ambush at Damastas Bridge; and finally the kidnapping of General Kreipe. Müller left the Cretans in no doubt that the abduction was one of the causes of the reprisal: 'since the abductors of General Kreipe passed through Anogia, using Anogia as a stopping place when transporting him, we order its RAZING to the ground and the execution of every male who is found within the village and within an area of one kilometre around it.'

In the early months of 1945, as the German occupation of Crete drew to a close, the use of destruction as a method of coercion came to know no bounds and was designed to implicate the entire occupying force in acts of terrorism. In his final report on the activities of SOE on the island, Tom Dunbabin, who is reported to have disapproved of the Kreipe operation, wrote that, in the end, the destruction was not limited to the Amari Valley, but 'was spread over the whole of western and eastern Crete. This was the last act of German barbarity for most of Crete.' He went on to analyse the German master plan as being to 'cover the imminent withdrawal by neutralising the areas of guerrilla activity, and to commit the German soldier to terrorist acts so that they should know there would be no mercy for them if they surrendered or deserted.

Seen in isolation, the abduction was exactly what Kreipe called it: 'a Hussar stunt' – dangerous, exhilarating and with elements of an undergraduate prank about it. But Kreipe's capture was one in the eye for the oppressors and a great morale booster for the islanders. Whatever it cost in life and property, many saw it as worth it. Even so, it is impossible to argue that the kidnap caused no reprisals. Moss's later action at Damasta Bridge made a difficult situation worse and left an uncomfortable legacy. Leigh Fermor and Ralph Stockbridge both regretted what Moss had done.

In 1951 Billy Moss published his book *Ill Met by Moonlight*, based on the diary he kept during the operation and the photographs he took. The book was later made into a film of the same name. Kreipe took exception to both claiming, among other things, that in the car he had not given Leigh Fermor his word to cooperate and not resist. He successfully took out an injunction to have the book and the film banned in Germany on the grounds that they defamed his character. Of the two SOE men he said: 'Paddy, I liked Paddy, but Moss, always with his pistol, it was childish'. He also claimed that, during the kidnap, Moss had hit him with a rifle butt. This is unlikely because Moss was on the opposite side of the car dealing with the driver and taking control of the vehicle, and he was not armed with a rifle.

One German who did read the book was a Dr Ludwig Beutin, who had been a German officer on Crete. Beutin wrote to Moss who did not tell anyone about the letter. Sometime after Moss's death, in 1965 at the young age of forty-four, Leigh Fermor came across the correspondence and wrote to Beutin. The doctor confirmed that the Germans knew about the resistance centres at Yerakari, Anogia and Asi Gonia, and that they had not found any secret radios. He explained that when Kreipe's replacement arrived on 8 May, he ordered the search for the general, which had been going on for over two weeks, to be scaled down. Troops were left guarding the coast but withdrawn from the mountains. 'The matter was closed to us,' wrote Beutin.

Leigh Fermor thought that this letter from Beutin proved that the massacres of August 1944 were nothing to do with the kidnap. Another account of the operation was written by Giorgios Harokopos, the young man who was taken on the boat with Kreipe, and to whose family Leigh Fermor had offered compensation. Harokopos's book contains some passages that do not stick to the Leigh Fermor party line, and this upset the Englishman. Leigh Fermor thought that Dr Beutin's evidence dealt with what he started calling the 'Calumnies of Harokopos'. There were other critical voices from within the fold: in 2011, Kimonas Zografakis, who had helped shelter the abductors, wrote an article in which he described Leigh Fermor as 'neither a great Philhellene nor a new Lord Byron . . . he was a classic agent who served the interests of Britain . . . anything else that the people of Greece attribute to him derives from either ignorance or Anglophilia, ignoring the terrible sufferings he caused our country at that time.' Leigh Fermor never stopped looking for corroboration that the kidnap had caused no actual harm to Crete. He was haunted too by the accidental killing of his Cretan friend Yanni, and by the killing of Fenske, Kreipe's driver.

Kidnapping a German general was a decisive event in the lives of everyone who took part. Almost thirty years later Leigh Fermor, most of the kidnap party and General Kreipe himself were reunited, in jovial mood, on a Greek television show. Leigh Fermor wrote up the story of the kidnap in various forms for the rest of his life, first in long hand, then in typewritten copies and finally in a bound, word-processed document entitled 'Abducting a General'.

In peacetime Leigh Fermor returned to the itinerant life of a travel writer. By the end of his life he had nearly fifty passports, all of them crammed with customs stamps and many of them the double-decker type issued to people who travel a lot. His friend Xan Fielding wrote of him: 'As delightful as his conversation, was the romantic attitude he adopted to his mission in Crete. Each of us I suppose . . . saw himself playing a role created only by his own imagination. I, for example, affected to regard myself as the Master Spy, the sinister figure behind the scenes controlling a vast network of minor agents who did all the dirty work. Paddy obviously scorned such an unobtrusive and unattractive part. He was the Man of Action, the gallant swashbuckler and giant slayer.'

Leigh Fermor died aged ninety-six on 10 June 2011, and was buried next to his wife, Joan. The legend of Leigh Fermor lives on in Greece.

The real heroes of the operation were the Cretans themselves. Ralph Stockbridge said of the islanders: 'Without their help as guides, informants, suppliers of food and so on, not a single one of us would have lasted twenty-four hours.' Some Axis soldiers based on the island came to see their army's actions for what they were: a German intelligence officer, Leutnant Albert Kirchen, wrote: 'From 1942 to the day of our departure from Crete the island was bathed in blood. Hundreds of Greek patriots were stood against a wall before our firing squads. It was a horror few other countries experienced . . . I remember that the *Geheime Feldpolizei* caught one Manolis Lambrakis . . . the torments that man underwent for about a month were truly horrific . . . yet hours before his execution he stood with his head held high and looked each of us in the eye as if challenging us.'

Of all the Cretans, Giorgios Psychoundakis achieved the greatest fame with his autobiography, published in 1955, *The Cretan Runner*, with an introduction by Patrick Leigh Fermor. After the war, Psychoundakis became the victim of an administrative blunder and was arrested and imprisoned as a deserter from the Greek army. On his release he was made to fight against the communists in northern Greece. After his return to Crete he scraped a living as a charcoal burner, and laboured on the new roads being built across the mountains, over which he had carried so many messages, so many miles. In spite of the success of his memoirs he was so poor that he could not afford pen and paper. When his friend and literary collaborator, the American social anthropologist Dr Barrie Machin, died, he left Giorgios a huge stack of cards and some pens. Psychoundakis immediately set about translating *The Iliad* into Cretan dialect, a task which took him three years and for which he was honoured by the Academy of Athens.

Psychoundakis, together with Leigh Fermor's 'right-hand-man' Manolis Paterakis, spent their last years employed as gardeners tending the German military cemetery outside the airfield at Maleme, where the Allies lost the battle for Crete and from where, as two young men, they had helped kick-start the island's resistance movement. The stories of these individuals symbolise the indomitable spirit of the Cretan guerrillas, the andartes.

The Kidnap Team
26 May 1944

Micky Akoumianakis

Ilias Athanassakis

Grigorios Chnarakis

Nikos Komis

Patrick Leigh Fermor (British SOE)

Antonios Papaleonidas

Manolis Paterakis

Stratis Saviolakis

William Stanley Moss (British SOE)

Giorgios Tyrakis

Mitsos Tzatzas

Antonis Zoidakis

Pavlos Zografistos (last minute addition)

Notes

A Note on Sources

The main sources I have used in the research for this book have been the collection of Second War War history in the Historical Museum of Crete (HMC), the huge private collection of the museum's curator, Mr C. E. Mamalakis (CEMA), and the Patrick Leigh Fermor archive in the National Library of Scotland (NLS/PLF). I was privileged to be given access to this archive before it was curated and I have used the box numbers that were in use on my visits. I have also consulted documents in the National Archive (NA) and the Imperial War Museum (IWM). The London Library was a valuable source of wartime memoirs both Cretan and British SOE. From other published material I found Anthony Beevor's *Crete: The Battle and the Resistance*, Alan Clark's *The Fall of Crete* and Geoffrey Cox's *A Tale of Two Battles: A Personal Memoir of Crete and the Western Desert, 1941*, very useful when writing my short account of what happened in the eleven days after the invasion. Finally, in the Leigh Fermor archive in the National Library of Scotland, there is a typewritten fragment of 'The Eagles of Mount Ida' written by the guerrilla fighter Giorgios Frangoulitakis, translated and annotated by Leigh Fermor.

1 An Island of Heroes

5   'Cretan mountain men': NLS/PLF, 13338/6, Black file, 'Fred Warner and Foreign Office Docs'.

'Blood vendettas over family honour': Mr C. E. Mamalakis, in a letter to the author, wrote: 'You would rather get cancer than be involved in a Cretan feud.'

'Cretans, especially those': ibid.

'In Roman times': Pendlebury, *Archaeology of Crete*, p. 6.

6   'The mountains hide a series': Grundon, *Rash Adventurer*, p. 247.
7   '*When will we have*': verses translated by Dr Stavrini Ionnadou, 2013.
7–8   'Before the Second World War': Pendlebury, p. 6.
8   '"with the speed of a cheetah"': Patrick Leigh Fermor in 'John Pendlebury and the Battle for Crete', *Spectator*, 20 October 2001.
9   'Pendlebury's home on Crete': see Powell, *The Villa Ariadne*.
         'When he was not moving': author interview with Mamalakis.
         'One, an Austrian woman': ibid.
         'Jan Knoch was a German tourist': ibid.
10   '"I know Crete"': Foreign Office SOE archive quoted in Grundon, p. 235.
         'His friend and fellow agent': Grundon, *Rash Adventurer*, p. 291.
11   'The military situation in Greece': see Beevor, *Crete: The Battle and the Resistance*, Kindle edition.
         '"From the first days"': *The Dixon Papers* quoted in Grundon, *Rash Adventurer*, p. 256.
12   '"The struggle needs blood"': Fielding, *Hide and Seek*, Kindle edition.

2 Defenders of Crete

15   'The general's desertion': author interview with Mr C. E. Mamalakis.
17   'But it also acted': filmed interview Giorgios Tzitzikas, *The Eleventh Day*, dir. Christos Eperson, Archangel Films, 2006.
         '"There was fear"': Tzitzikas, *The Eleventh Day*.

3 Operation *Merkur*

18   'On the same day': see Martin Pöppel, *Heaven and Hell: The War Diary of a German Paratrooper*.
19   'For the first': *German Airborne Troops 1936 – 45* Roger Edwards 1974. Purnell Book Services Ltd (Book Club Edition) p. 53.
         'Clumsy as it was': author interview Warwick Woodhouse, late Lt. Col. Royal Marines.
         'Before being allowed to jump': Kurowski, *Jump into Hell*, p. 18.
21   'The paratroopers piled their parachutes': Mamalakis, Private Collection.

22 'To stop it snagging': Pöppel.

'At last, each great, yellow-nosed Ju 52': Cox, *A Tale of Two Battles*, p. 69.

23 'One by one they lifted': Becker, *The Luftwaffe War Diaries*, p. 187. 'Feldwebel Wilhelm Plieschen took': Sutherland and Canwell, p. 61.

'Aircraft and gliders stretched': Gilberto Villahermosa, *Hitler's Paratrooper*, p. 89.

'In a leading glider sat': Becker, p. 193.

24 'Hundreds of canopies blossomed': Cox, p. 72.

'On the terrace': Beevor.

4 The Battle of Crete

25 'Blinded by the sun': Beevor, *Crete: The Battle and the Resistance*.

26 'Coloured clouds of parachutists': US Army Special Report No. 5 G-2/2657-231, The Battle of Crete.

'As far away as Paleochora': Beevor.

'At the northern port': Spurr, *To Have and to Lose*, p. 186.

27 'An agonised scream': ibid.

'A Greek, Captain Kalaphotakis': Beevor.

'Spurr shouted to a British': Spurr, p. 200.

28 'Twenty-six miles away': Clark, *The Fall of Crete*, p. 81.

29 'One of the villagers': MacDonald, *The Lost Battle: Crete 1941*, p. 177.

30 'Just over an hour': Clark, p. 83.

'By now the German commander': Kiriakopoulos, *The Nazi Occupation of Crete, 1941–1945*, p. 160.

32 '"I was enormously impressed"': Grundon, *Rash Adventurer*, p. 307.

'"You will give one"': ibid., p. 308.

'At headquarters he found': Tzitzikas, *Freedom and Glory (Memoirs 1939–1945)*, p. 39.

33 'Late on that first afternoon': Pöppel, *Heaven and Hell*, p. 55.

34 '"Today has been a hard one"': quoted in Churchill, *The Grand Alliance*, p. 254.

5 The Next Nine Days

36   'On the evening of 20 May': Beevor.

'On one wall': Heydte, *Daedalus Returned*, p. 111.

37   'Maleme was overlooked': Clark, *Fall of Crete*, p. 102.

'Very early in the morning': Beevor.

38   'An Allied artillery commander': ibid.

39   'they were forbidden': ibid.

'At Heraklion, a group': C. E. Mamalakis interview.

'one, Colonel Tzoulakis': ibid.

'Near the harbour': ibid.

'A fierce firefight': ibid.

'only his leg': ibid.

40   'A few miles south': Mamalakis interview.

'The battle lines in Heraklion': ibid.

41   'The sun set': Cox, p. 88.

'The bombers left': ibid., p. 90.

42   '"My son, we know"': Beevor, Kindle edition.

'The men were ordered': Mamalakis interview.

'"Nobody could get"': Fergusson, *The Black Watch and the King's Enemies*, p. 88.

'There was a stench': Gavin Long, *Greece, Crete and Syria*, p. 91.

42–3   'I never expected': NA/WO231/3.

43   'Brigadier Chappel left': NA/WO231/3.

'The remaining troops': Cox, p. 94.

'Every ridge promised': author interview with the late John Pumphrey, who fought and was captured in Crete. The interview, which was really a series of conversations, took place years before I had the idea for this book. Pumphrey was my uncle-in-law and his reminiscences have coloured my descriptions of the chaos that overtook the British Army on its retreat to the beaches on the south coast of Crete.

44   '"set up like an oasis"': Cox, p. 98.

'John Pendlebury never': Powell, *The Villa Ariadne*, p. 126. The precise details of the fate of John Pendlebury have been lost in the mists of time and the Cretan habit of mythologising events. Dilys Powell's account is the most complete, and I have used it in conjunction with an intereview with Mr C. E. Mamalakis.

6 The Occupation Begins

46 'In the meantime': Kurowski, *Jump into Hell*, p. 166.

'"Those who fought on Crete"': Theodore Papkonstantinou, *Die Schlacht um Griechenland*, 1966, quoted in Kaloudis, *Crete May 1941*, p. 42.

47 '"the murder of a German"': Stewart, *The Struggle for Crete*, p. 316.

'"It is certain"': General Student, order dated 31.5.41, quoted Memorandum, Canea, 1942; quoted in Beevor, Kindle edition.

48 'The victors needed': This account is based on the online record and photographed copy of Franz Peter Weixler's deposition to the Nuremberg Trial, *Goering Case*, translator Herma Plummer, Nov. 1945.

'One lay on the ground': Weixler photographs online and in CEMA.

51 'A few days later': Weixler, Nuremberg deposition.

7 Fortress Crete

52 'The streets were cleared': eyewitness account, CEMA.

53 'Although most of the Allied troops': Harokopos, *The Fortress Crete. 1941–1944*, p. 42.

54 'An engineer from Rethymnon': ibid., p. 64.

55 'At 22:00 hours on 26 July': NA/ADM236/30.

'*Thrasher* departed for Alexandria': Beevor, Kindle edition.

56 'A translator, Manolis Vassilakis': Harokopos, p. 49.

'The men split up': ibid., p. 52.

58 'I gazed and gazed': Psychoundakis, *The Cretan Runner*, p. 59.

'some were thrashed': ibid., p. 55.

'The behaviour of the villagers': Harokopos, p. 53.

59 'Escaping soldiers were led': Kokonas, *The Cretan Resistance 1941–1945*, p. 35.

60 'The Greeks call this period': Mazower, *Inside Hitler's Greece*, p. 89.

8 Ungentlemanly Warfare

61 'Churchill wanted Greece': *British Reports on Greece*, ed. Lars Baerentzen, Museum Tusculanum, Copenhagen, 1982, p. 41.

'SOE was a shadowy affair': the paragraphs describing the early history of the SOE are based on Foot, *SOE The Special Operations Executive, 1940–1946*, p. 4.

62   'In the early years': see Fielding, *Hide and Seek*.

63   '"Nobody who did not experience it"': Foot, p. 43.
      '"SOE personnel were always treated"': Beevor, Kindle edition.
      '"I found Tara, a whole villa"': W. Stanley Moss unpublished diary, IWM/05/74/1.

64   'Sophie's initial impressions': Tarnowski, *The Last Mazurka*, p. 216.
      'They soon welcomed': author interview with Candida Lycett Green and Daphne Astor.

65   'He described the days': ibid., p. 217.

66   'The inhabitants of Tara': ibid, p. 218.
      'Moss wrote in his diary': The diary of William Stanley Moss.
      'On the eve of an agent's deployment': ibid, p. 221.

9 The Cretan Resistance is Born

67   'For Colonel Michail Filippakis': eyewitness account, Clemenceau Filliakis, CEMA.
      'When he heard': ibid.

68   'A month later ': ibid.

70   'He was a': Leigh Fermor, typewritten MS, NLS/13338/32.

71   'Yerakari remained an important': Harokopos, *Fortress Crete*, p. 95.
      'The people were so hospitable': Beevor, Kindle edition.

72   'The letter stated': Harokopos, pp. 92–112.

73   'Fielding's relationship with Papadakis': Fielding, Kindle edition.
      'After several frustrating nights': ibid.

74   'One SOE agent wrote': Rendel, *Appointment in Crete*.
      'The three men made it': Kalitsounakis, CEMA.

75   'There were other dangers': Harokopos, p. 114.
      'There were no SS battalions': Beevor, Kindle edition.
      'Cairo sent a signal': NLS/PLF 13338/19.

77   'In his testimony Morakis': Harokopos, p. 120.

78   'The executioner was armed': CEMA.

10 A Terrible Tragedy

80   'In it he concluded': NLS/PLF 13338/4 'Crete'.
      'Bräuer was under no misapprehension': NLS/PLF/ 13338/6.

81 'The area commander for Rethymnon': ibid.

83 'A British officer in Cairo': Wood quoted in SOE report No. 1, NLS/PLF13338/19.

84 'Leigh Fermor believed': NLS/PLF 13338/19.
'"That Greece denounces the King"': NA HS5/671.
'Leigh Fermor always claimed': SOE Report, NLS/PLF/13338/19.

85 'In another of': NLS/PLF 13338/19.
'Any trained soldier': Geoffrey Matthews, late Irish Guards.
'This is called an "accidental discharge"': author interview with Geoffrey Matthews, late Irish Guards.

86 'Among the ten': Lefteris Kalitsounakis, eyewitness account, CEMA.
'who was very excitable': author interview, Adrian and Victoria Bartlett.

87 'Yanni's body lay in the open': Kalitsounakis, eyewitness account.

11 The Italians Change Sides

89 'The first meeting took place': SOE Report, NLS/PLF/13338/19.
'A message about the proposed': Harokopos, *Fortress Crete*, p. 205.
'Leigh Fermor says': SOE Report, NLS/PLF/13338/19.

91 'Leigh Fermor's signal ended': NA HS5/418.
'Bandouvas's headquarters were': SOE Report, NLS/PLF/13338/19.
'On 20 August, a huge drop': ibid.

92 'Bandouvas took the war': Beevor, Kindle edition.

93 'At first the troops': eyewitness accounts, CEMA.

95 'Bandouvas stood on the beach': Rendel, *Appointment in Crete*, pp. 64–6.

12 Operation Abduction

97 'It occurred to him': NA. HS5/732.
'He argued strongly': Sweet-Escott, *Baker Street Irregular*, p. 197.
'"I made myself extemely unpopular"': ibid.

98 'On Crete, Tom Dunbabin': Harokopos, *Abduction*, p. 63.
'Dunbabin then turned his attention': NA/HS5/732.
'Dunbabin sent word': Rendel, *Appointment in Crete*, p. 119.
'He told his new friend': 'Abducting a General', Patrick Leigh Fermor, handwritten MS, NLS/PLF/13338/31.

99   'Moss was spared the training': Moss, unpublished diary, IWM, 05/74/1.

'Moss's most enjoyable': ibid.

'"In our flat we had': Annette Street, 'Long Ago and Far Away', unpublished memoir, IWM 95/34/1.

'He wanted to take Billy Moss': ibid. In the next sentence Annette wrote: 'In fact when the operation came off Billy was invaluable.'

'His audience of two': David Smiley, quoted in Tarnowski, *Last Mazurka*, p. 219.

100   'When at last': The Diary of William Stanley Moss.

101   'They were delayed several times' ibid.

'On one occasion': ibid.

13 The Best Laid Plans . . .

103   'At about four': Rendel, *Appointment in Crete*, p. 130.

'The plane lumbered into the sky': Sortie report, Feb. 4/5, 1944 NA/Air 23/1443.

'onto the Omalos plateau': Rendel, p. 129.

104   'To Rendel's disgust': ibid., p. 130.

105   'Leigh Fermor's first': 'Abducting a General', handwritten MS, NLS/PLF/13338/31.

106   'Dear Annette, Well': Leigh Fermor letter to Annette Crean, IWM/Annette Street/95/34/1.

'It is absolutely grand': Rendel letter to Annette Crean, IWM/Annette Street/95/34/1.

108   'At dawn the guerrillas': Rendel, p. 138.

109   'Leigh Fermor found the waiting': SOE Report, NLS/PLF/13338/19.

110   'Half asleep, he sensed': Rendel, p. 140.

111   'The abbot offered them': ibid., p. 151.

112   'Through her brother': eyewitness account, CEMA.

113   'This time the captain': Moss, *Ill Met By Moonlight*, p. 27.

114   'Billy Moss was not prepared': ibid., p. 34.

'Moss was excited': Moss, unpublished diary, IWM, 05/74/1.

116   'Moss thought that': ibid.

'The party had to cross': Harokopos, *Abduction*, p. 82.

117   'They awoke the next morning': Moss, *Moonlight*, p. 40.

118   'John Stanley passed out': The Diary of William Stanley Moss.
      'Moss watched Rendel': Moss, *Moonlight*, p. 42.
120   'Manolis Paterakis recognised': Mamalakis.
121   'Moss came to realise': Moss, diary.
      'Like Manolis Paterakis': Mamalakis.
123   'Later, the women': Moss, *Moonlight*, p. 51.

14 First Base

124   'The next day they woke': Moss, *Moonlight*, p. 51.
      'The presence of the military hospital': author interview, Mamalakis.
125   'That evening they filled': Manolis Paterakis, eyewitness account,
      CEMA.
      'Outside Heraklion the bus': SOE report, NLS/PLF/13338/19.
126   'Military policemen with whistles': ibid.
      'Leigh Fermor found': Leigh Fermor, 'Abducting a General',
      handwritten MS, NLS/PLF/13338/31.
      'Back at the Zografakis': Moss, *Moonlight*, p. 54.
128   'A natural undercover agent': CEMA.
129   'The building was surrounded': ibid.
      'Micky's sister, Philia': Taxatake, with Kalogerakis, *The Legendary
      Capture of General Kreipe*, pp. 81–91.
130   'Leigh Fermor and Akoumianakis': Leigh Fermor, 'Abducting a
      General'.
      'While they stood': unnumbered photographs, *Kreipe Reunion*,
      NLS/PLF 13338.
131   'Micky had a friend': Mamalakis.
      'In the remote cave': Moss, *Moonlight*, p. 59.
132   'Chnarakis was grandfather': Harokopos, *Abduction*, p. 110.
133   'The Cretans crushed': Leigh Fermor, 'Abducting a General'.
134   'Ilias offered to go back': *Abduction*.
136   'In the late morning': Leigh Fermor, 'Abducting a General'.
137   'The briefing over': Manoli Paterakis, CEMA.
      'He was keeping a written': author interview with Mr C. E.
      Mamalakis.
138   'At dusk the twenty-five-strong': ibid.
      'A few minutes later': Moss, *Moonlight*, p. 73.
140   'Moss found the going': ibid., p. 75.

15 The Waiting

142   'A resistance worker in the city': Harokopos, p. 116.

143   'Later that night Leigh Fermor': Leigh Fermor, NLS/PLF/13338/31.

145   'Later that day Leigh Fermor': CEMA.
       The next day Zografistos': Harokopos, p. 119.

146   'Tyrakis wondered who else': Giorgios Tyrakis, eyewitness account,
       CEMA.
       'He and Micky Akoumianakis': Letter Giorgios Tyrakis to Mr C. E.
       Mamalakis, CEMA.

147   'Zoidakis appeared at around two': NLS/PLF/13338/31.

148   'At midday Pavlo': Harokopos, p. 129.

150   'The next day dawned': NLS/PLF/13338/31.
       'The two men agreed': ibid.

16 The Trap Springs

152   'That evening, in the officers' mess': P. Akoumianakis, CEMA.
       'Moss worried that': Moss, *Moonlight*, p. 96.

154   'Mitsos Tzatzas ran across': Manoli Paterakis eyewitness account,
       CEMA.

155   'Billy Moss, who': Moss, unpublished diary.

156   'Kreipe settled into the leather': NLS/PLF/13338/31.

157   'Through the windscreen': ibid.

158   'Zografistos saw something': Antonios Papaleonidas, eyewitness
       account, CEMA. Years after the war, Zografistos would show off
       the medal. He also had a gun stolen from Leigh Fermor.

17 Through the Checkpoints

160   'Kreipe began to shout': NLS/PLF/13338/31 & NLS/PLF/13338/1.
       'Leigh Fermor found': Powell. *The Villa Ariadne*, p. 177. In an
       interview with Dilys Powell Kreipe denied that he had given
       his word not to shout and said that he had successfully taken out
       an injunction preventing Moss's book *Ill Met By Moonlight* and
       the film of the same name being distributed in Germany on the
       grounds that it defamed his character.

161   'Moss drove fast': CEMA.
       'From somewhere on the terrace': ibid.

162   'Ahead Moss could see': author interview, Mr C. E. Mamalakis.

163 'From the back of the car': NLS/PLF/13338/31 & NLS/PLF/13338/1.

'Manolis and Giorgios slid': CEMA.

164 'There were more soldiers': CEMA.

'finally he decapitated him': author interview, Mamalakis.

165 'Leigh Fermor said all': NLS/PLF/13338/1.

'From the back of the car': Moss, unpublished diary.

166 'Ahead of them a familiar figure': CEMA.

168 'With the dawn': Moss, *Moonlight*, p. 108.

169 'He approached a woman': Giorgios Frangoulitakis, typewritten fragment, 'The Eagles of Mount Ida', translated and annotated by Leigh Fermor. NLS/PLF/13338/30.

'The Cretans had': ibid.

18 Radio Silence

171 'Tom Dunbabin lay low': Giorgios Frangoulitakis, typewritten fragment 'The Eagles of Mount Ida', translated and annotated by Leigh Fermor. NLS/PLF/13338/30.

173 'Paterakis recalled the time': author interview with Mr C. E. Mamalakis.

174 'Paterakis held his': Paterakis, CEMA.

175 'The graffiti were': the Cretans did not know that this Gothic script, known as *Schwabacher Judenlettern*, had been banned in Germany as being Jewish. On Hitler's orders Martin Bormann had issued a proclamation which contained the order: 'Authorities will refrain from using the Schwabacher Jew letters in future.'

'Leigh Fermor told': NLS/PLF/13338/30.

176 'Kreipe jolting along': Moss, unpublished diary.

177 'His name was John Lewis': He had entered into the Cretan spirit with gusto, at one point executing a spy by breaking the man's neck with this bare hands. Lefteris Kalitsounakis, eyewitness account, CEMA.

'Moss became more': Moss, unpublished diary, IWM/05/74/1.

178 'When he was asked': Giorgios Kalogirakis/Mamalakis interview, CEMA.

179 'Lo Mount Soracte': trans. Geoffrey Matthews.

180 'We had both drunk': NLS/PLF/13338/1. On the MS in the NLS

Leigh Fermor has written: 'I am not sure this is the location for this incident.' On his annotated and fragmentary translation of the 'Eagles of Mount Ida', Leigh Fermor says that the exchange took place several days later under some very dense pear trees in a 'sown field'. I think this is the most likely place. I have found it impossible to identify where in time and space the 'sown field' is, so have left the incident here.

'All the while Mandis Paterakis': Moss, *Moonlight*, p. 118.

19 Situation Ugly

181   'General Heinrich Kreipe': NA/HS5/671.

182   'The night duty officer': BBC internal inquiry into what happened to the SOE request for a transmission 8 May 1944. NA/HS5/671.

'At 7.45 the next morning': Miss Barker was an important figure in the BBC internal inquiry. Her trip from the World's End in SW3 is a fiction which I have used to give a feel for the state of London after four years of war, and the Blitz and later bombing. Miss Barker's journey is based on interviews with BBC employee Betty Willingale, who worked for the Corporation during the war and went on to become a distinguished television producer.

'*Festungskommmandant Generaloberst*': NA/HS5/671.

'At the same time': ibid.

183   'By now a frustrated': ibid.

184   'Dearest Paddy, the word': NLS/PLF/13338/6.

186   'The kapitan shook his head': Frangoulitakis, NLS/PLF/13338/30.

'The group set off in daylight': ibid.

'The general's state of mind': ibid.

187   'Tsikritsis showed the leaflet': ibid.

189   'They made their': Moss, unpublished diary.

192   'The Cretans worried': ibid.

193   'Skoutello was impressed': ibid.

194   'What are you doing': NLS/PLF/13338/1.

20 Marooned

196   'At the same time': Paterakis, CEMA.

197   'Giorgios Psychoundakis was with Barnes': Psychoundakis, *The Cretan Runner*, p. 268.

'the Germans set up': Frangoulitakis, NLS/PLF/13338/30.

198   'In the late afternoon': NLS/PLF/13338/5.

199   'In his diary he fumed': Moss, unpublished diary, IWM, 05/74/1.

'On 5 May, Tyrakis': NLS/PLF/13338/1.

200   'Eventually Psychoundakis tracked': Psychoundakis, p. 267.

'Moving a wireless station': Fielding, *Hide and Seek*, p. 133.

'Leigh Fermor wondered': Psychoundakis, p. 268.

201   'Psychoundakis returned the next day': NLS/PLF/13338/1.

202   'This was a comic improvisation': Psychoundakis, p. 269.

'At Cairo the SOE': NA/HS5/671.

21 Hide and Seek

204   'Dear Billy, All': NLS/PLF/13338/6.

205   'Moss wrote in his diary': Moss, unpublished diary.

'When Kreipe heard this': ibid.

'After this outburst': See Powell, *The Villa Ariadne*, p. 177. Kreipe did not like Moss. He told Dilys Powell that: 'Paddy, I liked Paddy, but Moss, always with his pistol, it was childish.' He also claimed that Moss hit him with a rifle butt during the kidnap moments. This is unlikely, because Moss was on the opposite side of the car dealing with the driver and taking control of the vehicle; he was not armed with a rifle.

'Manolis Paterakis began': Paterakis, CEMA.

206   'The brazen and criminal': Cooper, *Patrick Leigh Fermor*, Kindle edition.

207   'It was the local raki factory': Moss, *Moonlight*, p. 143.

208   'Leigh Fermor, Tyrakis': Harokopos, p. 164.

'Dear Paddy, have already': original signal NLS/PLF/13338/31.

211   'In the afternoon': Harokopos, p. 169.

22 Men of Darkness

214   'A few days before': Frangoulitakis, 'The Eagles of Mount Ida', MS, NLF/PLF.

215   'The SOE officers told': Harokopos, p. 185.

'They walked towards the rising moon': NLS/PLF/13338/31.

216   'Taking no chances': A few months later, Antonis Zoidakis
        was wounded and captured at exactly the same spot. German
        soldiers knocked him to the ground, tied his feet to the back of
        a lorry and drove off, dragging him for four miles. His flayed and
        unrecognisable body was left by the road, a warning to others.

218   'After a while he began': Moss, unpublished diary.
        'Moss took a': Moss, unpublished diary.

220   'The tensions of the last': Moss, *Moonlight*, p. 162.

222   'An hysterical, feminine': Moss, diary.
        'Leigh Fermor talked': Moss, unpublished diary.

223   'In an attempt to warm': Moss, *Moonlight*, p. 166.

23 Home Run

226   'Most of the men had fair hair': NLS/PLF/13338/31.
        'The party sat overlooking': ibid.

227   'You must be pleased': ibid.
        'They were in a tiny': ibid.

229   '"Bloody fools," replied Ciclitira': author interview with Paul
        Ciclitira.

230   'The men heading for Egypt': ibid.
        'Surprisingly many of the andartes': Paterakis, CEMA.

24 Returning Heroes

232   'The weary Cretans': Paterakis, CEMA.
        'Around mid-morning a klaxon': NLS/PLF/13338/1.

233   'The reception party watched': Moss, *Moonlight*, p. 182.

234   'They found the Cretans': author interview with Paul Ciclitira.

235   'The Cretans were moved': Harokopos, p. 226.
        'On 19 May a signal': NA/HS5/418.
        'The general's debriefing provides': NA/WO208/4208.

237   'A long time after': Sweet-Escott, *Baker Street Irregular*, p. 198.
        '"Oh we've got boxes"': Smith-Hughes letter to Leigh Fermor,
        NLS/PLF/13338/19.

25 Moss and the Battle of Damastas Bridge

239 'A modern doctor': I am grateful to Dr Richard Staughton MA, MB, BChir., FRCP, Emeritus Consultant Dermatologist, for this diagnosis.

'He received the medal': author interview with Prof. N. M. J. Woodhouse, MSc PhD.

240 'From the start Ilias': Athanassakis/Mamalakis, CEMA.

'In the end Moss received': ibid.

'The reality was that the letter': George Tyrakis/Mamalakis, CEMA.

'He returned to his': Moss, *A War of Shadows*, p. 20.

241 'On 7 August': Harokopos, p. 242.

242 'At the same time': Mamalakis.

'The group carried Hawkins': ibid.

'He carried a camera': ibid.

243 'The armoured car rumbled': ibid.

244 'The battle of Damastas Bridge': the remains of some of the men who died in the battle have recently been discovered in the area. One of them is thought to be the Russian Vanya – Mamalakis.

247 'When Moss got to Cairo': Moss, *Shadows,* p. 65.

26 Aftermath

248 'A captured German agent': Beevor, *Crete: The Battle and the Resistance.*

249 'General Benthack, who': ibid.

'When Ciclitira offered': author interview with Paul Ciclitira.

'In a surreal moment': ibid.

250 'In his final report': Lt. Col. T. J. Dunbabin, Final Report on SOE Missions in Crete, NA/HS5/724.

251 'Leigh Fermor and Ralph Stockbridge': Stockbridge interview with Mamalakis. There was an interesting incident when Mr Mamalakis was driving Stockbridge round Crete and told him that he had some SOE weapons in the boot of his car. Stockbridge's response was disapproving, he said: 'That was what Paddy and the SOE liked, not us in the ISLD.'

252 'His friend Xan Fielding wrote': Fielding, *Hide and Seek*, Kindle edition.

253 'a German intelligence officer': quoted in Harokopos, *The Abduction,* pp. 217–18.

Select Bibliography

Becker, Cajus, *The Luftwaffe War Diaries,* Doubleday and Co., New York, 1969

Beevor, Anthony, *Crete: The Battle and the Resistance*, John Murray, London, 1991

Buckley, Christopher, *Greece and Crete 1941*, Efstathiadis Group, Greece, 1995

Churchill, Winston, *The Grand Alliance*, Rosetta Books, Kindle edition, 2010

Clark, Alan, *The Fall of Crete*, Anthony Blond Ltd., London, 1962

Cooper, Artemis, *Patrick Leigh Fermor, An Adventure*, John Murray, London, 2012

Cox, Geoffrey, *A Tale of Two Battles: A Personal Memoir of Crete and the Western Desert, 1941*, William Kimber, London, 1987

Cruickshank, Donald, *SOE in the Far East*, Oxford University Press, Oxford, 1983

Davis, Wes, *The Ariadne Objective: The Underground War to Rescue Crete from the Nazis*, Crown, New York, 2013

Edwards, Roger, *German Airborne Troops 1936–45*, Purnell Book Services Ltd (Book Club Edition) 1974

Fairburn, W. E., *Get Tough*, Paladin Press, Boulder, Col., 1996 (1942)

Fergusson, Bernard, *The Black Watch and the King's Enemies*, Collins, London, 1950

Fermor, Patrick Leigh, 'Abducting a General', unpublished MS written over forty years and existing in handwritten, typewritten and word-processed formats, some bound and others not. NLS John Murray Archive/Leigh Fermor archive 13338/31

Fielding, Xan, *Hide and Seek: The Story of a Wartime Agent*, Paul Dry Books, Kindle edition, 2013

Foot, M. R. D., *SOE: The Special Operations Executive, 1940–1946*, Pimlico, London, 1999

Frangoulitakis, Giorgios ('Scuttlegeorge'), 'The Eagles of Mount Ida', unpublished MS in National Library of Scotland, John Murray Archive, Patrick Leigh Fermor

Grundon, Imogen, *The Rash Adventurer: A Life of John Pendlebury*, foreword by Patrick Leigh Fermor, Libri, London, 2007

Hadjipateras, Costas N., and Maria S. Falios, *Crete 1941, Eyewitnessed*, Efstathiadis Group, Athens, 2007

Harokopos, Giorgios, *The Fortress Crete, 1941–1944*, trans. Spilios Menounos, B. Giannikos & Co., Athens, 1993

—, *The Abduction of General Kreipe*, trans. Rosemary Tzanaki, V. Kouvidis & V. Manouras, Crete, 2003

Henssonow, Susan F., *Tara, Cairo: Gezira Island, Cairo, World War 2 Special Operations Executive*. Sophie Moss, Betascript Publishing, 2011

Hertz, *Exploring Crete*. S. Alexiou & Sons, undated

Heydte, Freiherr E. von der, *Daedalus Returned*, Hutchinson, London, 1958

Howarth, Patrick, *Undercover, the Men and Women of the Special Operations Executive*, Routledge & Kegan Paul, 1980

Kalogerakis, Georgios, *Yannis Dramoundannis 'Stephanoyannis' Chief of Anoyia Ano Milopotamo. 1941–1944*, Heraklion, 2008

Kaloudis, Pantelis, *Crete May 1941, The Fallschirmjägers Greatest Battle*, Albion Scott Ltd, 1981

Kiriakopoulos, G. C., *Ten Days to Destiny. The Battle for Crete 1941*, Franklin Watts, New York, 1985

—, *The Nazi Occupation of Crete, 1941–1945*, Praeger Publishers, Westport, CT, 1995

Kokonas, Nikolaos, foreword by Patrick Leigh Fermor and others, *The Cretan Resistance 1941–1945*, Graphotechniki Kritis, Rethymnon, Crete, 1991

Long, Gavin, *Greece, Crete and Syria*, vol. II of *Australia in the War of 1939 to 1945*, Series 1 – Army, Australian War Memorial, Canberra, 1953

Kurowski, Franz, *Jump into Hell German Paratroopers in World War II*, Stackpole Books, Mechanicsburg, PA, 2010

Langelaan, George, *Knights of the Floating Silk*, Hutchinson, London, 1959

MacDonald, Callum, *The Lost Battle: Crete 1941*, Macmillan, London, 1993

Macintyre, Donald, *The Battle for the Mediterranean*, Batsford, London, 1964

Mamalakis, Costas, *From* Mercury *to* Ariadne—*Crete 1941–1945*, Society of Cretan Historical Studies, Heraklion, 2010

Marks, Leo, *Between Silk and Cyanide: The Story of the SOE's Code War*, HarperCollins, London, 1998

Mazower, Mark, *Inside Hitler's Greece: The Experience of Occupation 1941–44*, Yale Nota Bene, Yale University Press, 2001

Mosley, Charlotte, ed., *In Tearing Haste: Letters Between Deborah Devonshire and Patrick Leigh Fermor*, John Murray, London, 2008

Moss, William Stanley, *Ill Met By Moonlight*, The Folio Society, London, 2001

—, *A War of Shadows*, Boardman, London, 1952

Pendlebury, J. D. S., *The Archaeology of Crete: an Introduction*, Methuen, London, 1965

Pöppel, Martin, trans. Dr Louise Willmot, *Heaven and Hell: The War Diary of a German Paratrooper*, Spellmount Publishers, Stroud, Gloucestershire, 2010

Powell, Dilys, *The Villa Ariadne*, Hodder & Stoughton, London, 1974

Prüller, Wilhelm, trans. H. C. Robbins Landon, *Diary of a German Soldier*. ed. H. C. Robbins Landon and Sebastian Leitner, preface by Correlli Barnett, Faber & Faber London, 1963

Psychoundakis, Giorgios, trans. and introduced by Patrick Leigh Fermor, *The Cretan Runner: His Story of the German Occupation*, Penguin Books, London, 1998

Rendel, A. M., *Appointment in Crete: The Story of a British Agent*, Allan Wingate, London, 1953

Spurr, Reg, *To Have and to Lose*, Society of Cretan Historical Studies, Heraklion, 2007

Stephanides, Theodore, *Climax in Crete*, Faber and Faber, 1946

Stewart, I. McD. G., *The Struggle for Crete: A Story of Lost Opportunity, 20 May–1 June 1941*, Oxford University Press, London, 1966

Sutherland, Jon, and Diane Canwell, *Images of War. Fallschirmjager. Elite German Paratroops in World War 11*, Pen and Sword, Barnsley, 2010

Sweet-Escott, Bickham, *Baker Street Irregular*, Methuen, London, 1965

Taxatake, Irene, with Giorgios Kalogerakis, *The Legendary Capture of General Kreipe*, The Prefecture of Heraklion, 2006

Tarnowski, Andrew, *The Last Mazurka: A Tale of War, Passion and Loss*, Aurum Press, London, 2006

Tzitzikas, Georgios Aristides, *Freedom and Glory (Memoirs 1939–1945)*, Society of Cretan Historical Studies, Heraklion, 2012

Villahermosa, Gilberto, *Hitler's Paratrooper: The Life and Battles of Rudolf Witzig*, Frontline Books, London, 2010

Woodhouse, C. M., *Something Ventured*, Granada, London, 1982

Zayas, Alfred M. de, *The Wehrmacht War Crimes Bureau, 1939–1945*, University of Nebraska Press, Lincoln, 1990

Acknowledgements

Luck played an important part in the capture of General Kreipe and luck has played its part in the writing of this book.

It was luck that took me to the Historical Museum of Crete on my first day of research in Heraklion where by chance I met the Curator, Constantinos E. Mamalakis, an expert on the history of Crete in the Second World War. In addition to the collections in the museum, Mr Mamalakis has a large private archive of documents, letters and artefacts. To his compendious knowledge of the events he brings a sharp eye for the archaeology of the war on the island and has possibly the most intimate understanding of the kidnap and its aftermath of anybody alive. Mr Mamalakis shared all this with me and words cannot express the depth of my gratitude.

Luck led me to the to the archive of Shaftesbury Young People where I met historian Simon Fenwick who had just finished some preliminary work on the Leigh Fermor papers. He too shared his knowledge with me and introduced me to David McClay, Senior Curator of the John Murray Archive at the National Library of Scotland. David and his team are making a magnificent job of curating Leigh Fermor's papers. He allowed me unlimited access to the archive and was very generous with the facilities of the library, giving me all the help I could possibly ask for. I am indebted to David and his brilliant staff, and to Simon for making the introduction.

The National Library of Scotland was only one of several great institutions that helped me. I am also grateful to the National Archive at Kew, the British Library, the London Library and the Imperial War Museum.

Luigi di Dio at Getty Images was very helpful, as was the estate of William Stanley Moss who kindly gave permission to use some of the photographs Moss took during the abduction, and to quote from his books and diary. I owe thanks too to the Estate of Sir Patrick Leigh Fermor.

I must thank Sofka Zinovieff and Manthos Lidakis for finding and introducing me to my two first research assistants, Irene Maris and Eirene Deritzaki. Among many other things, Irene and Eirene described the importance and depth of the godparent relationship. They introduced me to, and helped me to interview, many of the children and grandchildren of the kapitans and andartes, for which many thanks. Among the Cretans who talked to me I must thank Mr G. Kalogerakis, Mr C. Bandouvas, Mr N. Xylouris, M. G. Dramoudanis and Mr M. Lydakis. I list these kind people in the order in which I met them. Mr Dramoudanis, who is mayor of Anogia, laid on a delicious lunch of lamb barbequed on an open fire and a jeep to take us into the hills above the village. Thanks to Mr Dramoudanis, I visited the sheepfolds and saw the wild country that the kidnappers and General Kreipe travelled across in April and May 1944. The Cretans are a passionate people and their disputes can sometimes run for decades. It is not my intention to cause trouble and on a very few occasions in this book I have deliberately omitted a name or relationship. Wherever I went on the island I was greeted with wonderful generosity and hospitality.

In England I talked to the children of several SOE agents and must especially thank Paul Ciclitira, son of Major Dennis Ciclitira, and Nick Woodhouse, son of Colonel Monty Woodhouse, DSO OBE, who was sent to Crete in the first desperate months after the German invasion.

My friends have been encouraging and supportive and I must thank Victoria Hislop for her comradeship in the silence of the

London Library; Kirsty Tait and Jeremy Hardie for their unflagging interest and friendship; Adrian and Victoria Bartlet for their tales of Patrick Leigh Fermor, John Houseman and Micky Akoumianakis; Candida Lycett Green for her memories of Leigh Fermor; Daphne Astor who confirmed some aspects of his character; and Scarlett Sabet for her interest and encouragement. On the medical front Dr Peter Shephard shared some very interesting thoughts about the psychology of SOE agents; it was kind of Dr Richard Staughton to spend time pondering a modern diagnosis for the strange illness that afflicted Leigh Fermor during the stress of the escape phase. I must also thank two friends who shared their military experience: the indefatigable Geoffrey Matthews, late Irish Guards, who, at a time when he was very busy, gave me tutorials on weapons training and arms drill and helped me translate the Horace ode quoted by Kreipe; and Warwick Woodhouse, late Royal Marines and Royal Air Force Regiment, who has a passionate interest in all things to do with paratroopers. Warwick talked me through *Fallschirmjäger* parachuting techniques and equipment. Another military man to thank is the late Johny Pumphrey who, years ago, described his experiences as a soldier caught up in the battle of Crete and his time as a prisoner of war.

My agent, Victoria Hobbs, has been a model of good advice and support. My publishers, Bloomsbury, have provided their usual Rolls Royce service. I must thank the three editors who have worked on this book: Bill Swainson for his wise and scholarly advice; Anna Simpson whose clever and deft hand steered me calmly through the period from delivery to publication; and finally Kate Johnson who must be the best copy editor in the history of copy editors. Thank you too to Greg Heinimann for his cover; Martin Lubikowski for turning my rough sketches into clear, exciting maps; and proof readers Steve Cox and George Derbyshire, and indexer David Atkinson, for their meticulous professionalism.

Many people have helped me write *Kidnap in Crete* and I

apologise to anyone I have inadvertently forgotten. It goes without saying that any errors in the book are entirely my own.

Finally nearly twenty years ago luck led me to a strange gathering in Italy where I met my wife, Alexandra Pringle, who is not only my first reader, but my Commander-in-Chief and *sine qua non*.

Rick Stroud
London 2014

Index

A NOTE ON THE AUTHOR

Rick Stroud is the author of *The Phantom Army of Alamein: The Men Who Hoodwinked Rommel* and *The Book of the Moon*. He is also the coauthor, with Victor Gregg, of *Rifleman: A Front Line Life from Alamein and Dresden to the Fall of the Berlin Wall* and *King's Cross Kid: A London Childhood Between the Wars*. He lives in Chelsea, London.

@Rick_Stroud

A NOTE ON THE TYPE

The text of this book is set in Linotype Garamond Three, a type-face based on seventeenth century copies of Claude Garamond's types, cut by Jean Jannon. This version was designed for American Type Founders in 1917, by Morris Fuller Benton and Thomas Maitland Cleland and adapted for mechanical composition by Linotype in 1936.